Strategic Acts in the Study of Identity

Culture on the Edge: Studies in Identity Formation
Series Editor: Steven W. Ramey, University of Alabama

Culture on the Edge is devoted to studies—both monographs and collections of essays—that explore how social formation involves a series of strategies that present identity as static and uniform. Volumes in this series study identity formation as a sequence of interconnected historical practices, revealing ways that the image of stable selves and groups conceals the precarious and shifting nature of cultures.

Published:

Claiming Identity in the Study of Religion: Social and Rhetorical Techniques Examined
Edited by Monica R. Miller

Identity, Politics and the Study of Islam: Current Dilemmas in the Study of Religions
Edited by Matt Sheedy

Forthcoming:

Identifying Roots: Alex Haley and the Anthropology of Scriptures
Edited by Richard Newton

Strategic Acts in the Study of Identity

Towards a Dynamic Theory of
People and Place

Edited by
Vaia Touna

equinox

SHEFFIELD UK   BRISTOL CT

Published by Equinox Publishing Ltd.

UK: Office 415, The Workstation, 15 Paternoster Row, Sheffield,
        South Yorkshire S1 2BX
USA: ISD, 70 Enterprise Drive, Bristol, CT 06010

www.equinoxpub.com

First published 2019

British Library Cataloguing-in-Publication Data
A catalogue record for this book is available from the British Library.

ISBN-13   978 1 78179 072 4   (hardback)
          978 1 78179 073 1   (paperback)
          978 1 78179 816 4   (ePDF)

Library of Congress Cataloging-in-Publication Data

Names: Touna, Vaia, editor.
Title: Strategic acts in the study of identity : towards a dynamic theory of
  people and place / edited by Vaia Touna.
Description: Bristol : Equinox Publishing Ltd., 2019. | Series: Culture on
  the edge: studies in identity formation | Includes bibliographical
  references and index.
Identifiers: LCCN 2018025420 (print) | LCCN 2018045577 (ebook) | ISBN
  9781781798164 (ePDF) | ISBN 9781781790724 (hb) | ISBN 9781781790731 (pb)
Subjects: LCSH: Identification (Religion) | Identity (Psychology)—Religious
  aspects. | Identity (Psychology)
Classification: LCC BL53 (ebook) | LCC BL53 .S77 2019 (print) | DDC
  155.2—dc23
LC record available at https://lccn.loc.gov/2018025420

Typeset by S.J.I. Services, New Delhi, India
Printed and bound by Lightning Source Inc. (La Vergne, TN), Lightning Source UK Ltd.
(Milton Keynes), Lightning Source AU Pty. (Scoresby, Victoria).

Contents

SITE III: ACTS OF COMPARISON

APPENDIX

ACTS OF CLASSIFICATION

Contents vii

ACTS OF COMPARISON

Preface

"Show Your Work"

Vaia Touna

> I not only grant but insist that scholarship—like human speech in general—is interested, perspectival, and partial and that its ideological dimensions must be acknowledged, ferreted out where necessary, and critically cross-examined.[1]

In the Epilogue of his 1999 book, *Theorizing Myth*, Bruce Lincoln discusses the role of footnotes in scholarly works, and argues that they are similar to a teacher's demand of "show your work" on arithmetic tests. To "show your work," for Lincoln though, implies several salient notions—three of which he points out, which are all of particular interest and relevance to this volume. He writes:

> First, those who enter a field that constitutes itself as one of rigorous, disciplined inquiry do so in good faith. They pledge that their labor is honest, in token of which they "show their work" or "cite their sources." Second, they go beyond offering their results to an audience of consumers. They also display the process through which they arrived at those results for an audience of would-be critics, whom they accept as peers and superiors consistent with their control over the knowledge and principles that constitute the field. Third, they agree that if any challenges are forthcoming to their data, methods, or results, they will consider them thoroughly, defending or revising their positions as necessary, learning and/or teaching in the process. (209)

---

1 Bruce Lincoln, *Theorizing Myth: Narrative, Ideology, and Scholarship* (Chicago: University of Chicago Press, 1999), p. 208.

These three points, as I will discuss in the following pages, form the basis of this volume, which is part of a series that resulted from the collaboration of some members of Culture on the Edge—a group of scholars who work within the field of Religious Studies but who have a larger, shared interest in the study of identity or, as the title of this volume suggests, in the various strategic acts that make specific kinds of identifications possible.

The idea for a collaborative book started when the members of Culture on the Edge met as a group for the first time in March of 2012 at the University of Alabama. There were then seven of us (Craig Martin, Russell T. McCutcheon, Monica R. Miller, Steven W. Ramey, K. Merinda Simmons, Leslie Dorrough Smith, and myself), all of whom were working within the field of Religious Studies but each with diverse research interests.[2] At that first meeting, apart from our discussions based on our reading of Jean-François Bayart's book, *The Illusion of Cultural Identity* (2005), we also began crafting the idea of a collaboration that eventually resulted, in May of 2013, in the formation of a scholarly blog (edge.ua.edu)—at the time of writing the Preface of this book we had 987 posts on the site—and in two book series with Equinox Publishing (*Culture on the Edge* edited by Steven Ramey, and *Working with Culture on the Edge* edited by myself), both of which already include publications from individual members of the group as well as from other scholars who share our scholarly and theoretical interests.

Although the idea of collaborating on this book was among the first things that we discussed back in March 2012 at the University of Alabama, it has taken several years to materialize. In November 2012, when we met at the annual international conference of the AAR (American Academy of Religion), held that year in Chicago, we decided to read and discuss two papers that two members volunteered to write or had already written and were willing to share with the rest of the group;[3] one was by Craig Martin and eventually it became

2   For the history of the Culture on the Edge group see also the Preface of Russell T. McCutcheon, ed., *Fabricating Origins* (Sheffield, UK: Equinox Publishing, 2015), pp. ix–x.

3   Part of that conversation has been recorded for *The Religious Studies Project* by Andie Alexander, then a student in the Department of Religious

the Introduction to this book, and the other was by Steven Ramey, which became Chapter 1. Meanwhile, at that meeting we decided to begin work on our first collective book, *Claiming Identity in the Study of Religion*, published in 2015, and edited by former group member Monica Miller. In this volume the starting point of our conversation was six essays written by Russell McCutcheon, which served as identifiers of techniques, or so we argued, commonly used by scholars, and which each of the other members of the group then analyzed and identified in a piece of data closer to their own specific domain. The present volume, *Strategic Acts in the Study of Identity: Towards a Dynamic Theory of People and Place*, follows that initial book and falls within the spirit of our collaboration regarding our shared interest in the study of identity, or better put, in those "operational acts of identification" (borrowing the phrase from Jean-François Bayart), acts that constitute something as this or that. Thus, this book focuses on how the discourses related to those identifiers are negotiated, challenged, or changed, and by what means.

Important to note is that, in the six years from our first meeting to the publication of this volume, we engaged in conversation (in person and online), we read and discussed books, we wrote blogs that influenced our way of thinking (reading each others' posts was as important as writing our own)—in other words, we benefited from each others' views and individual work. This is evident in the following chapters, in a way that reminds me of Lincoln's advice to "show your work," so much so that I decided to begin this Preface with quotes from his work, followed by this brief background history of the group as a way to show the kind of (often unseen) processes that have been involved in the writing of this book.

Surely, like all scholarly works, the authors of the following main chapters—discussing topics such as the construction of the "nones" (Steven Ramey's main chapter at Site I), the idea of "creolization"

Studies at the University of Alabama, and now a doctoral student at the University of Emory, who has served from the outset of Culture on the Edge as the curator of its blog and now also as a contributing member. The recording can be found here: http://www.religiousstudiesproject.com/podcast/podcast-identity-or-identification/ (accessed January 24, 2018).

and "intentionality" in studies of Caribbean religions (Merinda Simmons's main chapter at Site II), or the discourses that construct particular boundaries and thus identities within modern women's movements (Leslie Dorrough Smith's main chapter at Site III)—have done so in a rigorous and disciplined manner. This is obviously the work that one can see in the footnotes and list of references in each chapter, but the work of this edited volume goes well beyond that. In a way, the very structure of the volume, in which the authors engage in a response/reply dialogue, brings the work in the footnotes into the main body of the book, thereby understanding footnotes also in the way Jonathan Z. Smith discussed: "a footnote is least interesting when it authorizes; it is at its best when it exposes, explores, and perhaps, mediates conflicts of interpretations; for me, the chief goal of scholarship."[4] This edited volume then takes Smith's point further by exposing, exploring, and mediating conflicts of interpretations not only in its footnotes but also through the dialectical structure of the book itself. For, each of the main authors is then challenged by a colleague and asked to mediate and critically cross-examine several issues in their reply—making the ongoing, collaborative nature of our project explicit. Given, of course, the fact that those main chapters were first drafted as papers several years prior to becoming part of this book, the authors were able to reflect upon their ideas and defend, revise, or point out in a critical manner issues pertaining to the very nature of scholarship.

As scholars we often confine ourselves to discussions only with those of our specific subfields, but what this book, like Culture on the Edge in general, demonstrates is the breadth and relevance that our work (though seemingly done specifically from within the field of Religious Studies) can have. The underlying connection between the members of the group, and I would say the very success, it seems, of Culture on the Edge (given the volume of engagement on our site), is a particular shift in our collective approach to the way we study the things we study, and more specifically the way we study so-called

---

4   Jonathan Z. Smith, "Reading Religion: A Life in Scholarship," in Willi Braun and Russell T. McCutcheon, eds., *Reading J.Z. Smith: Interviews and Essay* (New York: Oxford University Press, 2018).

"identities." For, as Craig Martin writes in the Introduction, "we propose avoiding the reification or hypostatization of [...] identities by focusing our analysis on *interested social actors who make identity claims*," that is, we understand "identities" not as fixed entities with some essential characteristics that transcend time and space but rather as the result of a variety of strategic acts.

What is particular about this book, as I already mentioned, is its very structure. In the Introduction Martin unpacks what those "operational acts of identification" or strategic acts are, and sets the table for the chapters that follow. The book is then divided into three sites, or what we might call three situations, each of which is representative of a specific strategic act: classification, appropriation, and comparison. Each site then consists of a main chapter, a response from another member of the group (who presses further the point of the main chapter while inviting its author to reflect upon their initial argument), and a reply from the author of the main chapter. Making our conversations explicit in this manner will, we hope, model for readers a process from which we have all benefited.

On Site I, in the main chapter Ramey looks at the constructive nature of groups. He unpacks the various discourses concerning the group now known as "nones" and argues that classifications employed by a variety of sources (scholarly, institutional, media, etc.) are never neutral descriptions of things but rather reflect various ideological assumptions and interests. In my response to Ramey's chapter I invite him to reflect upon the very idea of description, with which he also routinely engages throughout his chapter, in order to build or thicken his own argument. In his reply to my response Ramey argues that all descriptions, whether scholarly or not, are indeed contingent, although they can still be more or less convincing and valuable. Urging scholars to be more self-reflexive about the contingency of their descriptions prompts him to reflect and revise parts of his own chapter. What readers make of this response will be interesting to learn—making evident our hope that the collaboration extends well beyond the pages of the book.

On Site II K. Merinda Simmons's main chapter looks at academic discourses on hybridity and creolization in the context of Caribbean religious traditions. Martin then responds by challenging Simmons to think in terms of the material consequences of scholarly claims about syncretism by comparing what we sometimes call "cultural appropriation" to "subversive creolization or hybridity," suggesting that an alternative set of critical questions would provide a more sophisticated point of entry for cultural critique. Taking into account Martin's response, Simmons, in her reply, invites readers to consider that the problem is not with appropriation so much as it is with the authenticity claims contained therein.

On Site III Leslie Dorrough Smith's main chapter looks at scholarly discourses and how, depending on specific political interests, the same women's groups, through certain rhetorical techniques that Smith's chapter exposes, are described either as "feminist" or as "anti-feminist." McCutcheon's response to Smith asks her to consider the wider implications of the sorts of comparisons that are necessary for scholars to carry out their work—comparisons that are no less exemplified in her own chapter. In her reply to McCutcheon, Smith reflects upon the nature of the comparisons in her chapter and maintains that their similarities reveal the enduring life of certain unspoken biases in and conditions of scholarship today.

The book has one more particularity—the Appendix, which also falls within the idea of Lincoln's call for scholars to "show your work," that is, making evident how the authors progressed in their thinking, and the processes through which they arrived at the results they are discussing in their main chapters and responses. So, the Appendix presents a selection of posts that initially appeared on the Culture on the Edge site between the years 2013 and 2016. These are divided in three groups (corresponding to the Sites), and show how the authors worked through their ideas on issues of classification, appropriation, and comparison in various examples and a wide variety of situations. They shared those ideas with their colleagues at Culture on the Edge (and with whomever happened upon the blog), and benefited not only from their feedback but also from their peers' writing on similar issues though at different sites and in different situations. Of course our readers (i.e., those that follow us on the Culture on the Edge blog), and thus our "would-be critics," once again quoting Lincoln, played an important role in this process, often with comments under the posts but also on social media (such as Facebook or

Twitter) where those posts were shared. Their insightful comments, questions, and critiques (whether positive or negative) were part of the development of our ideas and therefore lie in the usually undisclosed past of this book's chapters. Lincoln's idea of "show your work" is thus certainly epitomized in the Appendix, and this is one of the main reasons I decided to included this section in the book. The pithy examples in the Appendix further exemplify and model a different way of approach and often at sites that would not necessarily be considered a source of "typical" scholarly data but, I think, it is in these apparently mundane examples that we can see how strategic acts construct particular kinds of identities that serve particular interests in the present—identities that, upon closer examination, are shown to be contingent, and always in flux. They are examples that we don't normally think about, perhaps, because we so often take for granted what we are familiar with.

Choosing the posts for the Appendix (five from each member of Culture on the Edge—although Monica Miller is not among the contributors of this volume, I decided to include her as well, as she significantly contributed in the first years of the group) proved to be not an easy task, given the abundance of posts from which I had to select; but choices needed to be made and therefore a couple of criteria were necessary. My initial criterion was, of course, the relevance of the posts to the volume's theme, but equally important proved to be the Culture on the Edge readership—that is, I included posts that were particularly favored by our readers (which I make explicit in the Editorial Notes [Ed. Notes:…] of the Appendix), such as, for example: Dorrough Smith's post "The Most Disgusting Picture Ever" with 6,538 views, or Ramey's "The Harm of World Religions" with 4,941 views.

As I wrote in the Preface of my book *Fabrications of the Greek Past*, I particularly benefited from my friends and colleagues in the Culture on the Edge group for though "their work may seem to have little to no relevance to my own work or at least to the dataset I happen to work, yet there was an overlap and communication on a theoretical level that made their work relevant to my own interests."[5]

---

5   Vaia Touna, *Fabrications of the Greek Past: Religion, Tradition, and the Making of Modern Identities* (Leiden: Brill, 2017), p. ix.

My hope is that readers will also benefit by becoming part of the dialogue that the members of Culture on the Edge initiated and which has produced this book. They may not, necessarily, be familiar or interested in the particular dataset that each bundle of chapter/response/reply is dealing with, but, ideally, the diversity of examples both within the main book as well as in the Appendix will allow a variety of readers to engage with the larger theoretical issue that those examples draw upon, and apply this to their own particular dataset.

Since the conceptualization of this volume to its realization, Culture on the Edge has seen, like everything, several changes. Among the most important was the dynamic of our group itself, which now counts 15 members from North America and Europe, scholars and PhD students who work within the field of Religious Studies (Russell T. McCutcheon, Steven W. Ramey, K. Merinda Simmons, Leslie Dorrough Smith, Craig Martin, Jason Ellsworth, Matt Sheedy, Martie Smith Roberts, Chris Cotter, Teemu Tara, Anja Basel, Richard Newton, Stacie Swain, Andie Alexander, Tara Baldrick-Morrone, and Vaia Touna). Since, the conversations at Culture on the Edge are ongoing my hope is that there will further such collective volumes that are even more challenging and edgy.

Finally, I want to thank all of those who made this volume possible, especially my friends and colleagues, old and new, at Culture on the Edge, in particular the series editor, Steven Ramey, for his support. The University of Alabama granted me a research leave semester, which allowed me to complete work on this volume. Special thanks go to Equinox Publishing and especially to Janet Joyce and Valerie Hall for their support and patience, and for understanding the benefit of this differently structured book. Of course, this work would not have been possible without the encouragement and support of my friend and colleague Russell McCutcheon, who was always willing to discuss and help me solve various issues that arose during the process of putting together this edited volume. Last but not least, I want to thank those who actively follow Culture on the Edge and who by engaging in our discussions and doing some ferreting of their own (thinking back to my epigraph) have made the conversations all the better.

Vaia Touna is Assistant Professor in the Department of Religious Studies at the University of Alabama. She is author of *Fabrications of the Greek Past: Religion, Tradition, and the Making of Modern Identities* (Brill, 2017). Her research focuses on the sociology of religion, acts of identification and social formation, as well as methodological issues concerning the study of religion and the past in general.

Introduction

On the Strategies of Identity Formation

Craig Martin

> There is no such thing as identity, only operational acts of iden-
> tification. The identities we talk about so pompously, as if they
> existed independently of those who express them, are made (and
> unmade) only through the mediation of such identificatory acts,
> in short, by their enunciation.
>
> —Jean-François Bayart (2005: 92)

Identity Magic

What if we, as scholars, told the following narrative? In the 1st century there was a man named Jesus who invented a magical spool of
invisible thread. He carried the spool with him everywhere he traveled as an itinerant preacher. When those who heard his message
accepted it, he would magically partition the invisible thread, handing
an end to each new follower. Jesus's disciples each carried an end of
this invisible thread, and everywhere they went they too distributed it.
Like the loaves and the fishes Jesus is said to have multiplied to feed
the masses, so was the thread multiplied and divided—like a complicated spider web—across the face of the ancient Mediterranean
world. In fact, the thread stretched not only across space, but across
time as well, although it has been divided innumerable times over the
last two millennia. Contemporary followers of Jesus in the Catholic,
Eastern Orthodox, and Protestant churches hold the thread today at its
various temporal and spatial termini.

Sadly, this is often precisely the story we tell, except instead
of "invisible threads" we talk about a mysterious thing called

"Christianity." Jesus invented this "Christianity," which spread to his followers who became "Christians" as they converted to his message, and which they subsequently spread—over two thousand years—from 1st-century Palestine to all corners of the globe. It is this myth we use to draw lines—or invisible threads—from the past to the present: this invisible thread that we call the "Christian tradition" connects persons in the 1st century with persons in the 21st century. Sometimes we tell the story slightly differently, with the magical spool having been invented by Yahweh, Abraham, or Moses, with its thread stretching unbroken from ancient Israel through the first and second temple periods, and through Christianity, therefore constituting the "Judeo-Christian tradition." Others stretch the invisible thread even further, stringing it through the three "Abrahamic religions," Judaism, Christianity, and Islam.

It is worth noting that different storytellers—or perhaps we should call them social and political architects—spin different stories. Martin Luther, for instance, likely would have been shocked by talk of the "Judeo-Christian tradition." For him and his contemporaries, Jews were "Christ killers." How did Jews go from being "Christ killers" (enemies of Christianity) to members of the "Judeo-Christian tradition" (and therefore allies of Christianity)? How does opposition turn into sameness? What competing criteria of identity and difference are at work in these contexts?

The contributors to this volume all take it for granted that cultural artifacts do not come prepackaged for us—that sameness and difference are not intrinsic to "things in themselves"—but rather that classification and identification are human *practices*. Identities and differences do not exist independently of their post facto production—and we as scholars can study the means by which they are made. Consequently, this book is not really about identity, but rather *acts* of identification.

Acts of identification are, arguably, much like acts of canonization —acts that fabricate what they presume to identify. Consider "the" Bible—the "the" is in scare quotes because it is clear there is not just one—which more or less all contemporary Bible scholars recognize to be the result of centuries of social work. In *Who Wrote the New Testament*, Burton Mack notes that "the Bible is taken for granted [by the public] as a special book" (1995: 1), but this special status mystifies the processes of social formation that went into its production. To begin with, the books that are included in the most popular canons today are only "a very small selection of texts from a large body of literature produced by various communities" (6).

> [O]ver the course of the second and third centuries, centrist Christians[1] were able to create the impression of a singular, monolinear history of the Christian church. They did so by carefully selecting, collecting, and arranging anonymous and pseudonymous writings assigned to figures at the beginning of the Christian time. (7)

These texts, Mack insists, were not accurate or faithful portrayals of the past, but myths that reimagined the past in ways that served the interests of those who wrote them (36). "Each group created Jesus, not in its own image exactly, but in the image appropriate for the founder of the school it had become or wanted to become" (46). In addition, there are many different canons made up of different selections of texts. Marcion, of course, initiated the canonization process: his Bible "contained ten (excised) letters of Paul and one abbreviated Gospel of Luke" (253). But other "church fathers"—such as Irenaeus—upped the ante by providing their own, alternative canons. Of course, the criteria of selection for each canon depended on each group's ideology. Marcion's criteria included the assumption that the ancient Israelite's god and Jesus's god could not be the same, and consequently he excluded the "Old Testament"; those with different assumptions employed different selection criteria. Mack hits the point home: "Even theologians know that the Bible did not fall from heaven, of course, and that the history of its production spans more than one thousand years. That knowledge has made it necessary for scholars to give an account of its formation" (276).

Thus there is not "the" or even "a" Bible. Rather, it appears that some people invented a wide variety of stories that reflected their

---

1   Note: the very idea of "centrist Christians" only makes sense given some logically prior act of identification which likely took place temporally after the moment in time which Mack is discussing.

social desires, later groups rewrote those stories in ways that served their subsequent mythmaking goals, and still later groups created a pastiche out of the texts available to them in ways that served local interests.[2] The key words in Mack's account include: produce, create, select, collect, arrange, mythmaking. "The Bible" is therefore not a thing that simply dropped from heaven and exists through time; rather, different groups ongoingly create bibles for themselves. However, despite this considerable sophistication with respect to bibles as multiple and diverse products of human social activity, Mack nevertheless speaks of "Christian" identity as if it were a thing that (almost) dropped from heaven and persists through time.

Mack describes Christianity as a thing that has desires (291), as something that has persisted "for almost two thousand years" (294), that intrudes on other cultures (295), that has its own "mentality" that apparently directs the behaviors of Christians (302). In addition, Mack speaks unironically about the "Judeo-Christian tradition" throughout the introduction and conclusion of his book, a "tradition" that has "the Bible"—the Bible Mack has just told us doesn't really exist—at its core.

Mack takes up the term "Judeo-Christian" but does not reflect as critically upon its invention as he does upon the formation of "the Bible." Others have done so, although in a variety of ways. In his classic article, "The Myth of the Judeo-Christian Tradition," Arthur A. Cohen suggests why social practitioners might have invented such a tradition. He states that Judaism and Christianity are essentially different religions, but that Christians experiencing collective postwar guilt about the Holocaust invented the Judeo-Christian tradition in order to ease their bad conscience (Cohen 1969: 76). While Judaism and Christianity might be similar in some respects and might be historically contiguous or genealogically related, that does not in and of itself constitute a common "tradition." In *Jews and Christians: The Myth of a Common Tradition*, Jacob Neusner concurs:

---

2   And this is to say nothing of the fact that even if we accept, for instance, that the gospel of Mark is part of "the Bible," we still have to invent that gospel out of competing extant copies of the said gospel.

Christianity and Judaism each took over the inherited symbolic structure of Israel's religion. Each, in fact, did work with the same categories as the other. But in the hands of each, the available and encompassing classification-system found wholly new meaning. The upshot was two religions out of one, each speaking within precisely the same categories but so radically redefining the substance of these categories that conversation with the other becomes impossible. (1991: 5)

Thus both Cohen and Neusner accept that there may be a genealogical connection between Judaism and Christianity, but a connection does not in and of itself make an identity. Norman Solomon, in *Judaism: A Very Short Introduction*, goes even further than Cohen and Neusner in denying such an identity between Judaism and Christianity. Modern Judaism, Solomon insists, is a product of the Talmud, which was written *after* the New Testament; if anything, Christianity came *before* Judaism, rather than vice versa: "When the Pope recently referred to Jews as the 'elder brothers' of Christians he got it wrong; we are both, of course, 'children' of the Hebrew scriptures, but in terms of our defining texts (New Testament, or Talmud) it is Christians who are the 'elder brother'" (1996: 21). For Solomon, then, the family tree runs from the Torah and splits first to Christianity and then later to Judaism.

I am interested neither in affirming nor denying the existence of a Judeo-Christian tradition. If identity formation is analogous to canonization, then what should perhaps interest us as scholars is not who is right, but rather how different groups imagine identities for themselves and others. Like Mack's work on the formation of "the Bible," perhaps our analysis of the formation of identities could use the following key words: produce, create, select, collect, arrange, mythmaking. Perhaps some postwar Christians fabricated the Judeo-Christian tradition by collecting or selecting some elements from the past, arranging them in a narrative, and thereby gerrymandering a "Judeo-Christian" identity. By contrast, it seems clear that Cohen is interested in selecting alternative elements from the past, arranging them in a different order, such that "Jewish" and "Christian" identities are set in competition with one another. We no more need to adjudicate the differences between their narratives any more than we need to say that either the Catholic or Protestant canon is the "real" canon. Different groups construct identities using the same words but in different ways.

Nothing predetermines how elements from the past will be collated or reorganized into new narratives. Lines of continuity, contiguity, connection, or similarity can be drawn in almost infinite ways. Consider my "self" and continuity: I could draw genetic lines through my parents and grandparents; I could draw lines connecting the matter in my physical body to the plants I've eaten and then to the water and sunlight that fed them; or I could draw lines connecting my ideology with that of my parents, American pragmatism, Friedrich Nietzsche, and Michel Foucault. I could group my "self" on the basis of similarity with all people whose names start with the letter "C," with all who were born in 1976, or with all who are professors of religious studies. The identities and connections I can draw up by imagining a continuity or similarity are innumerable. What is fundamental here is that it is *we* who do the drawing. The stuff of the world does not come to us organized according to a priori similarity and difference, continuity and discontinuity.

In *Symbolic Classification*, Rodney Needham writes:

> [I]n order to think about the world, and also to act upon it, we need to divide phenomena into classes. We have to group things together according to what we think are significant resemblances as, for example, when we discriminate a class of objects as edible mushrooms. And we need then to distinguish a contrasted class by a significant difference, as when we circumscribe a further class of objects as poisonous mushrooms. (1979: 17)

In addition to the fact that it is *we* who divide the world, it is noteworthy that we divide the world in ways related to our *interests*; animals with an alternative biology, for whom "poisonous" mushrooms are not poisonous, would have no need of such a distinction. "Judeo-Christian" is no less an interested category than "poisonous," and thus the crucial analytical question is no longer "Is there a Judeo-Christian tradition?" but rather "Whose interests are served by carving out or denying a Judeo-Christian identity?"

There is, of course, no means of escaping to a god's-eye-view from which to analyze, disinterestedly, identity formation. When we talk of "identity formation" we, as scholars, are also dividing the world into classes of things that interest us, employing a grid of classification that reflects our interests. To talk of "identity formation" requires us to fabricate something called "identity formation." If something distinguishes our claims from the claims of those we study, it is not that they are inventive and invested and we are not—rather, it is that we strive for constant reflexivity, to keep in focus both our objects of study and our contribution to their creation. Like a magician who shows his or her audience how a trick is done, we hope to produce a spectacle and simultaneously show how we produced it.

Many of those we would consider peers in the academy—even the most progressive ones—fail to achieve the level of reflexivity to which we aspire. It has become passé to suggest that "genders" and "races" are social constructions, and critical scholars no longer use "male" and "female" or "black" and "white" as if they referred to things that exist independently of their construction and performance. Why is it that we do not see the same critical reflexivity when it comes to talking about "Christianity" or "the Judeo-Christian tradition"? Otherwise critical scholars who would take it as obvious that people in different times and places construct and perform gender in various and competing ways nevertheless go on to talk about how a thing called "Christianity" moves across Europe, or influences culture or politics, or even mixes or becomes a hybrid with other religions.

We propose avoiding the reification or hypostatization of such identities by focusing our analysis on *interested social actors who make identity claims*. For this reason we prefer the term "identification" over "identity." As Rogers Brubaker points out in his book on "ethnic identity," using the term "'Identification' ... invites specification of the agents that do the identifying" (2004: 43). Again, our fundamental question will not be "what identity?" but rather "Who identifies whom as what, and to what end or with what interests in mind?" Brubaker continues:

> Apart from the general unreliability of ethnic common sense as a
> guide for social analysis, we should remember that participants'

accounts ... often have what Pierre Bourdieu calls a *performative* character. By *invoking* groups, they seek to *evoke* them, summon them, call them into being. Their categories are *for doing*—designed to stir, summon, justify, mobilize, kindle, and energize. By reifying groups, by treating them as substantial things-in-the-world, ethnopolitical entrepreneurs can, as Bourdieu notes, "contribute to producing what they apparently describe or designate." (Brubaker 2004: 10; quoting Bourdieu 1991: 220)

In addition, when we focus on those who perform acts of identification, it soon becomes clear that there are almost always *competing* identifications. Aaron Hughes suggests, for instance, that we cannot study "something called Islam precisely because no such thing can exist. Despite appeals to the contrary by either practitioners or scholars of the tradition, Islam, like any other religious tradition, is a series of sites of contestation" (2007: 54). Indeed, something like Islam cannot exist precisely *because of* the competing views of what "Islam" is. "In the case of social entities such as nations, classes, and states, we are not dealing simply with abstract notions, but with socially constructed beings: it is because there are narrating bodies that behave *as if* such beings existed, that they do *actually* exist" (Bottici 2007: 241). However, the competition between narrating bodies "results, not simply in a disturbance of identity, but in the absence of a possible story, that is, in the dissolution of a common identity" (242). While I am tempted to say that "all that is solid melts into thin air," it seems more accurate to say that "all that is solid melts into competing social agendas."

Of course, with such an approach it is arguable that we risk reifying or hypostatizing social actors and their interests. Are "social actors" not equally deconstructible? Are we reintroducing authors after the death of the author? I would argue that this is not the case because we freely admit that social actors and their interests could be further reduced to or redescribed in other vocabularies.[3] We do not take social

3   For Pierre Bourdieu, agents have a habitus that is structuring yet structured—ideally critical reflexivity keeps an eye on both the structuring capacity and the structures that shape the structuring capacity at the same time.

actors and identity formation to be a bedrock at the origin of things; rather, what interests us is those who *halt redescription*, those who resist attempts to dissolve or reduce the objects they've created into alternative discourses, or those who believe that the objects they've identified are transcendental signifieds. "Instead of being explanatory factors, [identities] must themselves be explained" (Bayart 2005: 95).

One further caveat: while it seems clear that interests drive identity claims, it is nevertheless also true that interests are themselves the product of identity claims. Put bluntly, a group cannot have collective interests without already having imagined itself as a group. If it served the interests of the Ku Klux Klan to imagine Jesus as a Klansman *avant le lettre*, as historian Kelly Baker points out in *Gospel According to the Klan* (2011), it is undoubtedly only because the group had already constructed for themselves white, Protestant, and Klan identities. In other contexts—for instance in contexts in which "white" fails to register as an identity—no such group interests could exist. By no means, then, do we identify "interests" as the bedrock underlying identity claims, and at which all analysis resists further reduction or redescription.

Strategies of Identification

In what follows I will attempt a partial catalogue of strategies social actors use to construct identities for themselves and others. Such a list is not intended to be comprehensive, but rather merely to focus on a few common strategies used by both practitioners of so-called "religious communities" and the scholars who reify the "traditions" they study. In addition, it should be clear that such strategies are never discrete—identity formation is a complex process and one would expect to see multiple, overlapping strategies operating at once.

Genealogy. Actors often form identities by drafting a genealogy and imagining the identity to be a product of a continuity or contiguity of elements. Much like the creation of "Abrahamic traditions" that have a supposed continuity from Abraham to Jesus to Muhammad and also to contemporary Judaism, Christianity, and Islam, those who utilize this strategy arrange a family tree of persons or cultural elements and draw identities around those they wish to include. However, it is always the case that not everything that is contiguous in history is included as a part of the identity drawn. Although Protestantism was temporally contiguous with late medieval Catholicism, it is doubtful that Martin Luther would have claimed that Lutheranism and Catholicism were "the same" on that basis; contemporary inter-faith activists with different interests, however, might suggest that Catholics and Protestants *are indeed* part of "the same" Christian tradition. Which contiguous elements are included in the family tree at stake—and which will be excluded as black sheep or bastards—depends on the interests of those drawing the lines of continuity.

Return-to-Origins Narrative. In order to construct an identity includ-ing some persons or cultural elements from the past and the pres-ent while *excluding* something that lies *between* the past and the present—from which one wants to disassociate oneself or one's group—a return-to-origins narrative might suffice. This is merely a variation on the genealogical strategy: by folding the family tree, one can connect the uppermost "branches" to the "roots," bypassing all contiguous elements in between. It is through such a strategy that the early Protestants, for instance, could draw a Christian identity straight from the Acts of the Apostles to the 16th century, bypassing the Roman Catholic and Eastern Orthodox communities they wished to exclude.

Nostalgic Teleology. Similar to a return-to-origins narrative, one could organize an identity around a nostalgic, teleological narrative according to which an essence unfolds over time in a way that returns to the latent essence at the origin. The progress and growth of an oak, for example, into a fully-fledged tree is judged against the imagined potential presumed to lie within the acorn from which it came. Of course, the shape of the origin/destination depends on the projection of a fabricated, nostalgic ideal onto the identity formation at stake, against which those who are said to share the identity can be judged negatively or positively.

Fabrication of History. If one cannot plausibly group together what one wants by either a genealogy or a return-to-origins narrative, one might simply fabricate the past most well-suited to one's social project. For example, those aiming at a universal shared essence among all "world religions" might draw a circle of identity around Jesus and those cultural traditions popularly identified as "Hinduism" or "Buddhism" simply by insisting that Jesus must have traveled to the "mystic East" during those years of his life about which the canonical gospels are silent. Thus one could create a contiguity where none apparently exists (at least according to the extant historical evidence), and thereby graft "Hinduism" and "Buddhism" into the "Abrahamic religions'" family tree.

Strategic Anachronism. Genealogies likely contain anachronisms designed to permit social actors to draw an identity around contiguous but remarkably dissimilar moments in the "tradition" they bring into relief. Past persons or cultural elements can be redescribed in contemporary terms such that they resemble the present or are useful for present purposes. Cecil B. DeMille famously suggested in the introduction to *The Ten Commandments* (1956) that the Moses story was about "whether man ought to be ruled by God's law, or whether they ought to be ruled by the whims of a dictator like Ramses. Are men the property of the state, or are they free souls under God? This same battle continues throughout the world today." Try as I might, I have been unable to find anything in Exodus about democracy and dictatorship, or about capitalism and communism, but for DeMille—who produced this film in the midst of the Cold War—the connection is obvious. What is obvious from a scholarly perspective, however, is that anachronistically projecting the conflict between the U.S. and the U.S.S.R. into the Exodus story allowed DeMille to line up the Israelites and the U.S. on one side, and the Egyptians and the U.S.S.R. on the other. In other words, the strategic anachronism permits him to portray his favorite "good guys" and most hated "bad guys" as part of a never-ending Manichean struggle—one in which it is clear who is good and who is not. Similarly, in *Gospel According to the Klan*, Baker notes that the Klan insists that Jesus was a Klansman *avant le lettre*, because—as a Jew, and since Jews are concerned with racial identity—he was of course concerned with his own "clan." Clearly, the discourses employed by the Klan in the 20th century—as well as the oppositional identifiers "white" and "black"—were unavailable to those who lived in the 1st century; nevertheless, "Collective memory is systematically unfaithful to the past, in order to satisfy the needs of the present" (Bayart 2005: 83).

Ahistorical Spirit. If a genealogy of contiguous cultural elements is impossible and the fabrication of them impractical, social actors might circle an identity around disparate groups via an appeal to an ahistorical or universal spirit that underlies the appearance of cultural elements at various times and places, much like Jung's collective unconscious. For instance, in the afterword to Christopher Moore's fictional biography of Jesus (*Lamb: The Gospel According to Biff, Christ's Childhood Pal*), Moore insists,

> While there are indeed astounding similarities between the teachings of Jesus and those of Buddha (not to mention those of Lao-tzu, Confucius, and the Hindu religion, all of which seem to have included some version of the Golden Rule), it's more likely that these stem from what I believe to be logical and moral conclusions that any person in search of what is right would come to, e.g., that the preferable way to treat one another is with love and kindness; that the pursuit of material gain is ultimately empty when measured against eternity; and that somehow, as human beings, we are all connected spiritually. (2002: 443)

That is, all those who teach what Moore identifies as the "golden rule" share an identity not because they are in the same historical genealogy, but because they manifest universal and ahistorical logical and moral conclusions. The appeal to an ahistorical spirit can be used to group together cultural elements across time and space that have nothing in common apart from a passing similarity (or a similarity one can anachronistically project).

Ad Hoc Classification. Similar to the above strategy, one could draw a circle around anyone or anything in history by applying a classificatory grid that groups things (present or past) according to whatever vocabulary is naturalized for the identifier. In his chapter in this volume, Steven Ramey discusses the creation of "nones"—i.e., people who don't identify with a religion—from the grid of classification employed in surveys that invite subjects to check-mark "Christian," "Muslim," "Jewish," etc. or "none." Arguably, the "nones"—the remainder of what doesn't fit the other categories—are more or less the result of the lack of imagination of those who write such surveys. There are lots of things that individuals are "not," but assuming a commonality on the basis of a negative identity is questionable. As one YouTube animator notes in his cartoons that mock Christians and the Bible, being called an "atheist" is somewhat like being called a "NonStampCollector."[4] I'm not a fan of polka music, but if I'm grouped together with all others who similarly don't prefer polka, this is not on the basis of my shared interests with them; it's the sheer result of the ad hoc grid of classification used by a classifier. As Ramey notes, this results in further naturalizing the importance of whatever identifier is at stake. When separating those who have "religion" from those who have "none," theism remains the "central classifier, reinforcing the centrality of religion."

Inconsistent Criteria of Inclusion. Last, one could organize an identity by inconsistently applying a criterion of inclusion. When dealing with an identity that carries a positive or negative valuation, one could include whomever one wishes to praise or sanction. As Leslie Dorrough Smith notes in her chapter in this volume, leftist feminist scholars may consider conservative women who advance women's rights in some way as feminist or not, based on nothing other than their personal sympathies toward the conservative women. These scholars might view women in so-called third world nations as feminists—with whom the scholars have common cause—if they advance women's rights in some respect, even if the women simultaneously accept patriarchal arrangements in the home. However, the same feminist scholars might deny the appellation "feminist" to conservative Christian women in the U.S. who also advance women's

---

4   That is, in fact, his username; see
https://www.youtube.com/user/NonStampCollector

rights in some way but accept patriarchal family relations. These scholars tend not to interrogate "the unspoken lines that designate which women will be called 'feminist' and which will be called 'conservative' or 'right-wing.'" The criterion of what counts as a "feminist" shifts depending on the sympathies of those applying the criterion.

Two Theories of Culture

How one thinks about identity may turn, in part, on one's theory of culture. A dominant folk theory of culture thinks of "culture" as something practitioners "have" or "follow," and which in some way determines the behavior of practitioners who share a common identity. This folk theory of culture is highly useful for rhetorical or propagandist purposes precisely because it assumes "that a culture is ... stable over time; it sees [culture] as closed in on itself and it assumes that this [culture] determines a specific political orientation" (Bayart 2005: 65). These assumptions permit those who use this theory to paint in broad strokes or stereotypes; it allows one to treat disparate groups "as if they were internally homogeneous, externally bounded groups, even unitary collective actors with common purposes" (Brubaker 2004: 8). Those who accept the folk theory of culture "believ[e] in the existence of identity related divinities, the primordial identities, that imperturbably traverse the centuries, each provided with its own core of authenticity" (Bayart 2005: 85).

An alternative theory of culture—the one assumed by the contributors to this volume—suggests that social actors have a practical sense or intuition that allows them to pick up, variously use, and discard elements of the cultural repertoire available to them. On this view, a "culture" or, better, "cultural repertoire" is more like a box of Legos than a set of beliefs that drive behavior. With a box of Legos one can build an indefinite number of things—nothing about the Lego blocks themselves predetermines the uses to which they will be put. On this theory of culture, nothing predetermines the behavior of those who share an identity.

In this latter view, the elements in any cultural repertoire are ambiguous, polysemic, and overdetermined in their symbolic and connotative content. In the "Christian tradition," a cross might bring to mind blood and sacrifice, or lilies and peace—consequently it might be used in a justification for going to war, or for protesting war. In addition, elements in a cultural repertoire can always be reappropriated or recycled for new purposes in new contexts. Indeed, "the main characteristic of the 'invention of tradition' is the recycling—whether instrumental or unconscious—of fragments of a more or less phantasmal past in the service of social, cultural or political innovation" (Bayart 2005: 36). Last, "reception of cultural phenomena, ideologies and institutions is never passive" (109). On the contrary, cultural repertoires "have no essential components that are inherently stable over time: old doctrines are replaced by new ones, existing rituals die out in favor of ritual innovations, and organizational structures are transformed. Innovations arise when the selection of religious elements from the repertoire changes, when existing elements are discarded or new elements are introduced" (Hammer 2009: 11).

This has particular bearing on scholarship that alleges some forms of culture are "hybrid" or "creolized." As K. Merinda Simmons notes in her chapter in this volume, when we suggest that some forms of culture result from social actors creatively mixing and matching two cultures to create a hybrid culture, we end up reifying the two source cultures we've identified, as if those source cultures weren't equally unstable. Simmons suggests that creolization "is not some unique or rare phenomenon but ... an endlessly ubiquitous one." In a sense, it's hybridity all the way down and, as such, we should consider source cultures "as every bit as contingent and subject to—if not constructed by—changes made over time and place."

Those employing the "cultural repertoire" theory of culture are unlikely to see any necessary continuity of behaviors among those who claim a shared identity, since those elements in the shared repertoire are so variably used. Knowing that someone or some group claims a shared identity or cultural repertoire tells us little to nothing about them. As Needham puts it, "It might be that the only common feature uniting the members of ... [a] symbolic class [is] that they belong together, to that class" (1979: 64). For this reason, the contributors to this volume agree that claims to a shared identity must be historicized in particular socio-political contexts, and in relation to different audiences. Claiming that one is a "Muslim" might have performed very different social work in 10th-century Iran than in 21st-century America, and even in 21st-century America such an identity claim can do different work depending on whether one is talking to an insider audience or outsiders, or whether one is speaking in New York or Alabama.

Last, it is worth noting that according to the theory of culture we assume, it is clear that not all identity claims are created equal—the effectiveness of some identity claims will depend on privilege and social power. Some groups will have the social or political power to determine their own self-identity; those with less power will have to accept the self-identity imposed upon them by others.

***

Acts of identification are strategic, and the means by which we draw lines between this and that, same and different, are complicated and often mystified. We therefore hope this volume advances critical reflexivity by encouraging scholars to look in two directions at once: both at our objects of study and at the discourses we use to create and manage those objects.

References

Baker, Kelly. 2011. *Gospel According to the Klan: The KKK's Appeal to Protestant America, 1915–1930.* Lawrence, Kansas: University Press of Kansas.

Bayart, Jean-François. 2005. *The Illusion of Cultural Identity.* Chicago: University of Chicago Press.

Bottici, Chiara. 2007. *A Philosophy of Political Myth.* Cambridge: Cambridge University Press. https://doi.org/10.1017/CBO9780511498626

Bourdieu, Pierre. 1991. *Language and Symbolic Power.* Cambridge, MA: Harvard University Press.

Brubaker, Rogers. 2004. *Ethnicity without Groups*. Cambridge, MA: Harvard University Press. https://doi.org/10.1017/CBO9780511489235.004

Cohen, Arthur A. 1969. *The Myth of the Judeo-Christian Tradition*. New York: Harper & Row.

Hammer, Olav. 2009. *Alternative Christs*. Cambridge: Cambridge University Press.

Hughes, Aaron W. 2007. *Situating Islam: The Past and Future of an Academic Discipline*. London: Equinox Publishing.

Mack, Burton L. 1995. *Who Wrote the New Testament: The Making of the Christian Myth*. San Francisco: HarperSanFrancisco.

Moore, Christopher. 2002. *Lamb: The Gospel According to Biff, Christ's Childhood Pal*. New York: Harper Collins.

Needham, Rodney. 1979. *Symbolic Classification*. Santa Monica, CA: Goodyear Publishing Company.

Neusner, Jacob. 1991. *Jews and Christians: The Myth of a Common Tradition*. London: SCM Press.

Solomon, Norman. 1996. *Judaism: A Very Short Introduction*. Oxford: Oxford University Press.

Craig Martin is Professor of Religious Studies at St Thomas Aquinas College. His research concerns theory and method in the study of religion and culture, specifically focusing on discourse analysis and ideology critique. His recent books include *Capitalizing Religion: Ideology and the Opiate of the Bourgeoisie* (Bloomsbury 2014) and *A Critical Introduction to the Study of Religion* (2nd Edition, Routledge 2017).

SITE I:
ACTS OF CLASSIFICATION

1. Nostalgia and the Discourse Concerning "Nones"

Steven W. Ramey

Discussions about those who respond to surveys as having no religion intensified when survey results reported an increase in these responses. The common identification of these respondents as "Nones" did not arise from the survey respondents themselves but involved sociologists and the media in the construction of a group from diverse respondents. This label traces back to the 1960s when Glenn Vernon encouraged greater attention to these respondents, and has been a topic of analysis ever since. Multiple surveys employ different questions and response options, and the characteristics of those identified as nones show significant diversity in practice and belief, yet many still gloss this variety as "Nones." Various organizations and institutions have used this newly constructed group for their own purposes. The formation of the nones also reflects various ideological assumptions such as individualism and nostalgia for a time with clear religious identifications. The attempt in this chapter is to understand the dynamics of the construction of the nones, which illustrates the ways identifications and groups come into existence.

Identifications, like the categories from which they arise, are not mere descriptions of people or objects within the world but construct and define those elements to which people pay attention. Often categories such as ethnicity and nationality become so naturalized that people forget about their constructed nature. This process of naturalization makes the ideological basis for the categorization, the ideas that form and maintain it, invisible to the participant in the ideological process, and those who accept the construction often project the category back into history, despite the constantly changing meanings and boundaries in the present.

The discussion of the category "Hindu" and its varied meanings historically is a commonly accepted example. From a geographical term it came to be a cultural/ethnic term, and the arrival of the British shifted it further into a label eventually defining a distinct religion. Imposing their notions of the category religion on the human activities in South Asia, the colonizers coined a new term, a new category, Hinduism, which classified human activities in a different fashion that reinforced particular assumptions of the British and began to inform the ways that many within South Asia identified themselves and their practices. The people so identified, along with most of the practices, existed prior to the coining of the term, but the ways that they were collected together, the emphases placed on one element against another, shifted with the imposition of European conceptions of what a true religion should be. Various reform movements among the people of South Asia accepted some of the British critiques to change the nature of what those identified as Hindus should do, thus naturalizing particular ideological elements that stemmed from the conception of religion that many colonizers held.[1]

As many people read elements of contemporary constructions of Hinduism back into earlier periods of the history of South Asia, it becomes difficult to conceive of Hinduism as a new category, a formation of the 19th century. It has become naturalized to the point that many people, both those who identify as Hindus and as non-Hindus, resist the assertion that "Hindu" as a religious category is a recent development. But the category Hindu is not unique in this manner. The categories identifying many communities develop within a particular historical context and reflect the ideological issues and concerns of that time.

Recent developments in the discourse relating to religion in the United States provide an opportunity to observe a similar process in the creation and naturalization of a new identification. Those who do not reference a religious affiliation in surveys include a diverse

---

1   For an overview of various disagreements on the history of the category "Hinduism," see Bloch, Keppens, and Hegde 2010.

collection of people who, in one fashion or another, do not identify according to standard religious identifications. Depending on the survey wording and the commentator, they have been described as the unaffiliated, non-religious, or nones—for "none of the above."[2] The category nones, which has become prominent recently in the public sphere in the United States, appears to arise in the late 1960s, when Glenn Vernon uses the term in an essay arguing for scholars to study those who declare no recognized religious identification (Vernon 1968). Over several decades, various works cite his essay and continue to develop a discourse surrounding the category nones, to the point that survey analysts and media outlets pick up the label and naturalize it. Some groups identify themselves as serving this (new) group, some individuals self-identify as Nones, and others see themselves competing against this community labeled nones. And thus, a new label, a new category comes into being, treating a range of disparate groups and individuals as a collective, and in doing so, naturalizing particular embedded ideological points.

The development of this collective correlates with the ongoing debate (both academic and popular) in the United States concerning the extent of the process of secularization and the future prospects for the continued dominance of particular social understandings commonly labeled as Christian. The construction of a group labeled nones also reflects a range of assumptions about individualism and the universal nature of the category religion that intersect with a particular

2   Throughout this chapter, I will apply a variety of labels to those who assert no religious identification/preference. In general, I will use the common label "nones" that has the broadest use. When describing a particular study or article, I will often employ the label that the particular author employs, sometimes as a precise term, sometimes not. As I note below, the label conflates a variety of different responses and meanings, as do many identifications. While in other writings I have proceeded differently, in this chapter I refrain from capitalizing "nones," as I use the label in a broad sense rather than a specific naming sense of a proper noun. However, when referencing people referring to themselves by the label, I will capitalize it as I understand them to intend it as a proper noun. The publications differ on their treatment of the capitalization of this label (e.g., Kosmin et al. 2009; Pew Research Center 2012a).

strand of American exceptionalism as a Christian or at least a religious nation. The formation of the nones also reflects various ideological assumptions such as individualism and nostalgia for a time with clear religious identifications. Understanding the dynamics of the construction of the nones illustrates the ways identifications and groups come into existence. Through the example of the discourse surrounding the nones label, the conception that categorizations are not simple descriptions but construct a particular world and the groups that inhabit it, drawing on a range of assumptions and ideological interests, becomes obvious.

Constructing the Nones

In his 1968 article, Vernon cites various studies referencing those without religious affiliation, but he does not attribute the nones label to any of those sources, even though he uses it as if it is a known term. He connects the term to "the last category, following 'Catholic, Jew ...', in a list headed by 'Religion'" (Vernon 1968: 219). In a footnote he references the varied conceptions of those whom he places into this statistical category, which includes "atheists, agnostics, those with 'no preference,' those with no affiliation, and also members of small groups and others who ... more properly belong in a residual or 'other' category" (219 fn 1). He emphasizes that his focus and call for further study is on those with no affiliation. However, in discussing other studies, he identifies studies that include "atheists," "militant secularists," "agnostics," implicitly equating these labels with his non-affiliation/nones label (221), though he later draws distinctions between nones as a broad category and labels such as atheist and agnostic (222). He further describes the "religious" activities of some nones, declaring, "It seems as inaccurate to consider all 'nones' to be 'of one piece' as it is to consider all Methodists to be alike in all religious matters" (224). This inconsistency of the category, as Vernon shifts between equating implicitly different categorizations and highlighting the problematic nature of employing such imprecise categories, has remained a characteristic of the discourse surrounding the unaffiliated. Unfortunately, not all have been as aware of the problem of different categorizations of nones as Vernon was in 1968, despite his own imprecision.

The imprecise nature of the categorizations of nones correlates with the central point of this chapter. The nones as a group did not exist prior to the construction of the category. The act of placing these various individuals into one category as if they formed a group suggests that their commonality existed before the creation of the category. Similarly, the language "'Nones' on the Rise" from the title of the Pew Research Center report implies an existence that has now expanded (2012a). Beyond the level of the individual analyst and published report, the diversity within the ways each analyst applies the term and the lack of consistency throughout the discourse highlight the homogenizing nature of the act of labeling. As I will demonstrate, the various references in individual statements, survey analyses, academic reflection, and media representations to those who do not identify with or state a preference for any religious label apply terms that may be technically different when compared to each other, yet readers and commentators, seeing the similarly applied labels, generally assume that these constructions represent a singular whole, despite the detailed analyses that highlight the diversity among those who are included within the category. Often, though, even the analysts themselves conflate the diversity into a single group.

Writing a decade after Vernon, Hadaway and Roof employ the term nones for those who reported that they "were raised having no religion," dividing them between those who still report no religious preference as adults, "stable nones," or those who have a religious preference and are thus "converts" (1979: 195). While the slippage between "having no religion" and "no religious preference" is limited, it is possible that some respondents to the General Social Surveys (GSS) of 1973–77 that Hadaway and Roof used could interpret those phrases differently. Considering the labeling at the time, Hadaway and Roof also connect their conception of nones with the category "unchurched" that the analysis of a late-1970s Gallup survey employed. Beyond the privileging of the frameworks of Christianity in that choice of labels, the conflation of "unchurched," "no religious preference," and "nones" illustrates further slippage (Hadaway and Roof 1979: 195).

More recent reports highlighting the significant increase in those who report no religious affiliation or preference are often relatively precise in their individual designations, even as they homogenize some respondents into a unified group. The scholars who analyzed the American Religious Identification Survey (ARIS) explicitly state, "'None' is not a movement, but a label for a diverse group of people who do not identify with any of the myriad of religious options in the American religious marketplace—the irreligious, the unreligious, the anti-religious, and the anti-clerical" (Kosmin et al. 2009: i). They, then, combine anyone who responded to the survey question "what is your religion, if any?" with any of the following: "none," "atheist," "agnostic," "secular," or "humanist," thus further acknowledging implicitly the analysts' agency in constructing the diverse grouping (Kosmin et al. 2009: ii). The report entitled "'Nones' on the Rise" from the Pew Research Center was even more cautious. Recognizing Vernon's concern in 1968 that the focus on a negative response about religious affiliation makes institutional membership the sign of being religious, the Pew report prefers the label "religiously unaffiliated" to the label nones "for those who tell us in surveys that they are atheists, agnostics, or have no particular religion"; however, since the report recognizes the terms used in popular discourse, it employs both terms, using quotation marks for the popular label "to indicate that it is a colloquialism" (2012a: 7). The end result is the same. In addition to reinforcing the developing popular label, they construct a group, choosing to include those who identify as atheist or agnostic and those who affiliate with no particular religion in a single group that remains highly diverse.

The point that these labeled groups are not pre-existing groups but constructions of the analysts remains. Kosmin et al. repeatedly use the third person plural when referring to those they label as "Nones" (which they also capitalize), which furthers the assumption that those who respond to one question in one of several ways form a cohesive group. However, they conclude, "Nones are the invisible minority in the U.S. today—invisible because their social characteristics are very similar to the majority," a similarity which they assert elsewhere is increasing, regressing to the mean as the minority grows (2009: 22, 2). Their invisibility reflects the point, according to the surveys, that those labeled as nones are as diverse on many questions as the general population, making their collection as a group even more obviously constructed. Similarly, the "considerable 'churn'" that Kosmin et al. found among their constructed group, with a significant number of people joining and leaving their ranks "quite frequently," further illustrates the absence of any group existing prior to the survey analysis, yet the analysts continue to homogenize the diversity under a singular group label (2009: 8).

These issues become even more apparent when the results of multiple surveys are combined. A 1985 study compared the religious preference question on the GSS to the 1957 Bureau of Census question about religion, in which those who responded to the question "What is your religion?" with atheist, agnostic, or no religion were all identified as nones. This analysis, therefore, conflates religious preference and various assertions of religious identification under the "none" label (Condran and Tamney 1985: 416–17). In an oft-cited 2002 study explaining the increase in those reporting no religious preference, Hout and Fischer similarly combined data from multiple surveys, including Gallup, GSS, the National Election Survey, and Pew surveys. Beyond the slight variation in the phrasing of questions in these surveys (between religious preference, religious affiliation, and simply religion), the Gallup survey alone does not include "no religion" as an option that surveyors read to respondents. The authors of the 2002 study use that variation to explain some of the different findings in the surveys (Hout and Fischer 2002: 166–7). Another study focusing on the reported number of Protestants suggests that surveys that list "Protestant" but not "no religion" in the options read to respondents generate about 3–5% more Protestants than surveys that list "no religion" among the options (Smith and Kim 2005: 213). Several analysts theorize that some respondents with a weak affiliation, such as "marginal Protestants," choose "no religion" when it is offered, another identification when it is not (Smith and Kim 2005: 218; Lim, MacGregor, and Putnam 2010: 615). The reason to combine these individuals into a group is the way that they answered a specific question on the survey, but the composite analysis of multiple surveys and the growing use of the label more generally combines responses that are not actually the same (as various analyses combine responses like atheist, agnostic, humanist, and no religion), that are not given to the same question (preference, affiliation, religion), and that are not provided the same articulated options. Moreover, each respondent may interpret their particular question and the available responses differently than another respondent to the same survey. Thus, the assertion of sameness reflects the assumptions of the analysts more than some intrinsic sameness among the respondents whom the analysts eventually group together. Despite the analytical caveats and footnotes, the end result is an assumption that the label references a group of people with characteristics that connect them beyond the way that they chose to answer a particular question on a particular survey.

The complicated nature of the constructed category is also apparent in various disagreements about who actually fits this group labeled nones. Some critics of the 2002 Hout and Fischer study question their labeling of some respondents with no preference as "religious" individuals and others as "secular" individuals based on responses to questions about belief and prayer, because this classification underreported secular individuals (Marwell and Demerath 2003: 314–15). Other scholars have used the diversity among those labeled "nonreligious" to argue the opposite, that scholars should conceptualize being "religious" more broadly to recognize that those without a religious affiliation or "traditional religiosity" actually remain religious (Baker and Smith 2009: 721). Another study contests the standard manner of determining who is unaffiliated, asserting that the narrative of the significant growth arises because changing attitudes towards denominational identity generate a subsequent misclassification of some Protestants (Dougherty, Johnson, and Polson 2007), though others contest their analysis (Smith and Kim 2007). Such disagreements correspond to my broader point that discussions of the unaffiliated are not simple descriptions of something external to those presenting the analysis but reflect a range of assumptions, selections, and interests that serve to construct the analysis and even the group itself.

The strategic nature of the practice of constructing a group is also apparent in the ways analysts have subdivided these groups. One study distinguishes between those who are "structural nones," who are generally lower-class workers who see religion as supporting management against them, and those who are "cultural nones," who reject particular beliefs associated with the religious institutions. This longitudinal study suggests that prior to 1960 most of those identifying as unaffiliated were "structural nones," and the "cultural nones" became more prominent beginning in the 1960s (Condran and Tamney 1985). In a fashion similar to Hadaway and Roof's distinction between "stable nones" and "converts," another study separates those who list no affiliation between "apostates" who left the religion of their childhood and "stable independents" who have been unaffiliated since childhood (Hayes 1995: 180). Yet another study references "liminal nones" for those who sometimes identify as nones and sometimes with a religious identification, in contrast to "stable nones" or "secular nones" who consistently identify as nones (Lim, MacGregor, Putnam 2010: 597). As these examples show, the diversity among those labeled nones is significant, allowing an array of different ways to group them, that could theoretically involve an aspect of their lives unrelated to beliefs and practices commonly defined as religious.

Complicating Characteristics

The absence of any pre-existing group is also evident within the demographic details of those labeled nones. The generalized description of the typical none is white, young, male, politically liberal, and well-educated, as each trait appears in significantly higher percentages among those labeled nones than among the general population. That composite image ignores the significant diversity, as some of those labeled nones are Hispanic, female, elderly, conservative, or limited in formal education; but also on many measures, the composite image of those labeled nones is "reverting to the mean" as the number who respond in ways identified as nones has increased (Kosmin et al. 2009: 2).

One area of characteristics that analysts have discussed significantly is belief and ritual practice. On many of these questions, the answers provided by those who respond with "no religion" (or similar response) differ statistically from those of the general population. The Pew Research Center notes, for example, that 68% of those whom they designate nones/unaffiliated "believe in a God or Universal Spirit," including 14% of those who identify themselves as atheist and 56% of agnostics, which contrasts to 91% of the general population (2012a: 48). Similarly, among the respondents to ARIS that the analysts labeled as nones, a bare majority were labeled either theists (27%) or deists (24%), compared to the large majority (70%) of U.S. adults whom they labeled as theists (Kosmin et al. 2009: 11).[3] People often respond to these numbers with surprise that the majority of those who report no religious identification largely believe in a higher power of some form, yet these figures also can be used to suggest that those labeled nones are distinct from the broader population. Of interest to me, however, is how diverse this constructed group is. If between one-half and two-thirds of this group believe in some higher power (depending on the survey analysis), then a significant portion of the group disagrees, making the group highly diverse on this question that many analysts and the general public identify as central to their conception of religion.

Similar issues arise with the discussion of regular practices that many associate with religion. The Pew report declared that 5% of those they labeled nones/unaffiliated, including 3% of atheists/agnostics, attended worship at least weekly, and an additional 22% report attending monthly or yearly. While this is significantly lower than the general population (37% attend weekly and 33% attend monthly or yearly), it challenges one of the main ways analysts (including Pew) have constructed this community, based on the lack of a relation to recognized religious institutions (2012a: 49). The Pew survey results showed a similar phenomenon concerning daily prayer, with 21% of

3   ARIS provided respondents five possible answers to their question about the existence of God, and the researchers assigned the provided responses to the following labels: "There is no such thing" represented atheist, "There is no way to know" signified hard agnostic, "I'm not sure" became soft agnostic, "There is a higher power but no personal God" was labeled deist, and "There is definitely a personal God" designated a theist (Kosmin et al. 2009:11). In relation to the question about constructed categories, the freedom with which the analysts assign these labels and interpret the survey responses in a particular fashion furthers the general point about whose assumptions become focal in these analyses.

those labeled nones/unaffiliated reporting daily prayer, compared to 66% of those who referenced an affiliation (2012a: 52). Looking at life-cycle rituals, the ARIS analysis suggests that 20% of nones antici-pate having a "religious funeral" and 43% had a "religious marriage," compared to 66% and 72%, respectively, for U.S. adults (Kosmin et al. 2009: 13). Showing that some of those grouped as the nones have prior and continuing levels of engagement with practices specifically labeled "religious," including institutional practices, these surveys of beliefs and practices confirm the diversity of this constructed group on questions that many associate with religion, making the conflation of labels like non-religious and unaffiliated highly problematic.

The data becomes even more complicated when respondents are asked about being "religious" or "spiritual." In the Pew survey, the majority of those labeled nones/unaffiliated responded that they think of themselves as either "religious" (18%) or "spiritual but not religious" (37%) (2012a: 44). Beyond illustrating the problem of equating the category nones/unaffiliated with nonreligious, the data illustrates the arbitrariness of the focus of the Pew analysts on one question. If researchers took the Pew question about being spiritual or religious as the basis for forming a similar group, calling them the "neithers" for neither religious nor spiritual, that grouping would be different from their nones/unaffiliated category, comprising 15% of the general population, 42% of those labeled nones/unaffiliated, and 8% of those asserting an affiliation (Pew Research Center 2012a: 44).

The 2013 Economic Values Survey, which included religious identification as well as various attitudes, further illustrates this point. The analysts labeled respondents as religious progressive, religious moderate, or religious conservative based on a series of questions that they had subdivided into three scales, theological questions (theism, biblical interpretation style, and the sanctity of tradition), social issues (same-sex marriage and abortion), and economic con-cerns (government intervention, wealth, healthcare, and the minimum wage) (Jones et al. 2013: 49). While those selections can obviously be debated (as can the selection within any of these surveys, as I am arguing), the end result is striking. While 82% of those whom the researchers labeled nonreligious (based on their responses to the three sets of survey questions) identified themselves as unaffiliated, 5% of the nonreligious identified as Catholic, and 4% as White Mainline Protestant (Jones et al. 2013: 50). Moreover, 18% of those whom the researchers labeled as religious progressives identified as unaffiliated, and likewise 3% of religious conservatives (Jones et al. 2013: 50). While it could be easy to read these results as problems with the labeling process in this study or the vagaries of statistical analysis, they reflect what the self-responses in other surveys about beliefs, practices, and identifications as religious or spiritual suggest: that the construction of the nones as a group is an arbitrary division rather than a description of an existing group.

While the diversity among those who report no affiliation or religious preference is significant (and more diverse than those who do report an affiliation on many questions), that diversity in itself does not undermine the existence of a group. For example, even on the denominational or local institutional level, people who report a religious affiliation often hold a range of beliefs, participate (or not) in a range of practices, and have various other ways of identifying themselves. What makes the case of the nones category more powerful is that, in addition to this diversity, these respondents generally did not maintain the same identification. Few of the respondents would have identified as a None or seen themselves as part of a group of nones prior to the survey analysis. Of course, as the later sections of this chapter analyze, some people have begun employing the "None" label for self-identification. The timing of that adoption, though, largely comes after the discourse on nones spread through the media. Thus, the construction of nones as a group is not simply an academic exercise involving the statistical significance and margin of error of survey results but has shifted both societal discourse and the self-identification of some.

Using the Nones

While scholars may primarily write for other scholars, the language, particularly the headline-ready nones label, has extended from Vernon through various analyses into the broader public discourse. As the Pew Research Center states, the popularity of the nones label in social science and the media prompted them to use the label, along with their preferred "religiously unaffiliated" label (2012a: 7). However, their decision to title their report "'Nones' on the Rise" and their release of the report through the media suggests an interest in drawing on that popularity to disseminate their findings and influence. They were particularly successful in this, as the release of that report generated further media attention to the label, as well as the attention of scholars such as myself.

The media attention encouraged some people to begin to identify themselves as Nones. More significantly, various organizations began to identify themselves as serving or representing this group, even though not one of these organizations seems to incorporate the full variety that the surveys suggest exist within it. When multiple secular humanist and atheist organizations, including the Freethought Society, Foundation Beyond Belief, and American Humanist Association, met together in January 2013 for the eighth annual Heads Meeting, they explicitly declared their intent to represent the interests of the nones politically and culturally (Merica 2013). A colleague also described a Unitarian Universalist community presenting itself as serving those whom they labeled nones, even though joining that community would mean the individual would no longer be labeled a none, at least based on the affiliation definition. When the *Huffington Post* included (in somewhat ironic terms) "The 'Nones' Get Organized" in its list of the of "Top Ten Religion Stories for 2013," the discussion focused primarily on the Sunday Assembly, a gathering of non-theists, that, therefore, represents a small portion of those labeled nones (Raushenbush 2013). These multiple organizations stepping in to organize this amorphously constructed group illustrate more than the homogenization within the dominant discourse, slipping from unaffiliated to non-religious or atheist. These organizational efforts also reflect the ways people, whether individually, collectively, or organizationally, apply these labels strategically, for themselves and for others, to promote their organizational and ideological interests.

The existence of this newly constructed group, with the survey enumerations, also became rhetorically useful for particular interests and ideologies. For example, Annie Gaylor, co-president of the Freedom From Religion Foundation, describes those she labels "nonreligious" as the second largest "denomination" in the United States (using Pew numbers for nones/unaffiliated). She further argues that atheism is a religion that must be taught alongside other religions if religious instruction takes place in public schools (Gaylor 2014). Both the denominational language and construing atheism as a religion place all people, whether identifying as nonreligious, atheist, or religious, as having a religion. This representation is ironic, as she uses it to oppose the incursion of "religion" in public institutions. Thus, the increase in the percentage of those declaring no affiliation has suggested for some individuals and organizations the decreasing influence of religion and the increase of people who, they assume, share their interests, even though the diversity of the survey data contradicts this assumption. In this fashion, groups like the Freedom From Religion Foundation construct their nonreligious category to support their own position, whatever the data (for all of its faults) might say.

In contrast, some news organizations discussed the increase in those labeled nones with individuals they recognized as religious leaders who often used the data concerning the group to promote their own perspectives. For example, Jim Wallis of Sojourners suggested that those labeled nones leave churches when they do not see the churches doing what Jesus taught, "loving their neighbors, caring for the poor, and being peacemakers in the world," and Samuel Rodriquez of the Hispanic Evangelical Association argued that those who report no affiliation want both a spiritual relationship with the divine and action towards social justice (Burke 2012). Pope Francis also declared that those who identify as nones should be allies of the church "to defend the dignity of man, in the building of a peaceful coexistence between peoples and in the careful protection of creation" (Speciale 2013). Similarly, Ellen Frankel argues for more flexible Jewish communities that allow people to engage in a variety of ways rather than "one-size-fits-all Judaism" (Frankel 2013). The prescriptions that these leaders generate to address the increase in those who respond with no affiliation or preference suggest social and institutional changes that largely happen to involve a more inclusive, socially liberal stance, partially in response to the discourse describing nones as liberal on social issues. However, many of these leaders advocated these ideas prior to the nones discourse gaining prominence. Much like the organizations promoting secularist ideas, these leaders used the constructed nones group to further their ideological positions. Doing a similar thing from a different theological position, Albert Mohler, the President of the Southern Baptist Theological Seminary, declared that the increase in those claiming no affiliation was "a healthy development," as it clarified the distinction between "authentic Christian faith and 'fuzzy fidelity'" (Mohler 2012). Whatever the theological or ideological perspective, many leaders and their organizations have used the nones category to strengthen their own ideological and theological positions often in relation to internal debate among those who identify with their respective religious label.

Those employing the malleable category nones for their own purposes extended beyond the leadership of both secularist and religious organizations. Discussions developed in 2012 surrounding the political mobilization of those labeled nones. Some commentators considered their role within the U.S. presidential election and ways the different campaigns perhaps intentionally downplayed themes commonly recognized as religious to cater to those described as nones (Berlinerblau 2013). Analysis of Barack Obama's electoral victory in 2012 suggests that he lost both the Protestant and Catholic votes in many states but prevailed by winning the votes of those labeled nones by overwhelming margins, leading an analyst with the Pew Research Center to declare the religiously unaffiliated to be "a very important, politically consequential group" (Halloran 2012). Beyond electoral politics, another commentator, who identifies himself as a None, draws on various anecdotes to suggest that the socially conservative views of some religious institutions, particularly surrounding homosexuality and abortion, have furthered the losses within these institutions, echoing the arguments of some of the religious leaders cited above (Signorile 2012). A 2013 article entitled "The Non-Religious Patriarchy" focuses on the "non-religious, atheist, and humanist movements," to question the lack of racial and gender diversity within these movements, which the author asserts remain dominated by the concerns of white males (Miller 2013: 211–12). Even though she later clarifies that the category unaffiliated includes more than the category atheist, her use of non-religious in the title, her own slippage in terms of labels, and the conflation of nonreligious and atheist with unaffiliated in the broader public discourse encourages readers to connect her ideological concerns with the nones label. The diversity among those labeled nones and the imprecision in descriptions of them make the label extremely useful in the pursuit of different ideological ends as well as in efforts to garner attention.

Scholars have used the discourse surrounding nones to address a variety of concerns. The Hout and Fischer study referenced above concludes, most notably, that the increasing association in public discourse of religion with socially conservative political positions in the 1990s was a major factor, along with demographic shifts, in the rise in numbers of those declaring no religious preference. Many who had a weak affiliation with religious organizations increasingly reported no religious preference on surveys as a type of political protest against the "Religious Right" (Hout and Fischer 2002: 188). As a professor at Harvard similarly asserted in the media, "These were the kids who were coming of age in the America of the culture wars, in the America in which religion publicly became associated with a particular brand of politics, and so I think the single most important reason for the rise of the unknowns is that combination of the younger people moving to the left on social issues and the most visible religious leaders moving to the right on that same issue" (Glenn 2013).

Other scholars have used the construction of nones as a group to explain other observations within society. In a study of the increase of survey respondents declaring that being Christian is important for being truly American, despite the growing diversity of religious identification in the nation, the analysts suggest that the changing composition within mainline Protestants (as more respondents with a weak affiliation begin identifying as nonaffiliated instead of mainline Protestants) has meant that mainline Protestants and "Other Christians" significantly increased the frequency with which they referenced "Christian America," closing the gap in such references between them and evangelical Christians (Straughn and Feld 2010: 298). Another study suggests that the increasing number of people identifying as unaffiliated is one of several factors in the eminent loss of a Protestant majority in the United States, exacerbated by the religious identification of recent immigrants and some potential misclassification (Smith and Kim 2005). Other scholars use their analysis of those labeled nones to argue over the process of secularization from various positions (Hout and Fischer 2002; Marwell and Demerath 2003; Lim, MacGregor, and Putnam 2010; Schwadel 2011). The vehemence of these debates and desire to explain the changing percentages suggest the significance that scholars and the broader public place on the conception of who is numerically in the majority and how religious society is.

The increase in those identified as nones has also generated a range of other questions that imply their existence is a problem to be explained, particularly in the context of the United States. The question of why people choose to not be affiliated has particularly arisen, both in the media and academia (NPR Staff 2013). Various scholars have studied the different aspects of disaffiliation from religious institutions (Hadaway and Roof 1979; Vargas 2012; Schwadel 2010). Embedded in such questions is an assumption that affiliation with a commonly recognized religious identification is normative, as those who choose to disaffiliate become particular objects of curiosity.

Deeper Ideological Concerns

While the questions asked and ways that organizations and individuals can use the group they label nones as a malleable symbol reflect particular ideological interests, the construction of the group within the context of survey data buttresses particular ideological interests that are less contested and more naturalized within contemporary society. The designation of a group as nones maintains the centrality and naturalness of religion. Everyone thus can be labeled according to their religious identification, even those who express no interest in religion, or affiliation with religious institutions, at least. In a similar fashion, the moniker atheist or agnostic still defines the person according to belief in the divine. Whether one believes in a divine being or not remains a central classifier, reinforcing the centrality of religion, even among those who actively reject religion. In this system, no one can escape being categorized according to a religious identification (either self-proclaimed or assigned to the person).

More specifically, the centrality of religious identifications through the design and analysis of these surveys maintains a specific conception of religious identification. Individual choice and freedom remain paramount in this designation; whether one actively chooses to affiliate or not is the defining point. Religious identification, then, is not a societal decision or an aspect of a birth, like ethnic identification is generally conceived. Thus, the conception of religion employed here correlates, as one might expect, with constructions prominent within American Christianity, perhaps more specifically American Protestantism. The historical narrative of the Great Awakenings that appear in various American history textbooks, for example, emphasize the influence of the individual freedom of choice to ascribe to particular religious beliefs and experiences. The centrality of belief in many of these surveys, with the analysts' frequent emphasis that many who respond as unaffiliated believe in a supreme being, further demonstrates that this construction reflects common American Protestant assumptions.

Such conceptions are not universal. Some within the context of South Asia suggest that people cannot convert to or from a Hindu religious identification, as that identification adheres according to birth. In the context of Japan, reports frequently emphasize people's participation in both Shinto and Buddhist life-cycle rituals without any sense that they convert between them. The assumption of a singular religious identification chosen/confirmed individually is not universal. Not only, then, does the construction of nones force survey respondents into a particular mold, but the application of the discourse surrounding nones globally universalizes these assumptions about religious identifications.[4]

This embedded ideological assumption, which the ongoing discourse continues to reinforce as natural, maintains particular societal relationships. Despite the increase in those identified as nones, the institutions that society considers religious remain central in the discourse and in the surveys themselves. Surveys that receive significant

4   The Pew Research Center report entitled "The Global Religious Landscape" declared that the unaffiliated formed "the third-largest religious group worldwide" (2012b: 1).

academic and media attention within public discourse typically do not ask people if they are members of amateur sports teams or fan clubs and then focus the reporting on those who opt out of any of those groups. It would seem odd to create a group, with the demographic data to support it, of the "anti-athletics" who do not participate in amateur sports teams or root for major sports teams. The naturalness of the unaffiliated designation, and the response that it generates, both reflects the centrality of religious institutions and individual choice and reinforces that centrality.

Some of the subsequent handwringing in the media and among institutional leaders concerning the increase of those labeled nones reflects a sense of nostalgia for a period in which religious identification was simpler and assumed. An image of the United States, in which most everyone identified as Protestant or Catholic (or Jewish in a few cases) and met at the local church on Sundays, remains, despite its idealized construction. The changes in reported identifications, then, correlate with concerns over increasing secularization and other current social issues, from crime and economic uncertainty to sexuality and drug use, that generate discomfort and fear for some. The disciplining of the unaffiliated into a religious identification at least allows the continued universality of that form of identification. The increase in the number of people who assert that being Christian is important for being truly American highlights both the connection of America with religion for some and the ways current changes in society influence some to become more strident in their proclamation of a Christian America (Straughn and Feld 2010). The various scholars who have debated the numerical dominance of Protestants and the counting of those identified as unaffiliated suggest that some see significance, or perhaps even a problem, in the predicted shift in the designation of Protestants as the majority (Dougherty, Johnson, and Polson 2007; Smith and Kim 2007; Smith and Kim 2005). Beyond the dispute over the data and how to explain it, the debate itself suggests the significance of religious identification in individual perception, public discourse (often hyped in the media), and academic discussions.

Asking those without a religious identification to place themselves into a religiously oriented category also reinforces a particular conception of America. One form of national identification is the unique significance of religion in the United States, sometimes termed American religious exceptionalism (Straughn and Feld 2010: 283; Tiryakian 1993; Warf and Winsberg 2008: 413–14). For example, during the Cold War, "under God" was added to the Pledge of Allegiance to maintain the U.S. contrast to the godless atheism of the Soviet Union. As Europe has become less overtly Christian, American religiosity has also served to distinguish the United States from European nations. Some of the discourse concerning nones directly references the United States as overtly religious (e.g., Hout and Fischer 2002: 165). Thus, this disciplining of those labeled nones, forcing them into a religious identification that reinforces the centrality of institutions deemed religious, intersects with concerns about a loss of American identity and cohesion. If a significant portion of the American population simply ignores religion, then the threat is not only to powerful institutions but also to America's distinctiveness.

This conception of individual choice further correlates with particular aspects of American sensibilities. Beyond the idolization of individualism and related freedoms, American society largely revolves around individual consumption from a smorgasbord of choice. Not only do various analyses of contemporary religious practices in the United States (not limited to these surveys) employ the language of the marketplace in relation to individual religious choice (Kosmin et al. 2009: i; Roof 1999; Wuthnow 1998), but the approach to practice and identification that the surveys validate also reinforces the training that we receive to be selective, informed consumers (who, above all else, consume things). This assertion is not intended as a critique of the language of the religious marketplace or capitalist consumption but as a consideration of the confluence of ideological positions within the discourse concerning nones. The survey form and language forces all respondents, those interested in religion and those not interested, into a frame of consumption as individuals who select their preference or affiliation, whatever their views of the concept religion and the consumption of spirituality. It becomes impossible to resist the demands of consumption.

Conclusion

In all of this discussion of nones as a newly constructed group that serves to mitigate the threat to national cohesion, the complex nature of identifications more generally should not be forgotten. To what extent are the complexities of "nones" as a group different from those of other labeled groups? Certainly, any grouping, whether alumni of a particular educational institution or members of a local congregation (not to mention a denomination) have a huge range of differences in terms of commitment to their community, beliefs, and practices. So the argument that those labeled nones are too diverse, too complicated to be lumped into a single group is only a part of the assertion.

One part of my own background that encouraged me to pursue reflections on the new label nones is my research on colonial India. While scholars often debate this point, many find convincing the assertion that a "Hindu" identification and a "Sikh" identification uniting different groups across the subcontinent as religious communities arose within the context of British rule in the 19th century. For one element, the census of India began enumerating people according to religious identification (as understood by the colonizers) (Oddie 2010; Jones 1981). Many of the respondents did not have a clear religious identification at that time, although some notions of Hindu intersecting with what the colonizers would term religion existed, but the process of enumeration and subsequent application of those numbers for particular benefits led communities to begin to take those labels seriously, argue over who was included and not in different classifications and enumerations, and begin to use the labels for themselves, according to their own interests. Some people presented themselves as representing a community that comprised smaller groups and individuals who might never have seen themselves as united before this time (Freitag 1989; King 2010; Oberoi 1994; Haan 2005).

The parallels to the discourse surrounding nones are quite powerful. I began to wonder if we in the U.S. were observing the creation of a new "religious" community and identification that would become naturalized over time. Consideration of these issues allows us to ponder the processes by which this construction of a collective identification may have happened before. While all such labels did not arise in response to the enumeration process defining distinct communities, evidence suggests that the early adherents of particular philosophies or followers of particular leaders did not always see themselves as starting a new religion or a new identification, let alone employing the label that is used today. The Israelites leaving Egypt (if the Biblical account is accurate), the early followers of Jesus, and the disciples of the Buddha, to name three groups, did not identify according to contemporary labels, if they identified according to any label at all. In other words, the labels that we commonly recognize as religious identifications are often strategic anachronisms, more recent terms applied back to the founder or earliest adherents according to the traditional narratives. The nostalgia for the old identifications, the stable categories of Protestant, Catholic, Jewish (and others) cloaks this constructed nature. Those labels themselves developed in particular historical moments, went through a variety of transitions, and became naturalized, homogenized categories, so that someone who identifies with a teacher of Zen Buddhism or with a United Methodist Church, for example, envisions themself as connected to people throughout the world who identify as Buddhist or Christian, respectively, as well as various devotees and leaders throughout history to whom they apply those labels. While those now labeled nones differ from those labeled Buddhist or Christian in these surveys because few among those labeled nones saw themselves as part of that community before the discourse became prominent, all of these groups are constructed fictions infused with various ideological interests.

Applying the label back in time, as a strategic anachronism, hides the work involved in maintaining the sense of unity under the label, despite the diversity that it entails. Recognizing how the process of community formation requires significant effort (that the naturalization of the community within the discourse cloaks) allows for a more dynamic consideration of the process of social formation and maintenance. Not only are nones constructed as a group, but those groups labeled as Greek Orthodox, Baptist, Theravadin, Jewish, Muslim, Hindu, etc., are all constructed communities naturalized through the application of identification labels. Like cultural identities (to paraphrase Jean-François Bayart 2005), identifications that we recognize as religious are illusions that have significant influence on individuals, communities, and society at large.

References

Baker, Joseph O'Brian and Buster Smith. 2009. "None Too Simple: Examining Issues of Religious Nonbelief and Nonbelonging in the United States." *Journal for the Scientific Study of Religion* 48(4): 719–33. https://doi.org/10.1111/j.1468-5906.2009.01475.x

Bayart, Jean-François. 2005. *The Illusion of Cultural Identity*. Translated by Steven Rendall, Janet Roitman, Cynthia Schoch, and Jonathan Derrick. London: Hurst & Company.

Berlinerblau, Jacques. 2013. "Who Are the Nones and Why Did They Vote for Obama?" *Huffington Post* (11 February 2013). http://www.huffingtonpost.com/jacques-berlinerblau/who-are-the-nones-and-why-did-they-vote-for-obama_b_2611842.html (accessed 1 November 2013).

Bloch, Esther, Marianne Keppens, and Rajaram Hegde (eds.). 2010. *Rethinking Religion in India: The Colonial Construction of Hinduism*. Routledge South Asian Religion Series. London and New York: Routledge.

Burke, Daniel. 2012. "Religious Leaders Respond to the Rise of the 'Nones'". NHCLC (16 October). http://nhclc.org/2012/10/16/religious-leaders-respond-to-the-rise-of-the-nones/ (accessed 27 May 2014).

Condran, John G. and Joseph B. Tamney. 1985. "Religious 'Nones': 1957 to 1982." *Sociological Analysis* 46(4): 415–23. https://doi.org/10.2307/3711157

Dougherty, Kevin D., Byron R. Johnson, and Edward C. Polson. 2007. "Recovering the Lost: Remeasuring U.S. Religious Affiliation." *Journal for the Social Scientific Study of Religion* 46(4): 483–99. https://doi.org/10.1111/j.1468-5906.2007.00373.x

Frankel, Ellen. 2013. "Jewish 'Nones' and the Question of Choice." *Huffington Post* (9 April). http://www.huffingtonpost.com/ellen-frankel/the-religiously-unaffiliated-and-the-question-of-choice_b_3033462.html (accessed 28 May 2014).

Freitag, Sandria B. 1989. *Collective Action and Community: Public Arenas and the Emergence of Communalism in North India*. Berkeley, CA: University of California Press.

44 *Strategic Acts in the Study of Identity*

Gaylor, Annie Laurie. 2014. "The Dangers of Religious Instruction in Public Schools." *Religion and Politics: Fit for Polite Company* (7 January). http://religionandpolitics.org/2014/01/07/the-dangers-of-religious-instruction-in-public-schools/ (accessed 8 January 2014).

Glenn, Heidi. 2013. "Losing Our Religion: The Growth of the 'Nones'." *National Public Radio Morning Edition, Losing Our Religion Series* (13 January). http://www.npr.org/blogs/thetwo-way/2013/01/14/169164840/losing-our-religion-the-growth-of-the-nones (accessed 14 January 2013).

Haan, Michael. 2005. "Numbers in Nirvana: How the 1872–1921 Indian Censuses Helped Operationalise 'Hinduism'." *Religion* 35(1): 13–30. https://doi.org/10.1016/j.religion.2005.02.003

Hadaway, C. Kirk and Wade Clark Roof. 1979. "Those Who Stay Religious 'Nones' and Those Who Don't: A Research Note." *Journal for the Scientific Study of Religion* 18(2): 194–200. https://doi.org/10.2307/1385940

Halloran, Liz. 2012. "Add This Group to Obama's Winning Coalition: 'Religiously Unaffiliated'." *National Public Radio* (9 December). http://www.npr.org/blogs/itsallpolitics/2012/12/09/166753248/add-this-group-to-obamas-winning-coalition-religiously-unaffiliated (accessed 30 May 2014).

Hayes, Bernadette C. 1995. "The Impact of Religious Identification on Political Attitudes: An International Comparison." *Sociology of Religion* 56(2): 177–94. https://doi.org/10.2307/3711762

Hout, Michael and Claude S. Fischer. 2002. "Why More Americans Have No Religious Preference: Politics and Generations." *American Sociological Review* 67(2): 165–90. https://doi.org/10.2307/3088891

Jones, Kenneth W. 1981. "Religious Identity and the Indian Census." In Norman Barrier, ed., *The Census in British India: New Perspectives*, 73–101. New Delhi: Manohar.

Jones, Robert P., Daniel Cox, Juhem Navarro-Rivera, E.J. Dionne Jr., and William A. Galston. 2013. *Do Americans Believe Capitalism and Government Are Working? Religious Left, Religious Right, and the Future of Economic Debate: Findings from the Economic Values Survey*. Washington, DC: Public Religion Research Institute and The Brookings Institution. http://publicreligion.org/site/wp-content/uploads/2013/07/2013-Economic-Values-Report-Final-.pdf (accessed 19 July 2013).

King, Richard. 2010. "Colonialism, Hinduism, and the Discourse of Religion." In Esther Bloch, Marianne Keppens, and Rajaram Hegde, eds., *Rethinking Religion in India: The Colonial Construction of Hinduism*, 95–113. Routledge South Asian Religion Series. London and New York: Routledge.

Kosmin, Barry A., Ariela Keysar, Ryan Cragun, Juhem Navarro-Rivera. 2009. "American Nones: The Profile of the No Religion Population: A Report Based on the American Religious Identification Survey 2008." Published by the Program on Public Values at Trinity College and the Institute for the Study of Secularism in Society and Culture. http://commons.trincoll.edu/aris/publications/2008-2/american-nones-the-profile-of-the-no-religion-population/ (accessed 8 November 2012).

Lim, Chaeyoon, Carol Ann MacGregor, and Robert D. Putnam. 2010. "Secular and Liminal: Discovering Heterogeneity Among Religious Nones." *Journal for the Scientific Study of Religion* 49(4): 596–618. https://doi.org/10.1111/j.1468-5906.2010.01533.x

Marwell, Gerald and N.J. Demerath, III. 2003. "'Secularization' by Any Other Name." *American Sociological Review* 68(2): 314–16. https://doi.org/10.2307/1519771

Merica, Dan. 2013. "'None' Leaders to Chart Path for More Political, Cultural Power for Religiously Unaffiliated." CNN (25 January). http://religion.blogs.cnn.com/2013/01/25/none-leaders-to-chart-path-for-more-political-cultural-power-for-religiously-unaffiliated/ (accessed 18 February 2013).

Miller, Ashley F. 2013. "The Non-Religious Patriarchy: Why Losing Religion HAS NOT Meant Losing White Male Dominance." *Cross Currents* 63(2): 211–26. https://doi.org/10.1111/cros.12025.

Mohler, Albert. 2012. "The Great Clarification: Fuzzy Fidelity and the Rise of the Nones." Individual blog (16 October). http://www.albertmohler.com/2012/10/16/the-great-clarification-fuzzy-fidelity-and-the-rise-of-the-nones/ (accessed 27 May 2014).

NPR Staff. 2013. "More Young People Are Moving Away From Religion, But Why?" *National Public Radio Morning Edition, Losing Our Religion Series* (15 January). http://www.npr.org/2013/01/15/169342349/more-young-people-are-moving-away-from-religion-but-why (accessed 16 January 2013).

Oberoi, Harjot. 1994. *The Construction of Religious Boundaries: Culture, Identity and Diversity in the Sikh Tradition.* Oxford and New York: Oxford University Press. (Reprint, Delhi: Oxford India Paperbacks, 1997).

Oddie, Geoffrey A. 2010. "Hindu Religious Identity with Special Reference to the Origin and Significance of the term 'Hinduism', c. 1787–1947." In Esther Bloch, Marianne Keppens, and Rajaram Hegde, eds., *Rethinking Religion in India: The Colonial Construction of Hinduism*, 41–55. Routledge South Asian Religion Series. London and New York: Routledge.

Pew Research Center. 2012a. "'Nones' on the Rise: One-in-Five Adults Have No Religious Affiliation." Pew Forum (9 October). http://www.pewforum.org/files/2012/10/NonesOnTheRise-full.pdf (accessed 15 October 2012).

Pew Research Center. 2012b. "The Global Religious Landscape: A Report on the Size Distribution of the World's Major Religious Groups as of 2010." Pew Forum (18 December). http://www.pewforum.org/2012/12/18/global-religious-landscape-exec/ (accessed 30 December 2012).

Raushenbush, Paul Brandeis. 2013. "The Top 10 Religion Stories Of 2013." *Huffington Post* (16 December). http://www.huffingtonpost.com/2013/12/16/religion-stories-2013-_n_4434068.html (accessed 20 December 2013).

Roof, Wade Clark. 1999. *Spiritual Marketplace: Baby Boomers and the Remaking of American Religion.* Princeton, NJ: Princeton University Press.

Schwadel, Philip. 2010. "Period, and Cohort Effects on Religious Non-affiliation and Religious Disaffiliation: A Research Note." *Journal for the Scientific Study of Religion* 49(2): 311–19. https://doi.org/10.1111/j.1468-5906.2010.01511.x

Schwadel, Philip. 2011. "Age, Period, and Cohort Effects on Religious Activities and Beliefs." *Social Science Research* 40: 181–92. https://doi.org/10.1016/j.ssresearch.2010.09.006

Signorile, Michelangelo. 2012. "'Nones' on the Rise: How Anti-Gay, Anti-Choice Churches Are Creating Their Own Demise." *Huffington Post* (15 October). http://www.huffingtonpost.com/michelangelo-signorile/nones-on-the-rise-how-ant_b_1966453.html (accessed 1 November 2013).

Smith, Tom W. and Seokho Kim. 2005. "The Vanishing Protestant Majority." *Journal for the Scientific Study of Religion* 44(2): 211–23. https://doi.org/10.1111/j.1468-5906.2005.00277.x

Smith, Tom W. and Seokho Kim. 2007. "Counting Religious Nones and Other Religious Measurement Issues: A Comparison of the Baylor Religion Survey and General Social Survey." *GSS Methodological Report No. 110* (April/Revised May). http://publicdata.norc.org:41000/gss/documents/MTRT/MR110%20Counting%20Religious%20Nones%20and%20Other%20Religious%20Measurement%20Issues.pdf (accessed 3 June 2014).

Speciale, Alessandro. 2013. "Pope Francis: 'Nones' Can Be 'Allies' For The Church." *Huffington Post* (20 March). http://www.huffingtonpost.com/2013/03/20/pope-francis-nones-can-be-allies-for-the-church_n_2917607.html (accessed 28 May 2014).

Straughn, Jeremy Brook and Scott L. Feld. 2010. "America as a 'Christian Nation'? Understanding Religious Boundaries of National Identity in the United States." *Sociology of Religion* 71(3): 280–306.
https://doi.org/10.1093/socrel/srq045

Tiryakian, Edward A. 1993. "American Religious Exceptionalism: A Reconsideration." *The Annals of the American Academy of Political and Social Science* 527: 40–54.
https://doi.org/10.1177/0002716293527001004

Vargas, Nicholas. 2012. "Retrospective Accounts of Religious Disaffiliation in the United States: Stressors, Skepticism, and Political Factors." *Sociology of Religion* 73(2): 200–23. https://doi.org/10.1093/socrel/srr044

Vernon, Glenn M. 1968. "The Religious 'Nones': A Neglected Category." *Journal for the Scientific Study of Religion* 7(2): 219–29.
https://doi.org/10.2307/1384629

Warf, Barney and Mort Winsberg. 2008. "The Geography of Religious Diversity in the United States." *The Professional Geographer* 60(3): 413–24. https://doi.org/10.1080/00330120802046786

Wuthnow, Robert. 1998. *After Heaven: Spirituality in America Since the 1950s*. Berkeley, CA: University of California Press.
https://doi.org/10.1525/california/9780520213968.001.0001

Steven W. Ramey is a professor in the Department of Religious Studies at the University of Alabama, where he also directs the Asian Studies program. He works on contested identifications in contemporary India and beyond and has published three books, *Hindu, Sufi, or Sikh* (Palgrave 2008), *Writing Religion* (University of Alabama Press 2015), and *Fabricating Difference* (Equinox 2017), along with a variety of articles.

2. Response to Steven Ramey

The Constitutive Discourse of Description

Vaia Touna

Descriptions, as Steven Ramey convincingly argued in his chapter, are never neutral, they are always selective, contingent, and invested with interests; yet, even in his attempt to demonstrate the constructive nature of discourses via the use of descriptions Ramey, unavoidably, engages in descriptions as well. So, in this chapter I want to press him further by asking: when are descriptions mere descriptions and when are they constitutive of a discourse themselves?

Descriptions always involve the use of categories—this is a myth and that is a scripture, or that ritual lasted a long time and this other one went by rather quickly, etc.—which, in the service of classification, allows us, as Mary Douglas wrote in her well-known book, *Purity and Danger* (1966), to "impose system in an inherently untidy experience" (4). It is often the case, though, that not only people in general but, many times, scholars as well take *their* categories and *their* descriptions as objective representations of realities, and the use of them as doing something different from theorizing. For example, in the Preface of his book, *Ancient Greek Religion* (2010), Jon D. Mikalson writes:

> And, finally, this book is largely descriptive, based on the ancient evidence that survives, and it limits discussion of modern theoretical interpretations of these complex subjects. Over the last hundred and fifty years a number of theoretical systems to explain major elements of Greek religion have come and sometimes gone. These theoretical approaches hold great interest in themselves, *but one needs to know what the Greeks*

themselves did and said about their religion before one can
adequately apply or evaluate the various theoretical systems to
explain it all. (xv; emphasis added)

Mikalson—like most all of us, probably—here distinguishes between theorizing and describing, seeing each as two different and, if not opposing then at least sequential processes by which knowledge is produced. Yet, in his effort to just describe what Greeks (that is, ancient Greeks) themselves thought of their religion, he uncritically (because unknowingly or unreflectively) imposes (on the ancient world he wishes to just describe), a category, i.e., "religion," which, as many scholars have argued, was utterly unknown to them; and therefore, in merely describing the features of this thing called Ancient Greek religion Mikalson imposes a modern classificatory system unfamiliar to the way ancient Greeks likely organized their own world (given that the Latin-based roots of our word had yet to be developed, let alone refined into the modern term that we take religion to be today). So, despite Mikalson's effort to avoid "interpretations of these complex subjects," the very use of the category "religion" is an interpretation itself and thus hardly an innocent description of the so-called facts on the ground;[1] his classification of this long-past world therefore tells

1   For example in Plato's *Euthyphro* we read: "πλείονος ἔργου ἐστίν πάντα ταῦτα ὡς ἔχει μαθεῖν· τόδε μέντοι σοι ἁπλῶς λέγω, ὅτι ἐάν μέ κεχαρισμένα τις ἐπίστηται τοῖς θεοῖς λέγειν τε καί πράττειν εὐχόμενός τε καί θύων, ταῦτ᾽ἔστι τά ὅσια, καί σώζει τά τοιαῦτα τούς τε ἰδίους οἴκους καί τά κοινά τῶν πόλεων· τά δ᾽ἐναντία τῶν κεχαρισμένων ἀσεβῆ, ἅ δή καί ἀνατρέπει ἅπαντα καί ἀπόλλυσιν" (14b). Mikalson translates the passage as follows: "if someone knows how to say and do in his prayers and sacrifices what is pleasing to the gods, these things are religiously correct (ὅσια) and save private households and the common interests of the city. But the opposites of those pleasing things are religiously incorrect (ἀσεβῆ), and they overthrow and destroy everything" (2010: 23) Mikalson translates two ancient Greek terms (ὅσια and ἀσεβῆ) as relating to religion, when these terms seem to have a more complex meaning in the ancient world, meaning that involves proper behaviors not only towards gods but generally towards others, of knowing, for example, one's own position within various social relationships. But once the term "religion" or "religious" gets inserted into the translation of the ancient text it is difficult to see anything but religion in the ancient world, and consequently religious behaviors.

us more about his world and how we in the present (i.e., his readers) divide and organize our social world rather than that of the ancient Greeks—which perhaps makes evident just how thorny a problem it is to distinguish description from theory.

The problem we encounter when just trying to name and describe the ancients, I would suggest, is not any different from the way the category "nones" functions in interpretations of surveys inasmuch as it imposes an interpretation and identity on the respondents, and eventually assists those interpreting them to construct a reality, a group—that of the nones—which scholars then seek to describe as self-evidently existing while only later attempting to explain them. Again: the problem of description and theory arises.

With this in mind, reading Steven Ramey's chapter, "Nostalgia and the Discourse Concerning 'Nones,'" made perfect sense and accorded with my own understanding of how categories (and, through them, scholarly descriptions) actively constitute what we take to be "the past." So his analysis of the constitutive nature of this category, "none," was welcome, especially given what seems to be the rather uncritical use of the term by many in either the media or academia (inasmuch as they now seek to understand how the nones will vote in this or that election). But then, to press the problem of description and theory a little further, in a self-reflexive manner, I started thinking about Ramey's *own* descriptions, that is, to what degree they were also deeply implicated in constituting, rather than describing, the world as he sees it. In fact, I found myself asking: Did I agree with or was I persuaded by Ramey's chapter because he accurately describes a process of a constructed identity—that of the nones—or is it because he and I share a certain kind of intellectual, even social, affiliation that, upon first reading his chapter, I failed to see the work of his own descriptions in the constitution of not just his argument but also his data and conclusions? So, as may be evident at this point, I'm not going to be discussing the category "nones," for Ramey has certainly convinced me about its constructed nature; rather, what I want to explore in this brief response, and thereby invite Ramey to elaborate upon, is: when are descriptions mere descriptions and when are they constitutive of a discourse themselves? To rephrase, making the self-reflexive turn of current scholarship quite explicit: how does his analysis of those who describe the traits of nones apply to his own analysis of the traits of those whom he describes as being scholars of the nones?

Before I proceed, I wish to make clear that I'm not trying to be cute or play a game of "gotch'a" with Ramey, for this is a problem that I see not just throughout scholarship but in my own work as well—perhaps an unavoidable one (more on this below). So, for those of us who trouble the seemingly commonsense distinction between "mere" description and subsequently theory—and it is a distinction with which, as my opening makes clear, I have great difficulty—where does that end?

Now, unlike Mikalson, who takes his very modern category "religion" and projects it into the ancient Greek world as if the category was native to the "Greeks themselves," Ramey examines exactly the opposite; how certain categories like "the nones" (similarly to how the category "religion" is used by many scholars) come to be naturalized as if they are describing self-evidences. For instance, in his opening paragraph Ramey writes: "Identifications, like the categories from which they arise, are not mere descriptions of people or objects within the world but construct and define those elements to which people pay attention." I surely could not agree more with this opening line. In fact, in my own work I looked exactly at how categorization, and therefore description, construct certain kinds of identities; yet, what I want to press further here, and thereby tweak a little, is that descriptions construct and define not only "those elements to which people pay attention" but also those elements *scholars* want people to pay attention to.

To be more specific, a few lines later, after Ramey recognizes the role of description in the constitution of identities, and before going on to explore exactly that in his example of the constructed nature of the category "nones," he writes:

> The discussion of the category "Hindu" and its varied meanings historically is a commonly accepted example. From a geographical term it came to be a cultural/ethnic term, and the arrival of the British shifted it further into a label eventually defining a distinct religion. Imposing their notions of the category religion on the human activities in South Asia, the colonizers coined a new

> term, a new category, Hinduism, which classified human activities in a different fashion that reinforced particular assumptions of the British and began to inform the ways that many within South Asia identified themselves and their practices.

Here, as most would undoubtedly read him, Ramey seems to simply be describing what was happening in India during the 19th century; in fact, in his conclusion to the chapter he further supports such a description: first by pointing to other contemporary scholars who have made a similar argument, but also in his descriptions of the perceptions people in India had of the term "religion." As might now be obvious, I'm curious about the status of these claims, given what I'm calling the problem of description and theory: are they descriptive or constitutive?

Even in his description of the history of the "discourse surrounding the category nones," as with any narrative, Ramey (again, inevitably?) makes his own choices in creating his account. For example, consider the origin of the term, located as it is in the late 1960s (what we might study as an origins discourse driven by contemporary interests?), or when, for instance, he describes how the construction of the group "reflects a range of assumptions about individualism and the universal nature of the category religion that intersect with a particular strand of American exceptionalism as a Christian or at least a religious nation." Not unlike my own above critique of Mikalson's work, perhaps, one might conclude that this description bares all the marks of the author's own time, when concern has been focused on examining liberal individualism and the historical limitations of the category religion—a focus that may tell us little about those being studied and everything about the one carrying out the study.

At this point I should be explicit and note that it would be a mistake to think that I'm critiquing Ramey here since this is actually a common practice among many scholars who tried to expose how certain identities got naturalized by 18th- and 19th-century scholars, starting with no less figures than Michel Foucault and Hayden White. In fact, I consider myself to be part of this trend. On many occasions in my own recent book, *Fabrications of the Greek Past,* I *described* how scholars (for example, in the 19th and early 20th century) have interpreted Euripides' tragedy *Hippolytus* (even in the opening to this very response I have made a similar move, *describing* Mikalson's work). For instance, I examined how André-Jean Festugiére, writing in 1912, presented the main character of the play by employing anachronistically the term "personal religiosity," both in his interpretation of the play itself as well as in his description of its lead character. For it seemed to me that Festugiére, projecting backwards in time his anachronistic category "personal religiosity," was constituting/ fabricating a certain kind of reality for the ancient world—one that was appealing to him and readers in the early 20th-century world. But, in my *description* of this early 20th-century scholar—that is, Festugiére—did I not also *constitute* Festugiére as an item of discourse, doing so with my own so-called descriptions of his work? In fact, to make my point of how scholars fabricate the past writing from a certain historical period, and thereby make evident their own disciplinary present position, I too made choices in writing that book— choices about which scholars to use and therefore to describe. So in a way I too, writing from a specific historical period and influenced by my own disciplinary rules and interests, was implicated in the fabrication of the broader discourse of an ancient play. For, taking my own theoretical interests seriously (and, yes, self-reflexively) means that I may have to inquire what the relationship is—if any at all!— between the Festugiére of my book and the actual (and now past) human being. For if, as others have instructed us, the author is truly dead, then the distinction between innocent or accurate description, on the one hand, and subsequently theorizing those descriptions, on the other, falls apart. All we have are readings of readings, always at an indeterminate distance from some actual situation on the ground that could be said to have been observed accurately.

Or, as Steven Ramey rightly observes: "Often categories ... become so naturalized that people forget about their constructed nature"— and I think that scholars forget about the constitutive nature of their own discourses, especially those with which they happen to be in agreement.

To give another example: in my effort to understand better how the past is constituted through present-day discourses, my current project involves participant observations and interviews with archaeologists and residents of a community in northern Greece, where there is/was an archaeological dig. In my preparation for the interviews I had to submit my plan to our campus's IRB (Institutional Review Board), an application that, once approved, would guarantee that my research would not pose potential harm to the people I would be interviewing. Among the things that I had to submit was a list of questions that I intended to ask the interviewees. In devising these questions I soon enough realized (as ethnographers before me have for some years, to be sure) that there is a complex way by which scholars constitute their object of study by presenting it as if they are merely describing people through their disengaged observations, and interviews. For the idea of listening carefully, in a non-judgmental way, to the people on the ground seems to secure a more accurate, objective way to proceed with one's research, in order to have a better (i.e., accurate, not biased or skewed) understanding of them. Yet, I realized while I was preparing those questions for my research, the fact that I had to prepare questions for the IRB process already signaled that I was not simply listening to the people on the ground but, rather, that I was perhaps deeply implicated in crafting the conclusions to be reached by this research, long before I started. In asking local residents and archaeologists these prepared questions about how they conceive of that thing we call "the past," I could, in fact, be subtly forcing them to think of a category and a topic that they might not have thought of, at least not prior to talking with me on a hot Greek summer afternoon. For before I even started describing and then analyzing their responses to my questions, I had already set my own criteria that had informed the questions I would ask as well as what segments of their long answers would be used to answer my own theoretical questions (for, as anyone who has conducted fieldwork knows all too well, not everything participants say will be of relevance). So, long before I started the interviews about that thing we call "the past," and long before I started describing those people's discourses, I myself as well as my institution had already been implicated in making possible, maybe even shaping or creating, any eventual description.

Now, to draw this to a close, in hopes that Ramey will see my response as a friendly invitation for him to help me to complicate my own work, I simply ask: is description itself a problem? And if so, then when or in which cases? Is this problem something we cannot avoid? And if so, how do we acknowledge, and then overcome it in our own work? Does my initial "failure" (is it even a failure?) to see Ramey's descriptions as themselves constituting a discourse along with its various objects have something to do with our shared social worlds and intellectual interests (we are interlocutors in this book, after all, and work in the same Department, both being members of the same research collaboration—our overlaps are therefore considerable)? Is this similar to the way the category "nones" eventually becomes a useful tool for the individuals and groups it at first constituted? Is this "granting of the problem" a form of implicit authorization that we, as scholars, should be identifying for our readers in order to not just proceed with *our* work but, perhaps, scrutinize it as well? For if we take seriously our critique of how scholars construct realities though identification processes, one justification for which is their use of the categories by which they come to identify/describe phenomena in the world, then shouldn't we recognize (or, if we already see it, then at least admit) that there is *no* special or privileged position from which a scholar can see and then describe things *as they really are*? But, as my final question to Ramey, what are the implications of reaching the point of such a realization, and would such an acknowledgment help shape our own work?

Or would it be the end of it?

References

Douglas, Mary. 2002 (1966). *Purity and Danger: An Analysis of Concept of Pollution and Taboo*. London: Routledge.
https://doi.org/10.4324/9780203361832

Festugiére, André-Jean. 1954 (1912). *Personal Religion among the Greeks*. Berkeley and Los Angeles: University of California Press.

Mikalson, Jon D. 2010. *Ancient Greek Religion*. 2nd Edition. UK: Wiley-Blackwell.

Touna, Vaia. 2017. *Fabrications of the Greek Past: Religion, Tradition, and the Making of Modern Identities*. Leiden and Boston: Brill of the Netherlands.

Vaia Touna is Assistant Professor in the Department of Religious Studies at the University of Alabama. She is author of *Fabrications of the Greek Past: Religion, Tradition, and the Making of Modern Identities* (Brill, 2017). Her research focuses on the sociology of religion, acts of identification and social formation, as well as methodological issues concerning the study of religion and the past in general.

3. Reply to Vaia Touna

Situated Descriptions

Steven W. Ramey

Building on Vaia Touna's response to my chapter on the construction of the nones, I argue that our academic descriptions should reflect the contingent nature of descriptions that Touna emphasizes. Any description of past actions, an item, or a scholar's work makes selections and emphases that create the object of its discussion. Rather than arguing that some descriptions are true and others are false, I suggest that descriptions can be more or less convincing and valuable. I propose three ways of analyzing any description's incompleteness, including its correspondence to evidence, the coherence of the connections presented, and the classifications employed. Then I propose three strategies to be more self-reflexive about the contingency of descriptions and their role in constituting the object of their discourse, and I demonstrate some of those strategies by rewriting a paragraph of my original chapter in which I failed to acknowledge the limited nature of the narrative.

Descriptions are always theory laden.
—Hans Penner (1989: 42)

In the quote above, Penner asserts the same point that Touna has argued. Assumptions about what makes certain elements distinct from others, how those things relate, and what things are significant —in essence, a theory of how the world functions (whether articulated or not)—determine what people include in any particular description. The creation of descriptions involves choices that construct the objects of the description, and thus the world; they do not simply describe the world in a form that existed before the description. As

Touna notes, a reader's response often depends on whether the narrator's theoretical conceptions and assumptions match those of the reader. Touna extends this point further in her response to my original chapter in order to highlight how our descriptions of other scholars and commentators, and even our descriptions of each other, are not simple descriptions but construct the other interlocutor and their assertions according to our own theoretical assumptions.

To push this further, when Touna describes my writing and thus constitutes me as her object of discourse, that constituted object is not the same me as the one writing this reply. Not only is the same thing true of my description of her, but my own self-descriptions (whether in critique or defense) are also not the same self who wrote the original piece. As Judith Butler explains, the "I" that narrates her own life is not the same "I" that has become the object of that narration—the narrating I constructs the narrated I (Butler 2005: 39).

Such assertions, while not new, push me to reconsider my own descriptions in this volume in a broader, critical sense. It is easy to apply the critical analysis of descriptions to others whose assertions appear problematic from the perspective of our own theoretical assumptions, but it is more difficult to hold ourselves and those whose ideas we generally accept to the same critical standards that we use for those whose approach and assertions we find problematic. In fact, our discussions of the work of other scholars, whether Glenn Vernon on the "nones" or Jon Mikalson on "ancient Greek religion," are historical narratives that we have created. We choose which parts of their work to isolate as distinct and significant and how those parts connect to other elements. So while Touna discusses the ways the historical narratives construct their own objects, she is correct to see that such a principle applies to our own work. Her questions bring to the fore important clarifications and challenges surrounding our consistent use of the assertion that descriptions constitute objects of discourse.

Nevertheless, I see value in the descriptions that we develop to analyze other descriptions. One starting point is a consideration of the purpose of our descriptions and critical analyses generally. A point that Touna and I agree on, I believe, is the value of questioning assumptions and challenging things taken-for-granted that, perhaps, should not be. In the response, Touna challenges the assertion that religion is universal and can be found in ancient Greece, among other places; my focus in the original chapter is to challenge the assumption that the nones (and other groups) exist prior to the discourse that constructs them.

Seeing the value in such analyses that challenge naturalized descriptions, I do not consider all descriptions to be equally problematic, even though every description is incomplete. I simultaneously reject a realist position that judges each description based on its relation to the real event in the past, as if those events are knowable and distinguishable without someone's descriptions. Problematic, though, is perhaps not the correct term for descriptions. Rather, they are contingent, strategic, selective. The central mistake is to treat any description as natural, given, unconstructed, or even worse, to present our descriptions as natural and the descriptions of others as contingent.

For example, Partition is the common name given to geopolitical actions surrounding the independence of India and Pakistan in 1947 and the massive human migration and suffering related to the division of British India into two independent nation-states. We can debate the specifics of any narrative account of that period, the beginning and end of Partition, the precipitating causes, or the best way to distinguish actions as separate events that we then classify and connect to others, but understanding that those debated descriptions create the object of their description does not deny that many people moved and suffered, with violence and death being a component of those events commonly labeled as Partition. Drawing the distinction that these actions constitute a separate event, excluding things that came before as well as other acts of migration or violence in other areas of the world, constitutes Partition as a distinct event, individuates it from other stuff that happens. No description or historical narrative can fully convey the past, what "really" happened, but that does not deny that people did things.

In the same way, the assertion that our perceptions and discussion of objects constructs those objects, relating them to other constructed objects, does not imply that the objects being described, delineated, and grouped together only exist in discourse. Rather, their individuation as distinct objects, related to other objects in particular ways (differentiated, compared, hierarchized), is what is constructed. Theories that approach the world assuming that descriptions simply reflect distinctions that pre-exist the discourse hide this process, as "realism naturalizes historically specific matrices of individuation" (Martin 2017: 21).

The multiple eyewitness accounts of any event reflect this issue, as people attend to different details, connect different actions together, interpret the same statements differently. No one has the complete account that can adjudicate between these competing perspectives. In fact, the same individual when observing an object will have different perceptions of it depending on her physical position in relation to it, the lighting, etc., so an account from the same person of an object is neither stable nor complete (Edmund Husserl, quoted in Martin 2017: 5). Yet, any individual's selective, strategic presentation of a description can be egregious in its exclusions. Complicating the commonly assumed binary of true and false, accurate and inaccurate, is necessary to advance this analysis of descriptions and "reality," as any assertion of reality is filtered through observations and the theoretical assumptions informing those observations.

In relation to our objectives and construction of narratives, analyzing narratives on three specific points—correspondence, coherence, and classification—moves us beyond the binary of true and false. The first two points draw on the work of Hayden White in relation to historiography (1985), and the third is specific to both my analysis of the discourse that constitutes the nones as a group and Touna's analysis of the discourse describing "ancient Greek religion." Any description that addresses what others have written and said, like those that Touna and I present, are types of historical narratives. Recognizing the constructed nature of historical narratives in a literary form, as Hayden White (1985) has argued, contributes to this form of evaluation of different components of narratives/descriptive accounts. These focal points provide a nuanced means of differentiating the quality of competing descriptions and narratives. Everything is not equally valuable.

The first distinction is the correspondence between details in a description and observable, documented, or commonly accepted information. On a very basic level, asserting that Mohandas Gandhi,

Jawaharlal Nehru, and Muhammad Jinnah interacted corresponds to not only the synchrony of their lives, but also records that describe their interactions in the period leading up to India's independence. These records, however, never tell everything. "The incompleteness of the archives coexists right alongside the abundance of documents" (Farge 2013: 54–5). While we know these three interacted, the details of their interactions and the others involved are harder to determine. Many things that happen are never recorded, or individuated, in the records; everything recorded is not preserved; and everything preserved is not legible (Farge 2013: 56–63). The historical records themselves are descriptions, and thus, are "always theory laden."

That said, a narrative placing Mohandas Gandhi, Plato, and Susan B. Anthony meeting in a Starbucks does not correspond to the commonly accepted information and documentation related to these famous figures. Both narratives reflect the choices of the author concerning whose actions to highlight, and thus neither is an unfiltered description, yet their connection to verifiable information differs considerably. That second narrative may have value as an allegory (building on White's use of literary forms), but a literal reading of the narrative as factually accurate is a challenge. Although the records that allow the first narrative to be considered factual themselves are incomplete, as those preserving the accounts make their own selections about which elements are important and whose actions are forgotten, common notions of evidence allow us to be confident that some interactions took place between Gandhi, Nehru, and Jinnah, giving the first narrative greater, though significantly incomplete, correspondence to the documented past than the second narrative.

In a similar way, taking a hypothetical passage that asserts, "While some people maintain that *the Civil War was not about slavery*, the evidence in Confederate statements themselves demonstrates otherwise," and describing it as denying that the Civil War was about slavery, based on the seven italicized words attributed to others but then rejected, is not a reading that corresponds to a literal interpretation of the statement when read in full. That full statement certainly relies on a particular interpretation of Confederate assertions through which the author selects elements and constructs meaning to create the description. Yet, the author's position, while also interpretable, cannot be easily read to say the opposite of a plain reading of it. To argue that the author denied the role of slavery in the Civil War requires either a sloppy or disingenuous reading to attack the author, or a convincing argument why the literal reading of the full passage misses an important component of the author's statement. To take on commonly accepted narratives, assumed information, and straightforward readings, as I suggest scholarship often attempts to do, requires precise argumentation and evidence from the person creating the challenge to make the narrative or description convincing.

Evidence, therefore, remains of value, despite the assertions that the evidence is incomplete and selective and that narratives/ descriptions construct their objects of study. Considering some of the material of my first essay and Touna's response, her assertions about the anachronistic nature of applying the category religion to ancient Greece relies on scholarship about the etymology of the word "religion," the ways that it shifts at different times, and the absence of a clear equivalent for the category in many languages, including ancient Greek (see, for example, Smith 1998). Similarly, the survey data that some used to construct the nones, including the variations within the data between different surveys and the diversity of beliefs and practices reported by people who identified as unaffiliated or not religious, provide a different type of observable data that supports the description of the constructed nature of the nones as a group. These readings are selective descriptions and interpretations, but they correspond well to a significant body of admittedly selective evidence. In contrast, my assertion about the British construction of Hindus as a group in the 19th century requires greater manipulation of the available evidence and ignores much of the complexity of the process, as I will detail below. Thus, my simple presentation of this narrative as an example of the process of group construction from identifications is more problematic (except for those who already agree) because it simplifies a narrative as if it were unconstructed.

Beyond the selection of particular elements to describe/events to narrate, another component of the descriptive process is constructing particular relationships between elements to make a coherent narrative. This process of generating coherence (in White's term) is an important component of any description or narrative, including all of the examples that I have discussed above. Unlike the particular verifiable (though themselves selective and incomplete) facts, these relationships suggest a causality and motivations that are not readily observable or verifiable. Which details the author of the narrative puts in relation to each other and the motivations and intentions projected onto actors in the narrative determine its coherence and the narrative it tells. This element of interpretation, therefore, generally becomes convincing based on its adherence to preconceived notions of causality and motivation. Like the selection of details to include, such assertions of relationships between details draw on the theory that the author and the readers bring to the narrative construction. Thus, when we move beyond somewhat discrete details in the record, we very quickly move towards an arena that is beyond the available evidence and reflects the interpretation of the narrator, whether she is an eyewitness or a contemporary scholar.

In the process of constructing a coherent narrative, different narrators can employ a variety of literary forms to organize the details and sequence of events in a form that connects with the expectations of readers. While White's approach details four tropes (comedy, romance, satire, and tragedy; see White 1985: 70), other literary forms also influence the construction and reading of historical descriptions. The narrative featuring Gandhi, Plato, and Susan B. Anthony, alluded to above, could be read as an allegorical account, which might convey something valuable to engage particular aspects of history differently. The narrative might have an internal coherence, despite the lack of correspondence. Such an assessment does not conform to the typical construction of history as providing accurate descriptions of reality, but the allegorical narrative could convey (depending on the reader's own assumptions) something accurate in the midst of its lack of correspondence to the commonly accepted timelines of these figures. In both the notions of correspondence and coherence, a strict dichotomy of truth and falsehood is not as useful as a spectrum from more demonstrable and convincing to less demonstrable and convincing.

A different mode of consideration of descriptions that is particularly relevant to the work that both Touna and I undertake is the question of classification. Classifications can relate to the issue of correspondence, as some elements within the historical record, or some people whose stories we consider, employ particular classifications for themselves. At other times, others, including those composing the narrative of the past, apply the classifications, making their success a matter of coherence between the details of the narrative and the assumptions of the traits of the classification from authors or readers.

Classifications are distinct from some of the other details that become the basis for assessing correspondence or coherence. Classifications are rarely uncontested in the way that the basic time periods and locations for Gandhi, Susan B. Anthony, and Plato are typically accepted. For anyone self-identifying, others often contest the identification. In the realm of contemporary identifications, for example, people frequently debate whether a particular politician is a true Democrat or Republican (whatever that person might claim), whether a Protestant, a Catholic, or a Mormon is truly Christian, whether an attacker is a terrorist or not, etc.

When dealing with the past, the challenge of classifications becomes even more apparent, as classifications such as religion have not been universally used throughout time. Moreover, where they have been used in the past, the common sense of that term has shifted (Smith 1998). Similar assertions can be made of the classification of historical periods. What constitutes the Vietnam War, both in terms of its starting point and the range of military action in Southeast Asia that fits within that category? While it is possible to analyze how someone employs a category, whether a contemporary colleague or a historical source, and to surmise what interests that application of the label furthers, simply accepting someone's self-identification or application of a label to another as fact is problematic. The application of a label then, such as describing particular actions, ideas, and artifacts as comprising ancient Greek religion or treating those who respond that they do not have a religious affiliation as a group, is clearly open to contestation and critique. A description that analyzes the application of a label, therefore, is more valuable than simple assertions of a classification itself.

That said, we obviously take things for granted ourselves, leaving ample room for anyone to question our narratives and descriptions. My discussion of the construction of Hinduism overstates its certainty, ignoring the complexity and contestation surrounding that assertion, as if the contestation did not exist. For example, my description simply declares that the term Hindu shifted from a geographical to a cultural/ethnic term, and then under the British began to be used as a religious term. While this point is not unique to my take on South Asia (Pandey 1990; King 1999), it depends on particular interpretations of evidence of the ways people at various times understood an identification as Hindu and when their understandings shifted. The ways people used and shifted their meanings is difficult to demonstrate conclusively and universally within the textual evidence from the period. Scholars, in fact, debate these shifts and the time when the term Hindu began to be used as a religious identification. I also highlighted the actions of the British without taking account of the contributions of some of the local leaders to the process, not to mention the shifting notions of "Hindu" that generate a range of interpretations of what the use of the term meant to people at that time. These assertions were not simply a straightforward description of what happened but a selective emphasis on certain details to further my authorial concern of paralleling the construction of the nones as a group to the construction of Hindus. The challenge is to present a shortened narrative that illustrates the point without undermining the larger concept of the limits of description and narrative generally. To follow Touna's assertion, I should not simply give my prior self a pass because I generally agree with him.

If we value the questioning of assumptions, then facing questions ourselves is an experience that should be invited, rather than resisted. One challenge to address in this, however, is how, within the descriptions themselves, to make that openness to the limitations of our own descriptions apparent while presenting a convincing enough description to be able to challenge the broader assumptions. My three suggestions below draw on the three forms of analysis that I have outlined, though in reverse order.

An explicit assertion of the contestation of labels and acknowledgment of whose application is operative highlights the contingent nature of those classifications. As a previous version of me has argued in the first volume in this series, it is vital to acknowledge the process of applying labels that illustrates that the label is not some universal or transhistorical description that we are applying according to an uncontested norm (Ramey 2015). Rather, we choose how to apply the label or repeat someone's application of it. Acknowledging our own agency within the categorization process then becomes vital to avoid the problem that Touna has highlighted, the ease in which we selectively apply the criticism that descriptions selectively construct objects.

The question of coherence produces a significant imperative to consider how we construct our own narratives. While a decisive narrative that fits the expectations of readers by employing particular tropes and hiding the process of its own construction can be effective to convince readers of a specific point, such an approach is similar to the familiar aphorism, winning the battle but losing the war, as it fails to address the larger question over the nature of historiography and description. For this standard approach places our work into a competition for the most coherent narrative and fails to challenge the limitations of narratives and descriptions in general. If we take our purpose to be challenging preconceptions and accept the postmodern critique of historical narratives, then continuing to produce the same type of descriptions undermines our larger assumptions and goals. The theory that operates within our own narrative descriptions too often is not the theory that we claim to hold. Farge asserts that scholars should avoid imagining a complete narrative for individuals whose partial stories they encounter in the archives, aiming instead for "writing that illuminates the circumstances of his appearance in the archives and takes into account whatever remains obscure about his existence, getting as close as possible to that which will always be missing" (Farge 2013: 77). We could take Hayden White's assertion about literary tropes and historiography a step further and consider the postmodern literary forms as a means to construct our descriptions and narratives in a manner that highlights these limitations of any single coherent narrative and the power of multiple perspectives. Exactly how to balance this approach with the desire to create a convincing intervention in a specific debate, whether over the construction of the nones or ancient Greek religion, is a point that needs further development. However, the tension between constructing tidy narratives and the messiness of life presents a significant challenge, so that those who recognize the messiness and limitations of narratives should be willing to interrogate the common preference for a tidy narrative that many of us also hold.

Asserting "Descriptions are always theory laden" (Penner 1989: 42) calls for scholars to present our own arguments in a more nuanced and self-reflexive manner that engages the limits of correspondence more explicitly. The nuance arises with our recognition of the distinctions among the particular details and data, as some are generally accepted or verifiable, and others are more speculative. Furthermore, self-reflexivity involves acknowledging our role in the selection of details from the myriad sources of information to include in our descriptions. Acknowledging these points provides a richer and more precise discussion of the issues that we present, as all forms of evidence are not equal. Our purposes and the theory that underlies our description should be made explicit, as informing our choice of which details to discuss, which things are distinct and significant, and what elements relate to each other.

If we take these points seriously, we should highlight our own processes of description and narrativization. Rather than hiding the process, making visible the selections that we make as to details, relations, and classifications reinforces the point that we have made about those whom we criticize, that the process is closely tied to the scholars making the assertions. Making explicit the theory-laden nature of our descriptions and the ways that it serves particular interests, then, reinforces that broader point that all descriptions are theory laden. Through such a process, the description and critique become significantly more consistent with our broader approach and purpose.

My original chapter and Touna's response both serve to highlight several points evident within the data available to us and consider the implications of taking that evidence seriously for how we discuss both those who do not identify with a religion and activities in ancient Greece. In contrast, my assertions about the construction of Hinduism are more contested. Regrettably, I ignored the larger contestation surrounding the details of the shifting understanding of the label Hindu in an effort to draw a simplified parallel to the construction of the nones. In my shortened description I also placed the agency predominately with the British, when even some scholars who generally agree with my assertions emphasize the interaction between some of the

British colonizers and their Indian informants and interpreters. While I maintain that the general point remains valuable as a way to view the development of the concept of Hinduism, and thus the parallel that I drew to the construction of the nones as a category also remains useful, the description that I presented previously is significantly more problematic as an authoritative description than the other assertions I and Touna made. Thus, a rewrite of the description to adhere more closely to the principles that I have outlined is warranted, as both a correction and a demonstration of an alternative, more sophisticated description.

To take the identifier Hindu as an example, many scholars have described the shift in meaning from a geographical identifier from the time of Alexander the Great towards an ethnic identifier that eventually takes on the connotations of a religious identification. While the period when the term took on a religious connotation is a matter of debate, a common description that I find most convincing posits that British colonizers, in their interaction with leaders in India, imposed the category of religion onto India and interpreted the cultural identifier of Hindu as a religious category, eventually coining the term Hinduism around the turn of the 19th century. Administrative actions, including the British Indian census later in that century, applied the identifier as a religious label, and some have seen this as contributing to the definition of a group across British India as Hindus with a common religious identification (Jones 1981). Many whom the British identified as Hindu adopted that identifier themselves. This process of construction collected together both people and particular emphases as a bounded group, people and practices that, in many descriptions, were not grouped in this exclusive fashion previously. Even those who trace the religious connotation back prior to the British generally acknowledge that the label Hindu has shifted in meaning. Taking seriously the shifting meanings of the term Hindu and acknowledging the apparent influence of an increasing association of the label with the European category of religion suggests that the construction of the nones as a group is not a unique event but a contemporary example of a general process in which group and category formation has significant effects on a people.

The preceding paragraph, while less authoritative and lengthier in its description, better represents the contestation over my example than the slightly briefer description in the original article. The revised description does not employ all of my recommendations, particularly the application of postmodern literary forms to narrativize history in a way that acknowledges the multiple perspectives and the complexity, even absurdity, of experience. Implementing all of the suggestions is obviously not required, as different approaches make sense in differing contexts. The brevity of a paragraph overview makes the self-reflexivity and acknowledgment of labels more reasonable than the application of alternative literary forms. What is vital is that we take Touna's challenge seriously to bring our approach to description and narrativization in line with our analytical critiques of the narratives and descriptions of others.

References

Butler, Judith. 2005. *Giving an Account of Oneself*. New York: Fordham University Press. https://doi.org/10.5422/fso/9780823225033.001.0001

Farge, Arlette. 2013. *The Allure of the Archives*. Translated by Thomas Scott-Railton. New Haven: Yale University Press. https://doi.org/10.12987/yale/9780300176735.001.0001

Jones, Kenneth W. 1981. "Religious Identity and the Indian Census." In Norman Barrier, ed., *The Census in British India: New Perspectives*, 73–101. New Delhi: Manohar.

King, Richard. 1999. *Orientalism and Religion: Postcolonial Theory, India, and the "Mystic East"*. London and New York: Routledge.

Martin, Craig. 2017. "'[T]he thing itself always steals away': Scholars and the Constitution of Their Objects of Study." Unpublished manuscript, PDF, last modified November 2017.

Pandey, Gyanendra. 1990. *The Construction of Communalism in Colonial North India*. Delhi and New York: Oxford University Press.

Penner, Hans. 1989. *Impasse and Resolution: A Critique of the Study of Religion*. New York: Peter Lang.

Ramey, Steven W. 2015. "Accidental Favorites: The Implicit in the Study of Religion." In Monica Miller, ed., *Claiming Identity in the Study of Religion: Social and Rhetorical Techniques Examined*, 223–38. Sheffield, UK: Equinox Publishing.

Smith, Jonathan Z. 1998. "Religion, Religions, Religious." In Mark C. Taylor, ed., *Critical Terms for Religious Studies*, 269–84. Chicago: University of Chicago Press.

White, Hayden. 1985. *Tropics of Discourse: Essays in Cultural Criticism.* Baltimore: Johns Hopkins University Press.

Steven W. Ramey is a professor in the Department of Religious Studies at the University of Alabama, where he also directs the Asian Studies program. He works on contested identifications in contemporary India and beyond and has published three books, *Hindu, Sufi, or Sikh* (Palgrave 2008), *Writing Religion* (University of Alabama Press 2015), and *Fabricating Difference* (Equinox 2017), along with a variety of articles.

SITE II:
ACTS OF APPROPRIATION

4. Strategizing Subjectivity

Creolization and Intentionality in Studies of Caribbean Religions

K. Merinda Simmons

This chapter looks at academic discourses on hybridity and creolization in the context of Caribbean religious traditions. A major emphasis in these discourses is the perceived strategic and subversive patterning of hybrid belief systems by slaves in the Caribbean under Christian colonial rule. Using the text Creole Religions of the Caribbean: An Introduction from Vodou and Santería to Obeah and Espiritismo, *by Margarite Fernández Olmos and Lizabeth Paravisini-Gebert, as a point of departure, I argue for scholarly consideration of the implications of the articulated impulses of projects like this, projects that are prevalent in academic discussions of identity and migration within African diasporas.*

When the levees broke and New Orleans faced the aftermath of Hurricane Katrina, news outlets struggled to grapple with the many layers of devastation and articulate a cohesive and compelling narrative for those who looked on from elsewhere in the country. What surfaced was an optimistic refrain praising the "spirit" of the community —the people's resilient spirit, their spirit of determination, and so on. Not long after the disaster came fiction writer and journalist Tom Piazza's book with HarperCollins, *Why New Orleans Matters* (2005). With admittedly more eloquent rhetorical flare, the book echoed what many heard from journalists and commentators: namely, New Orleans has a distinctive spirit, and it is vital that we appreciate and recognize it so that we will make sure the city is rebuilt. The description of the much-celebrated book suggests that, along with "explaining how its people ... transcend those conditions [of corruption, racism, and injustice] ... he asks us all to consider the spirit of this place and all the things it has shared with the world: its grace and beauty, resilience and soul."

Piazza spent only a handful of weeks writing the manuscript. It scurried to press in the winter of 2005, just months after the storm blew through the Gulf. The impulse to write an unabashed love letter to the city while feelings of loss, outrage, nostalgia, and hope swirled is an understandable one. However, the basic point—to galvanize goodwill toward a city in desperate need of rebuilding—is offered through a description of the city's singularity, its unique "spirit." That spirit, argues Piazza, touts an outlook of gratitude in the face of uncertainty —a worldview that proves difficult for Americans more generally on account of our busy and over-scheduled lives. Of course, the rush that does not seem to affect or sully New Orleanians is also indicative of a level of privilege lacking in the impoverished regions of New Orleans which apparently generate the tenacious spirit Piazza praises. This romanticized look at certain underprivileged communities— namely, for Piazza's purposes, people of color and the poor—is nothing new in American post-disaster discussions fueled by well-intended onlookers and media who talk about the collective "spirit" of a community that unites against the odds and teaches a lesson in values to the rest of the country.

The irrepressible spirit of New Orleans, Piazza claims, comes from African and Caribbean religions that offer a deep and abiding gratitude among their participants, as well as the complex cultural strands that are woven together to form the city—cohesive in its heterogeneity. This branding, of course, has far more to do with the needs of those offering it than it has to do with what or whom they discuss. Indeed, "New Orleans" as we know it is a product of the discourses surrounding "it." The features one chooses to highlight (whether jazz, voodoo, beignets, or systems of public transportation) are certainly not obvious or natural elements—they are tools that help in the manufacturing of a particular image. If successful, that image, then, is mistaken for "the thing itself." This is also quite often the case for scholarship that does indeed purport to offer deep ethnographies of various peoples and places. In attempting to get at the origins of this or that social phenomenon, scholars mistake their academic interests for authentic narratives about the group or region they study. This is frequently the case in scholarship on the Caribbean, as academic projects embark on recovery efforts of their own. Where postcolonialism and neoliberal politics in the academy meet is a vein of analysis wherein the Caribbean is said to be valorized in its marginalization and unified in its hybridity.

In this chapter I look at academic discourses on hybridity and creolization in the context of Caribbean religious traditions. Specifically, I use the text *Creole Religions of the Caribbean: An Introduction from Vodou and Santería to Obeah and Espiritismo* (*CRC*), by Margarite Fernández Olmos and Lizabeth Paravisini-Gebert, as a scholarly point of entry, looking particularly at their Introduction in which they outline their methodology and approach to the topic. Its second edition having been printed in 2011, the book is described both in its Introduction and on its cover blurb as offering an introduction to beliefs and rituals in the Caribbean by "trac[ing] the historical-cultural origins of the major Creole religions" (3). A major emphasis in the text is what the authors understand to be the strategic and subversive patterning of hybrid belief systems by slaves in the Caribbean under Christian colonial rule.

Scholars of religion would do well to consider the implications of the articulated impulses of projects like this, projects that are prevalent in academic discussions of identity and migration within African diasporas. I am particularly interested in the ways in which the work typified by *CRC* not only traces a linear narrative and timeline of religious development from Africa to the Caribbean but also suggests an active shaping of this development by strategic and intentional creole agents. Viewing creole religious systems as a subversive response of Caribbean slaves to their colonial oppressors, Fernández Olmos and Paravisini-Gebert cast "spirituality" and "cultural practices" as elements that are manifested and expressed by diasporic subjects. In this way, this popular turn in scholarship continues to position "religion" as an internal, experiential phenomenon even as it appeals to "hybrid" and socially constructed subjectivities. Furthermore, hybridity in such discourses—echoing thinkers like Stuart Hall[1]—substantiates

---

1   I am thinking specifically of his essay, "Créolité and the Process of Creolization" (2004) in which he states the following: "I would argue that

a cohesive and identifiable Caribbeanness. Analytical attempts—widespread in postcolonial studies—to showcase a distinctive and yet hybrid subject or community often nonetheless retain a notion of knowable and self-evident subjectivity.[2] This is a problematic trajectory, I will argue, for scholars of religion and postcolonialism, as it keeps the conversation locked into defensive modes of positioning Caribbean identity as synonymous with Caribbean intentionality.

Like so many schools of thought and scholarly trends based on a particular region, academic work on the Caribbean often attempts to articulate an exceptionalism narrative for the cultural history of the space. In the case of scholarship about the Caribbean, thinkers take account of the myriad languages, belief systems, rituals, and colonial histories with the rhetoric of "creolization" and "hybridity."[3] The heterogeneity of the islands and the people who live on them is, in fact, what many find distinctive about the space. After discussing briefly their personal identifications with Caribbean homes and diasporic communities, Fernández Olmos and Paravisini-Gebert suggest in their Preface to the first edition of *CRC*:

> [T]he Diasporic condition—which is so fundamentally Caribbean—is today a global concern, linking, through the encounters of peoples and cultures engaged in transnational

the process of creolization ... is what defines the distinctiveness of Caribbean cultures: their 'mixed' character, their creative vibrancy, their complex, troubled, unfinished relation to history, the prevalence in their narratives of the themes of voyaging, exile, and the unrequited trauma of violent expropriation and separation" (29).

2   See work, for example, by Jean Bernabé, Patrick Chamoiseau, and Raphaël Confiant, especially their co-authored essay "In Praise of Créolité" (2010) in which they argue, "We cannot reach Caribbeanness without interior vision. And interior vision is nothing without the unconditional acceptance of our Creoleness ... . We declare that Creoleness is the cement of our culture and that it ought to rule the foundations of our Caribbeanness" (83).

3   For some representative examples of this kind of scholarship, see the following two anthologies on the topic: *The Creolization Reader: Studies in Mixed Identities and Cultures*, edited by Robin Cohen and Paola Toninato (2010) and *Creolization: History, Ethnography, Theory*, edited by Charles Stewart (2007).

movement, the ongoing (re)construction of identities that is itself a form of global creolization. Religion is one of the crucial elements of that ongoing process for the peoples of the Caribbean. (ix–x)

Thus, *the* Diasporic condition is seen as, while global and transnational, a singular signifier, fundamentally descriptive of a unique Caribbeanness.

But how are imperial nations and agents any less creolized or diasporic? Surely the authors would not suggest that European colonizing forces were fixed points in sociocultural mappings of imperial identities and politics. So then are we left to classify "diasporas" (or, in so many scholarly cases, a singular, capitalized Diaspora) exclusively as displacements? The potential uses and heuristic conveniences of such a move are understandable. The trouble comes, however, in naming and categorizing displacements. Where are the lines of forced migration, refugee journeys, exiles, and other types of emigration drawn? Here we run up against the basic fact of the matter: there are always scholars drawing those lines and choosing how to present them. That their presentations suggest the lines of demarcation to be innocuous, descriptive, phenomenological facts is suggestive not of the cultures they attempt to describe but instead of their own interests and motivations in describing them.

Fernández Olmos and Paravisini-Gebert slip easily into an essentializing presentation of the Caribbean, despite their articulated interests to the contrary. Even when the essence offered is a complex or hybrid one, the intellectual move is no less problematic. Regarding creolization in relation to the larger region, they suggest, "The complex dynamics of encounters, adaptations, assimilation, and syncretism that we refer to as creolization are emblematic of the vibrant nature of Diaspora cultures" (3). That essentializing move is often in service of a seemingly progressive political move to "recover" lost voices and identities. As they note in their Introduction, "the development of a complex system of religious and healing practices ... allowed enslaved African communities that had already suffered devastating cultural loss to preserve a sense of group and personal identity" (3).

The debate over whether African slaves retained or lost their traditions or cultures is by now a well-rehearsed one, typified most famously, perhaps with the Herskovits-Frazier debate.[4] And though scholars have since made interventions into this debate by challenging the idea of a linear cultural transference, instead focusing on permeable boundaries and ebbs and flows, the basic point of the debate remains present in current scholarly trends.[5] But the question of what was kept or lost seems demonstrably not the point. After all, one cannot go back in time and get to the "truth" of the matter. Any descriptive history is a claim offered in the present and, as such, refers to current interests. Projecting those concerns backwards for scholarly purposes in the present day may nicely lend a politically desirable currency for the work at hand; however, doing so also effectively creates objects of speculation out of the very "identities" thought to be being recovered.

While such theoretical problems easily surface, scholars are often intent on offering origin narratives. If we simply go back and tell the story in the right way, this line of thought would have it, we can recuperate the tale of what *really* happened. Thus, the authors of *CRC* have as a primary motivation historicizing where the religions they discuss came from, how, and why. They describe their intent early on in their Introduction: "This book traces the historical-cultural origins of the major Creole religions and spiritual practices of the region—Vodou, Santeria, Obeah, Espiritismo—and describes their current-day expression in the Caribbean and its Diaspora" (3). The prospect of knowable origins from which lineages can then be traced

---

4   E. Franklin Frazier (beginning with his *The Negro Family in the United States*, 1939) suggested that slaves arrived to the New World as blank slates, their rituals and traditions having been stripped from them during the Middle Passage. Melville Herskovits, on the other hand, in his classic *The Myth of the Negro Past* (1941) held that slaves retained significant parts of the cultures from which they were taken.

5   See the summary in Roland Littlewood's essay "History, Memory and Appropriation: Some Problems in the Analysis of Origins" (1998) of responses to Herskovits from Roger Bastide (1979) and James Clifford (1988).

is an enticing one for scholars invested in recuperating a presumably authentic narrative. However, to emphasize origins—to suggest as Fernández Olmos and Paravisini-Gebert do that "Caribbean Creole religions developed as a result of cultural contact"—one must identify the actors on respective sides in a narrativized history of cultural contact (3). And despite the productive nod toward the *development* of these traditions (as opposed to thinking of them as a sort of natural or stable state), "Creole religions" for the authors is a signifier pointing to real things in the world rather than discursive moments wherein a choice is made to distinguish "religion" from other categories. There, precisely, is the point: such identifications are always choices, but all too often scholars treat the decisions they make as neutral descriptions of their objects of study.

The authors make clear their interest in correcting a certain historical account and offering a truer alternative early on. In the Preface to the book's first edition, they describe the hard work of the project:

> Our most difficult task has been that of gleaning from the complexity and deeply etched nuances of those materials our own authentic, candid, yet comprehensive account intended for nonexperts with an interest in these fascinating and significant, although frequently misrepresented, cultural and religious practices. (x)

With authenticity as their aim, the authors plainly state here one of the more problematic aspects of intellectual recovery efforts. Namely, they want to correct what they deem to be the misrepresentations of religious practices to an intended audience of nonexperts. Certainly, complicating stereotypes and reductive narratives for students and scholars new to a topic is a productive endeavor. However, the new narrative taking the place of the old one is no less reductive if it still purports to describe the nature of the Caribbean, no matter how dynamic that ostensible essence might be.

Elsewhere in their brief Preface, they suggest that "The introductory nature of this work offers wonderful opportunities for showcasing the common roots and comparative aspects of religious practices that are quite unique and dynamic" (ix). Thus, the authors rightly name their introductory framework as a mode of comparison work.

Like any other project of drawing delineating lines between a this and a that—in this case, between those things identified as "creole religions" and what, implicitly, are non-creolized religions—the work is not about the items being compared or the commonalities identified as distinguishing characteristics in them but is rather about the scholars making the comparisons.

J.Z. Smith's *Drudgery Divine* is useful here. Along with a critique of labeling something "unique,"[6] Smith calls our attention to the *process* of comparison—a process not at all to do with the substance of seemingly naturally occurring things in the world but rather with the scholarly interests of those classifying and comparing:

> In the case of the study of religion, as in any disciplined inquiry, comparison, in its strongest form, brings differences together within the space of the scholar's mind for the scholar's own intellectual reasons. It is the scholar who makes their cohabitation —their "sameness"—possible, not "natural" affinities or processes of history. Taken in this sense, "genealogy" disguises and obscures the scholar's interests and activities allowing the illusion of passive observation. (1990: 51)

What we are left with, then, in reading descriptive accounts of Caribbean religious histories, is just that: a critically removed genealogy from which the interests of the scholars offering them are conveniently but conspicuously absent.

This is but one important way in which so much seems easily taken for granted in the name of "introducing" a subject. Assumed is a synonymy between introduction and descriptive survey, rendering invisible the work scholars do that allows various groups or practices to be compared or contrasted in the first place. However, there is no reason I can see for an introduction to be any less critically nuanced than a more thoroughgoing investigation of a topic.[7]

6   Smith notes, in many discourses within religious studies, "'Unique' becomes an ontological rather than taxonomic category; an assertion of a radical difference so absolute that it becomes 'Wholly Other', and the act of comparison is perceived as both an impossibility and an impiety." (1990: 38)

7   We might again turn to J.Z. Smith, who in "The Necessary Lie: Duplicity in the Disciplines" (2007) suggests: "We're really lying, and lying

The authors cite Aisha Khan, agreeing with Khan's assessment that "[h]egemonic and abiding, prejudices, stereotypes, and presumptions are notoriously slow to become corrected—in either popular or scholarly imagination" (xi). And while they offer their work as a "contribut[ion] to a better informed perception," the ease with which they hold to a knowable "Caribbean" whose casting can be an authentic one is indicative of the very prejudices and presumptions that are slow to be corrected indeed (xi). However, since the presumption here is seemingly progressive in its motivations, attempting to recover marginalized histories of Caribbean cultures and traditions, the reductive logic does not register as such. Instead, certain claims appear problematic or reductive while those of the authors appear savvy and forward-thinking. The competing claims are, however, merely two sides of the same coin.

The seeming progressive politics present in this type of scholarship are established with the stated motivation of recuperating narratives that have traditionally been ignored or marginalized by canonical histories then taken as the exhaustive authority on a particular time period or people. The Introduction of *CRC* begins with several anecdotes about various rituals and practices identified as religious that make quotidian appearance in the lives of a few people taken as a representative sampling from the so-called Afro-Caribbean and its diasporas. These stories, the authors suggest, "speak to the continuing power of the Afro-Caribbean spiritual traditions that have sustained the peoples of the region and beyond for centuries" (2). Thus, there is immediately set up a connection between spirituality and sustaining ability.

---

in a relatively deep fashion, when we consistently disguise, in our introductory courses, what is problematic about our work. For example, we traditionally screen from or students the hard work that results in the production of exemplary texts, which we treat as found objects. We hide consistently the immense editorial efforts that have conjecturally established so many of the texts we routinely present to our students as classics, not to speak of the labors of translation that enable many of them to read these texts." (74) Though he is speaking specifically about pedagogy in introductory courses here, there is productive resonance for *CRC*, whose authors hope the book finds use for students coming to the topic for the first time.

While this may seem an innocent descriptive move, it is troublesome in its unavoidably speculative analysis. It is nonetheless a familiar refrain. After a natural disaster, media outlets cannot but lavish praise on the "spirit" of the people in the affected region—their resilient spirit, their spirit of community. In the face of widespread devastation, well-meaning reporters and politicians trot out liberal humanism in the mode of complimenting a group of people, noble in their victimized state.

Postcolonial scholarship interested in creolization, however, tends nominally to attempt avoiding hackneyed distinctions between us and them. The work coming out of this discourse broadly posits itself as complicating easy definitions of "culture" and "identity," doing so with an emphasis on the interlocking systems—linguistic, historical, racial, and others—that create communities resisting a single identification.[8] These communities and cultures are thus said to be "creolized," "hybrid," and/or "syncretic." The defining heterogeneity is often cast as a distinctive and unique element. This is where a more nuanced discussion invested with the moves of poststructuralist criticism might enter. Specifically, the irony of a *distinctive* heterogeneity is one worth serious consideration. Too many conversations about creolization keep up and running stable spheres of acculturation and/or subjectivity that overlap or intersect. In this model, there is a sort of "add culture and stir" recipe for something identified as creole. The same trend is present in diaspora discourses, suggesting—even if ever so implicitly—a single and clear point of origin and return. In so many cases within diaspora studies, "Africa" serves as a romanticized whole from which disparate postcolonial communities emerged. Despite our insistence on not homogenizing a singular "Africa" from the many languages, countries, and political investments that make "it" up, scholars focusing on migration and postcolonialism too often still talk freely about "the African diaspora" or "African religions."

---

8   See Sabine Mabardi, "Hybridity in Cultural Theory: Encounters of a Heterogeneous Kind" (2010) in which the author offers historical analysis of hybridity as a critical concept, putting it in a larger conversation employing terms such as syncretism, bricolage, *mestizaje*, creolization, transculturation, among others.

Nathaniel Samuel Murrell's *Afro-Caribbean Religions: An Introduction to Their Historical, Cultural, and Sacred Traditions* (2010)—another introductory survey text aimed at a historical ethnography of so-called Caribbean religious traditions—is a case in point. Murrell's first sentence in the Introduction sets the table: "Religion is one of the most important elements of Caribbean culture that links Afro-Caribbean people to their African past" (1). Murrell casts two tropes that bookend the sentence—"religion" and an "African past"— as stable and naturally occurring. He goes on to outline what he sees as the connective elements of what he calls Afro-Caribbean religions:

> These diverse religious traditions share several commonalities: They show strong African connections and harbor African cultural memory; they are religions of the people, by and for the people; they are nontraditional and creole faiths shaped by cultures; they are an integral part of the Caribbean colonial legacy; and they continue to generate international interest and inspire a huge body of literature worth of academic study. (1)

Thus, by deploying taken-for-granted notions like "Africa," "the people," "cultures," and "colonialism"—all enormous in their complexity and variance depending on their context in scholarship—scholars fall into the very essentializing traps they try to avoid. What we might do instead, Russell McCutcheon (2007) suggests, is to embark on our studies with less nostalgia and more critical analysis: "In place of this quest for the authentic heart of Africa ... I suggest that we become a little more self-conscious about what it is we do when we do this thing we call scholarship" (236). The same goes for studies of African diasporas in the Caribbean. Scholars can do this, according to McCutcheon, through an emphasis on discourses: "I *am* suggesting that recognizing that all we have are discourses by means of which banal stuff become such things as artifacts, will help to dispel the rush to culpability and the search for complete understanding that drives so much of our work as scholars in our post-colonial world" (236).

In the second edition of *CRC*, the authors do make as a point of revision a more thorough analysis of the scholarship surrounding creolization and diaspora. A telling passage from the Preface notes that academia has seen a dramatic rise of interest in Caribbean Studies and Diaspora Studies:

> The term creolization has been a contentious one, an issue we hope to address in this second edition, which brings up to date the scholarship on the religions themselves and also expands the regional considerations of the Diaspora to Mexican American and other U.S. Latinos who are influenced by Creole spiritual practices. The increased significance of material culture—art, music, literature—and the healing practices influenced by Creole religions are also taken into account. (xi)

In updating the discussion on creolization scholarship, the authors nonetheless keep intact "the religions themselves," as something set apart from other forms of socialization and practices. Similarly, the popular phrase "material culture" appears as implicitly distinguished from other forms of culture. The question of what might constitute "immaterial culture," of course, is left unaddressed. All the while, the authors present phrases like "Creole spiritual practices" and "Creole religions" as clear and identifiable ends in themselves—different, presumably, from ordinary religions. What postcolonial scholarship and ethnographic studies of religion would benefit from is a serious consideration of "creolization" as a discursive tool used to identify particular geocultural regions in the world and distinguish them from others. As such, "it" is not some unique or rare phenomenon but an endlessly ubiquitous one, entrenched in spaces marked "dominant" or "imperial" every bit as much as in the identified margins. If we press this vein of criticism, scholars would not think of "religion" as some stable entity able to be divvied up into those that are creolized and those that are not. They would, instead of studying how religions spread to this place or that and the subsequent shapes they took, take a cue from Russell McCutcheon (2007) and "consider studying why naming part of their social world *as* religion has caught on so widely among diverse human communities" (233).

Even in scholarship where criticism is a significant part of the discussion, the temptation to talk about religion and culture as knowable realities often proves a powerful one indeed. In *The Creolization Reader: Studies in Mixed Identities and Cultures* (2010), for example, editors Robin Cohen and Paola Toninato attempt to offer a more theoretical look at the topic of creolization rather than jumping directly into descriptive ethnography without preliminary analysis of the terms being used. Engaging with Stephan Palmié (2007), they state their own take on the term "creolization": "We concur that creolization should refer to something tangible (namely real social and historical experiences), but suggest that there are many places where such experiences can be found and legitimately described as creolization" (7). Thus, even while broadening the scope of the discourse, suggesting that it not be limited to one specific region or group, Cohen and Toninato defer to notions of realness (where historical reference is concerned) and legitimacy (where classifications of creolization are concerned). And—just like that—would-be savvy scholarship slips into old claims about authenticity.

Thus, scholars who discuss creolization as a distinct and special occurrence, happening only in isolated cultures or spaces, must inevitably rely on an essentialist reading of the cultures into which they read it. The authors of *CRC* offer the following definition and assessment: "Creolization—that is, the malleability and mutability of various beliefs and practices as they adapt to new understandings of class, race, gender, power, labor, and sexuality—is one of the most significant phenomena in Caribbean religious history" (4). Here, then, is the question scholars should be asking if taking serious account of poststructuralist turns that would reject a knowable center to what many call "religion" or "religious history": which of the things we have come to know as religions did *not* adapt to new understandings of class, race, gender, power, labor, and sexuality? The important work done in feminist and race theory that posits neither gender nor racial identification as a fixed point or biological reality is key here. If we read "identity" as a social (and socializing) act, there is no belief or practice not already infused with the political maneuverings of something called "race," and so on. Further, the ways in which categories like "race" and "gender" become identified and thus knowable are never isolated moments or events. They are only ever classified according to their context—or, to put it another way, according to their proximity to other tropes.

With these ideas in mind, an exploration of the rest of the discussion about creolization and other terms in the book is telling. Quickly the point becomes one about cultural resourcefulness and the subversive reestablishment of a group's "original" or "traditional" beliefs and practices. That these moves are ostensibly subversive is enough rationale with which to claim a certain brand of scholarly anti-essentialism. The authors state their intentions thus:

> In our approach to the creolized religious systems that developed in the region in the wake of colonization, we seek to avoid essentialist definitions of religious experience, opting instead for a practice- or experience-based presentation and analysis, rooted in particular historical circumstances. Although the Creole religions vary in their origins, beliefs, and rituals, all of them demonstrate the complexities and the creative resourcefulness of the creolization process. (4)

A specific and linear history is accordingly established here. First there was colonization, and then new, creolized religious systems appeared in its aftermath. Despite the problematic simplicity of this analysis, more problematic still is the universal claim made in the name of anti-essentialism. The admitted variance among creole religions gives way to "all of them" showcasing not only the complexities but also "the creative resourcefulness of *the* creolization process" (emphasis mine).

As I have suggested elsewhere, an emphasis on experience is no indication of anti-essentialism (Simmons 2015). Often, it is exactly the opposite. Many scholars in cultural and identity studies rely on the feminist aphorism of the personal being political. The quick read given to that idea, however, results in phenomenological presentations of experiential narratives as obviously significant ends-in-themselves. The authors of *CRC* suggest that they dodge essentialism by offering "a practice- or experience-based presentation and analysis, rooted in particular historical circumstances" (4). The seeming specificity of experience-based data is no guarantee for avoiding essentializing claims, however. In fact, more often than not, they serve as two sides of the very same coin. If the personal is always political, little is gained by simply offering up this or that experiential narrative or personal account. What scholars are actually talking about—though they seem remiss to admit it—are the political moves that make a sphere called "the personal" possible. Nevertheless, too much work in Caribbean studies and certainly in anthropological studies of religion try to get at the "thing itself"—in this case, creole religious practice as manifested in the lives of participants. Describing and analyzing that, scholars in this vein would suggest, recuperates voices that were rendered silent by the imperial ventures of colonialism and subsequent institutional racism in the academy. In this way, experience and the scholarly motives of recuperation intersect.

The broad strokes regarding how to discuss various systems of belief and rituals within and after the context of the transatlantic slave trade, then, have had to do with issues of cultural retention and loss. *CRC* outlines the basic scholarly conversation regarding these issues, summarizing the positions of well-known thinkers in the field Melville Herskovits and Edward Kamau Brathwaite:

> Melville Herskovits challenged prevailing assumptions regarding the survival of African influences in the New World in his *Myth of the Negro Past* (1941), demonstrating in great detail that African culture has survived and indeed thrived. In the 1970s, Edward Kamau Brathwaite in his essay, "The African Presence in Caribbean Literature" and in *Folk Cultures of the Slaves in Jamaica*, claimed that the Middle Passage "was not, as is popularly assumed, a traumatic, destructive experience, separating the blacks from Africa, disconnecting their sense of history and tradition, but a pathway or channel between this tradition and what is being evolved, on new soil, in the Caribbean." (5)

Herskovits and Brathwaite are representative of an influential strand of scholarship that holds to an African cultural presence that diasporic populations maintained despite the Middle Passage. This argument still resonates with politically-minded scholars today. The seeming progressivism of the intellectual move, however, too often maintains a nostalgic view of a monolithic Africa. Further, it resorts to unavoidably speculative claims where the category of "experience" is concerned. All the while, the taxon "religion" retains a traditional and ironically conservative definition as something housed within the realm of personal experience.

Contemporary scholars take poststructuralist and postmodern moves only so far as to suggest culture is not a stable *thing* but rather a system of exchanges—conflicts and convergences. The popular description of such exchanges as fluid is thought to productively untangle a hegemonic tether to linear histories in the Anglosphere; however, the term serves only to demarcate what—if we are to take those same postmodern turns seriously—is not special or unique at all. Hegemony is not the absence of the cultural fluidity that fascinates scholars. Indeed, to suggest as much is only to reify the dominance that postcolonialists attempt to deconstruct. It is not the stable, neutral space *against which* other cultures and groups might be defined or distinguished. Instead, we must view cultural hegemonies as every bit as contingent and subject to—if not constructed by—changes made over time and place.

However, scholars seem nonetheless inclined to delineate spheres of power out of a well-intended but intellectually problematic conflation of advocacy and analysis. Thus, Fernández Olmos and Paravisini-Gebert cite anthropologist Aisha Khan's definition of creolization as a "means of revealing the successful and creative agency of subaltern or deterritorialized peoples, and the subversiveness inhering in creolization, which contradicts earlier notions of cultural dissolution and disorganization" (quoted in *CRC*, 6). In this model, agency is something dwelling internally that is *revealed* in one way or another. Additionally, subversiveness rests somehow inherently within creolization. Herein lies the analytical rub. To suggest that subversive creativity can lie beneath the surface of this or that group without essentializing that very group is to—as Khan has done—set apart certain communities as warranting a different sort of analysis. Identifying these communities as "subaltern or deterritorialized" is the necessary move for scholars to then claim that the descriptive ethnographies on which they embark are recuperative and not essentializing, progressive and not conservative, cutting-edge and not traditional.

This kind of scholarship relies on a particular understanding of identity—namely, as something existing already internally that gets subsequently performed or enacted. Thus, a discussion of religions in such a framework is cast in a traditional sense of being performed from the inside out. "Belief" functions for these scholars as a deeply held feeling or state of being and, as such, plays a rather conservative role. Utilizing "belief" in this way is also what allows for the confident—while ultimately speculative—claims about the strategic use of religious systems on the part of diasporic subjects. In this way, the presumed anti-essentialist heterogeneity "inherent" in creolization nonetheless engenders a simplistic and rather essentializing dichotomy between dominant and marginalized, as well as belief and performance. Authenticity claims are thus allowed, it would seem, as long as they are tied to conversations about strategy and subversion on the part of marginalized groups.

Fernández Olmos and Paravisini-Gebert introduce the notion of strategic religiosity early on as a touchstone of their research and argumentation. Describing their project as an introduction to African-based religions that took root in the Caribbean after European colonization, they explain that the text "shows how Caribbean peoples fashioned a heterogeneous system of belief out of the cacophony of practices and traditions that came forcibly together in colonial society" (2). Their basic claim is as follows:

> Creolized religious systems, developed in secrecy, were frequently outlawed by the colonizer because they posed a challenge to official Christian practices and were believed to be associated with magic and sorcery. They nonetheless allowed the most oppressed sectors of colonial Caribbean societies to manifest their spirituality, express cultural and political practices suppressed by colonial force, and protect the health of the community. (3)

We can glean much about the approach identified here just by looking at the active verbs in these sentences. Presenting spirituality as something that participants manifest, express, and use to protect their communities, Fernández Olmos and Paravisini-Gebert resort to a relatively recent and broadly conservative notion of religion, even as they stack creolized religions in contradistinction to Christianity. Namely, they implicitly suggest a kind of religious identity held deep within the individual that is then expressed or transmitted externally into the social world. In so doing, they distinguish categories of the religious and social, even as they purport to offer an analysis of the societal underpinnings of something called "Caribbean religions." Suggesting that creolization has become synonymous with hybridity and syncretism in current strands of scholarship about globalization, the authors discuss syncretism as one of the ways in which strategy comes to the fore: "The strategies of religious syncretism— the active transformation through renegotiation, reorganization, and redefinition of clashing belief systems—are consistent with the creolization process." (9) I will not belabor the relatively longstanding and, to my mind, quite right complaints about the term "syncretism" within the academic study of religion (Stewart and Shaw 1994). More to the point in this chapter is the issue of how scholarship uses notions of strategic practices to serve current academic and political interests.

Fernández Olmos and Paravisini-Gebert cite several scholars who associate syncretism with strategic resistance to dominant spheres. Andrew Apter, for instance, argues the following:

> The syncretic revision of dominant discourses sought to trans-
> form the authority that these discourses upheld ... the power and
> violence mobilized by slave revolts and revolution were built
> into the logic of New World syncretism itself. The Catholicism
> of Vodou, Candomblé and Santeria was not an ecumenical
> screen, hiding the worship of African deities from official perse-
> cution. It was the religion of the masters, revised, transformed,
> and appropriated by slaves to harness its power within their uni-
> verses of discourse. In this way the slaves took possession of
> Catholicism and thereby repossessed themselves as active spiri-
> tual subjects. (quoted in *CRC* 11)

Scholars are right to reject an analytical model that would see Catholicism as a simple overlay of fundamentally African systems of belief. However, likewise simplistic is a speculative analysis of the motivations that ostensibly guided the incorporations and alterations of various beliefs and rituals in the daily lives of Caribbean slaves. Such a scholarly pursuit is akin to early anthropologist E.B. Tylor's assessment of what he supposed the response might be from "primitive" people to the phenomenon of dreaming (Tylor 1873). The attempts made by early humans to account for natural phenomena (like experiencing altered realities in dreams), he argued, might well have stoked the animistic "belief in spiritual beings"—the essence, as he saw it, of what came to be known as religion.

Tylor's insistent interest in uncovering the origins of religious belief and the assumptions made about the rationales of the "savage philosopher" have made his work problematic for scholars thinking critically about religion, as well as the methods that motivate ethnographic study. It is, therefore, fascinating to find references to contested notions like "animistic beliefs" and the "spirit world" in the eleven characteristics that the authors of *CRC* offer as shared by all creole religions. Giving cause to their list, they argue, "Despite notable differences among African-based Caribbean Creole practices, a general overview of the Creole religions reveals that they share a number of fundamental features" (12). Again, the impetus toward introducing and describing a survey of creole religions does the scholarship a disservice here. The list is but one example that undercuts the assurance that the text avoids and rejects essentialism. Inasmuch as the importance of recuperating (much less the ability to recuperate) is taken for granted, there is no irony embedded in the claims of anti-essentialism alongside a list of shared "fundamental features" or the inherent qualities of creolization.

Similarly, they suggest without irony, "Religious and cultural development follows many paths; a true understanding of magic and its place in a society requires an appreciation of cultural context"—the notions of a *true* understanding and a cultural *context* apparently not contradicting one another. To help get to that "true understanding," the authors invoke James Frazer's *The Golden Bough: A Study in Magic and Religion* (1890), a text whose tenets, they suggest, are followed by "the logic, structure, and 'technology' of magic in Creole religions" (13).[9] Another early anthropologist and Intellectualist like

---

9   They utilize Frazer's concepts of "homeopathic" and "contagious" magic, wherein homeopathic magic follows the "law of similarity in which like produces like and an effect resembles its cause, so that one can produce any effect by imitating it," and contagious magic follows the law of contact, "namely, that things which have once been in contact continue to act upon

Tylor, Frazer's own essentialist quest for origins took magic to be the evolutionary antecedent to modern religion. While Fernández Olmos and Paravisini-Gebert call attention to what Yvonne P. Chireau identifies as the "contested notions of belief,"[10] they nonetheless suggest that there are correct and incorrect ways to understand categories of magic and religion: "On some level, magical thinking is common to all societies, but magic as a religious and spiritual practice is a category that is perhaps the most misunderstood, maligned, feared, and sensationalized of all identified with African-derived religions" (16). In their model, "magic" and "religion" name real things in the world: magic exists, simply waiting for scholars to come along and name it.

As argued above, what scholars choose to name, locate, or compare suggests much about their own academic projects rather than the natural substance of their objects of study. In the discourses of postcolonial and diaspora studies, some scholars have critiqued what they see as a reliance on so-called Western traditions and scholarship. Fernández Olmos and Paravisini-Gebert cite Silvio Torres-Saillant's *An Intellectual History of the Caribbean*, in which Torres-Saillant discusses what he sees as the turn to paradigms of globalization and a broader postcolonial context within Caribbean studies. This turn, he suggests, is the result of a problematic attempt to legitimize the field within the academy. Fernández Olmos and Paravisini-Gebert summarize his position: "Caribbeanists relied on the pillars of Western tradition as they did prior to the rise of anticolonialism in the region, reaffirming the 'centrality of Western critical theory'" (6). Beyond the problems embedded in what amounts to a standpoint theory brand of analysis and leaving aside the simplicity with which the term "Western" is deployed here, what I find ironic about this idea is that the same Caribbeanists who do not want to rely on Western academic models nonetheless still rely on Western taxonomies and conceptions—like the term "religion"—to launch their critiques.

---

each other at a distance, a 'magical sympathy' that exists between a person and any severed portion of his or her person" (13–14). Their reading works with Frazer's abridged text (1922).

10 They cite her *Black Magic: Religion and the African American Conjuring Tradition* (2003).

In this manner, the very scholars who want to problematize dominant intellectual traditions that have historically marginalized the Caribbean as a place worthy of academic inquiry also want to utilize the tools of those same traditions, as if the terms are not themselves value-laden and endlessly fraught. We might turn again to McCutcheon's "Africa on Our Minds":

> Of course, using the local [such as the terminology "religion"] *as if* it were universal, and doing so for *our* analytic purposes, to satisfy *our* own curiosities and *our* interests, is the inevitable situation in which we find ourselves inasmuch as we, as scholars, are situated human beings with no choice but to grapple with issues of familiarity and strangeness, similarity and difference, nearness and distance, etc. However, doing so because of our confidence in the universal reach of these purposes, curiosities, and interests is best understood ... as that form of ideology that goes by the name of imperialism. (2007: 233–4)

It is in this way that savvy scholars promoting what they see as progressive scholarship that advocates as it analyzes make similar intellectual moves to what we see on the evening news after a disaster in an underprivileged region. Nostalgically talking about what makes the space and its people unique and special, scholars get swept up in the naïve fantasy that their own designations name real things "out there." In so doing, they do not recuperate the marginalized but perpetuate the hegemonic—the very inverse of their articulated aims. Rather than talking about the spirit of this or that group, then, we would do far better to think critically about what machinations are at work in constructing the semblance of a stable group ... with a spirit.

References

Bastide, Roger. 1979. *The African Religions of Brazil: Towards a Sociology of the Interpretation of Civilizations.* Baltimore: Johns Hopkins University Press.
Bernabé, Jean, Patrick Chamoiseau, and Raphaël Confiant. 2010. "In Praise of Créolité." In Robin Cohen and Paola Toninato, eds., *The Creolization*

Reader: Studies in Mixed Identities and Cultures, 82–88. New York: Routledge.

Chireau, Yvonne P. 2003. *Black Magic: Religion and the African American Conjuring Tradition*. Berkeley, CA: University of California Press.

Clifford, James. 1988. *The Predicament of Culture: Twentieth Century Ethnography, Literature and Art*. Cambridge, MA: Harvard University Press.

Cohen, Robin and Paola Toninato. 2010. "The Creolization Debate: Analysing Mixed Identities and Cultures." In Robin Cohen and Paola Toninato, eds., *The Creolization Reader: Studies in Mixed Identities and Cultures*, 1–21. New York: Routledge.

Cohen, Robin and Paola Toninato (eds.). 2010. *The Creolization Reader: Studies in Mixed Identities and Cultures*. New York: Routledge.

Fernández Olmos, Margarite, and Lizabeth Paravisini-Gebert. 2011. *Creole Religions of the Caribbean: An Introduction from Vodou and Santería to Obeah and Espiritismo, Second Edition*. New York: New York University Press.

Frazer, James. 1922. *The Golden Bough: A Study in Magic and Religion* (1890). New York: Macmillan.

Frazier, E. Franklin. 1939. *The Negro Family in the United States*. Chicago: University of Chicago Press.

Hall, Stuart. 2004. "Créolité and the Process of Creolization." Reprinted in Robin Cohen and Paola Toninato, eds., 2010, *The Creolization Reader: Studies in Mixed Identities and Cultures*, 26–38. New York: Routledge.

Herskovits, Melville J. 1941. *The Myth of the Negro Past*. Boston: Beacon Press.

Littlewood, Roland. 1998. "History, Memory and Appropriation: Some Problems in the Analysis of Origins." In Barry Chevannes, ed., *Rastafari and Other African-Caribbean Worldviews*, 233–52. New Brunswick: Rutgers University Press. https://doi.org/10.1007/978-1-349-13745-9_10

Mabardi, Sabine. 2010. "Hybridity in Cultural Theory: Encounters of a Heterogeneous Kind." In Robin Cohen and Paola Toninato, eds., *The Creolization Reader: Studies in Mixed Identities and Cultures*, 247–56. New York: Routledge.

McCutcheon, Russell T. 2007. "Africa on Our Minds." In Theodore Louis Trost, ed., *The African Diaspora and the Study of Religion*, 229–37. New York: Palgrave Macmillan.

Murrell, Nathaniel Samuel. 2010. *Afro-Caribbean Religions: An Introduction to Their Historical, Cultural, and Sacred Traditions*. Philadelphia: Temple University Press.

Palmié, Stephan. 2007. "On the C-Word Again: From Colonial to Post-Colonial Semantics." In Charles Stewart, ed., *Creolization: History, Ethnography, Theory*, 66–83. Walnut Creek, CA: Left Coast Press.

Piazza, Tom. 2005. *Why New Orleans Matters*. New York: HarperCollins Publishers.

Simmons, K. Merinda. 2015. "'Well Isn't That Special?': What We Talk about When We Talk about Identity." In Monica Miller, ed., *Claiming Identity in the Study of Religion: Social and Rhetorical Techniques Examined*, 19–27. London: Equinox Publishing.

Smith, Jonathan Z. 1990. *Drudgery Divine: On the Comparison of Early Christianities and the Religions of Late Antiquity*. Chicago: The University of Chicago Press.

Smith, Jonathan Z. 2007. Afterword: "The Necessary Lie: Duplicity in the Disciplines." In Russell T. McCutcheon, *Studying Religion: An Introduction*, 74–80. London: Equinox Publishing.

Stewart, Charles (ed.). 2007. *Creolization: History, Ethnography, Theory*. Walnut Creek, CA: Left Coast Press.

Stewart, Charles and Rosalind Shaw (eds.). 1994. *Syncretism/Anti-Syncretism: The Politics of Religious Synthesis*. New York: Routledge. https://doi.org/10.4324/9780203451090

Torres-Saillant, Silvio. 2005. *An Intellectual History of the Caribbean*. New York: Palgrave Macmillan.

Tylor, E.B. 1873. *Religion in Primitive Culture*. London: John Murray.

K. Merinda Simmons is Associate Professor of Religious Studies and Graduate Director of the Religion in Culture MA program at the University of Alabama. Her books include *Changing the Subject: Writing Women across the African Diaspora* (Ohio State University Press, 2014), *The Trouble with Post-Blackness* (co-edited with Houston A. Baker, Jr., Columbia University Press, 2015) and *Race and Displacement* (co-edited with Maha Marouan, University of Alabama Press, 2013). She is working on a monograph tentatively entitled *Sourcing Slave Religion: Theorizing Experience in the American South*, as well as two co-authored books: *Race and New Modernisms* (with Andy Crank, Bloomsbury) and *Gender: A Critical Primer* (with Craig Martin, Equinox). She is the editor of the book series *Concepts in the Study of Religion: Critical Primers*.

5. Response to K. Merinda Simmons

When Is It OK to Borrow? Discourses on Syncretism and Cultural Appropriation

Craig Martin

Leftist criticisms of "cultural appropriation" negatively value a cultural phenomenon that is structurally analogous to what other leftist discourses laud as subversive creolization or hybridity. This chapter compares the two phenomena and their competing evaluations in political discourses and suggests that an alternative set of critical questions would provide a more sophisticated point of entry for cultural critique.

In "Strategizing Subjectivity: Creolization and Intentionality in Studies of Caribbean Religions," K. Merinda Simmons draws attention to the moral valences attached to analyses of what is variously called "syncretism," "creolization," "hybridity," or the cultural production of "diasporic" communities. As Simmons notes, scholars who study "creolization" tend to reify the apparent "source" cultures from which so-called creole hybrids are formed. Creolization, we are to understand, draws on "authentic" African or Caribbean cultural traditions. In addition, the adaptation of these "authentic" traditions is described as subversive of the imposed, colonial hegemonies within which the creolizers live. Often, in such scholarly analyses, "the point becomes one about cultural resourcefulness and the subversive reestablishment of a group's 'original' or 'traditional' beliefs and practices" (see p. 86 in this volume). Analysis of hybridity therefore reinforces the notion of an originary source and simultaneously points to the genius of agents who cleverly adapt the authoritative past to the present. Arguably, such work employs the identification

strategy of creating a nostalgic teleology: creolization is a manifesta-
tion of the creative spirit of immigrants, realizing the potential they
bring from their authentic culture of origin. This praise of subversive
hybridity perhaps comes naturally to scholars with left-leaning political sympathies, at least for those who work to recover the agency
of those whose power has been circumscribed so effectively, but it
comes with costs; as Simmons notes, "[t]he seeming progressivism of
the intellectual move, however, too often maintains a nostalgic view
of a monolithic Africa" (p. 87). While attempting to avoid essentialist
accounts of subjects of African descent, such scholars ironically reify
the "Africa" from which they create new, hybrid cultures. In sum,

> the presumed anti-essentialist heterogeneity "inherent" in creo-
> lization nonetheless engenders a simplistic and rather essential-
> izing dichotomy between dominant and marginalized, as well as
> belief and performance. Authenticity claims are thus allowed,
> it would seem, as long as they are tied to conversations about
> strategy and subversion on the part of marginalized groups.
> (p. 89)

Of course, the production of syncretic forms of culture by dominant
rather than marginalized groups may be valued differently.

Consider, for instance, the increasingly popular discourse on "cultural appropriation" that we today find in academia but also throughout popular culture. Also hailing from the left, critiques of cultural
appropriation deride as theft those "hybrid" combinations of culture
apparently "owned" by marginalized groups—groups that are themselves essentialized in the critique of appropriation. Structurally,
we seem to be working with an identical phenomenon as described
above: some individual or group borrows from an authentic form of
culture, creatively mixing and matching with elements from another
culture. The primary difference between the discourses on "syncretism" and "cultural appropriation"—a difference that helps us account
for the opposite moral valuations attached to the analyses—seems to
be whether those doing the borrowing are members of a dominant or
marginalized group.

Consider a few examples of recent criticisms of "cultural appropriation." In an article from *The Atlantic* titled "A Food Fight at Oberlin

College," columnist Conor Friedersdorf draws attention to complaints at Oberlin by students who object to "cultural appropriation" in their school's cafeteria (Friedersdorf 2015). According to one complaint, the food service

> has a history of blurring the line between culinary diversity and cultural appropriation by modifying the recipes without respect for certain Asian countries' cuisines. This uninformed representation of cultural dishes has been noted by a multitude of students, many of who have expressed concern over the gross manipulation of traditional recipes.

According to another complaint,

> [t]he sushi is anything but authentic for Tomoyo Joshi, a College junior from Japan, who said that the undercooked rice and lack of fresh fish is disrespectful ... . "When you're cooking a country's dish for other people, including ones who have never tried the original dish before, you're also representing the meaning of the dish as well as its culture," Joshi said. "So if people not from that heritage take food, modify it and serve it as 'authentic,' it is appropriative."

Much like the praise of creolization, these condemnations of appropriation essentialize the apparent source culture—implicitly deploying a return-to-origins narrative strategy. Asian cuisine is apparently truly Asian only when it appears in its "authentic" form, without modification, manipulation, or adaptation. However, rather than seeing such syncretic dishes as clever, subversive hybrids that widen American cuisine in creative, unforeseen ways, here they're derided as immoral or unethical imposters of the "real" thing.

Similarly, in the *Huffington Post* commentary titled "Is My Yoga Cultural Appropriation? What to Do About It," Susanna Barkataki condemns the uncredited cultural appropriation of Indian yoga as just another form of colonization (Barkataki 2016). Surprisingly, the commentary begins by noting that yoga itself is an unstable referent: "Yoga has always been syncretic ... . It began in what we now call Indus Valley Civilization, and it predated even what we now know as any formal religious practice. It has been changed, reinvented, shaped and reshaped over time. It is partly this re-imagining that makes it exciting." However, despite this acknowledgment, there is apparently an essence to yoga that, when left out, makes it inauthentic and unethical. Appropriation, as she goes on to outline, involves the:

> [p]ower to pick and choose what we take from a culture and to leave the rest behind.
>
> For example, physical practice, or asana, is one of the eight limbs. So in the Western world, in a lot of places where we see yoga practiced, primarily what is being practiced is one of the eight limbs—asana.
>
> Practicing just one of those eight limbs without practicing the rest is not practicing the full range and depth of what yoga has to offer.
>
> If someone from the dominant culture does a teacher training and choses [sic] not to focus on or is unaware of the complexity of yoga's true aim or the roots of the practices, they are culturally appropriating yoga.
>
> By remaining unaware of the history, roots, complexity and challenges of the heritage from which yoga springs and the challenges it has faced under Western culture, they perpetuate a re-colonization of it.

Here it seems that unless one adopts (i.e., reproduces and thereby authorizes) the whole—a reified whole, to be sure—one is reproducing the violence of colonialism.

This last claim sits uneasily with the earlier qualification that yoga is—and has been—always changing. If it is always changing, then there is no such "whole" to appropriate, let alone reproduce. On the contrary, in the author's own words the "it" under consideration has been "changed, reinvented, shaped and reshaped over time." What makes this adaptation different from all of its apparent predecessors? Perhaps only the status of those doing the adapting—not an insignificant factor, to be sure. However, since there is no account of who did the appropriation of yoga throughout Indian history—was it by brahmins or untouchables?—we don't have a basis for that judgment. Perhaps yoga was *always* appropriated and modified by elites, in contest with yet other elites.

In the end, despite such qualifications, the author recommends recognizing the authentic sources of full, authentic yoga (deploying the often-used imagery of roots and branches):

> The best way to decolonize our practice is to honor its roots. Of course yoga is always evolving. It's just a matter of honoring where things came from.
> If we are a yoga practitioner—ask our teachers for more than asana. Going deeper, asking and taking the time to learn and practice more.
> Practice and teach as many of the limbs as possible. So we can experience and the full range that yoga has to offer.

The return-to-origins narrative identifying the essence at the source could scarcely be any more explicit. And, much as with the creolization discourses analyzed by Simmons and the critique of the appropriation of Asian cuisine discussed above, this discourse reifies, and thereby to some extent dehistoricizes, the apparent source culture. For this critic, if we're going to borrow from India, we need to recognize and respect the essential differences of the donor culture, and avoid appropriating the merely convenient parts rather than the whole—we must return to the imagined, *entire* origin, it seems. Despite the nod to the idea that yoga is continually reshaped—not a thing-in-itself but an ongoing process—at the end we return to an essentializing dichotomy.

One more striking feature of the discourse on "cultural appropriation"—despite its apparent critique of colonialism and hegemonic powers—is its ironic reliance on certain capitalist assumptions about ownership of culture and identity, assumptions that rely on the idea that culture is a form of intellectual property. For instance, according to a report from *The Guardian*, the U.S. clothier, Urban Outfitters, was sued by the Navajo Nation for appropriating the Navajo name in the marketing of its products: "Urban Outfitters reached a settlement with the Navajo Nation after illegally using the tribe's name for a collection that included 'Navajo hipster panties' and a 'Navajo print flask'" (Woolf 2016). The appropriation of the Navajo name was criticized in part because the products did not represent "authentic" and "unique" Navajo culture: "These and the dozens of other tacky products you are currently selling referencing Native America make a mockery of our identity and unique cultures." However, despite their disgust at the items marketed, the Navajo Nation was able to come to an agreement with Urban Outfitters, allowing them to license the trademarked Navajo name in the sale of such products:

> The tribe registered the name Navajo as a trademark in 1943, according to court documents.
>
> In a press release Thursday, Navajo Nation president Russell Bagaye said: "We applaud [Urban Outfitters] for acknowledging the validity of the Navajo Nation trademark and are glad we have settled this matter."
>
> "We expect that any company considering the use of the Navajo name, or our designs or motifs, will ask us for our permission," he added.
>
> Both sides settled for an undisclosed amount but have entered into a "supply and license agreement", which says that the Navajo and Urban Outfitters plan to collaborate on a line of Native American jewelry.
>
> "We are pleased we've reached an agreement with the Navajo Nation," said Urban Outfitters general counsel Azeez Hayne in a statement. "We take the rights of artists and designers seriously, both in protecting our own and in respecting the rights of others."

Again, on this view "culture" is apparently an intellectual property that some people own and that others can either steal or legally acquire, given the trade of other sorts of capital.

Arguably, depending on our interests, we could tell this story in one of two ways. On the one hand, perhaps the Navajo Nation is syncretically and subversively adopting capitalist discourses for their own, counter-hegemonic ends? Or, on the other hand, perhaps the Navajo Nation is guilty of cultural appropriation, wrongfully adapting Euro-American elements of capitalist culture for their own purposes, passing it off as if it were their own, but without full attribution? Such stories differ not in their core claims: either narrative involves the adoption and adaptation of cultural elements from an alien "source" culture. Rather, they differ only in the underlying moral valuation attached.

One final example: in 2017 the white painter Dana Schutz was widely criticized for her painting—which appeared in a special display at the Whitney Museum of American Art—depicting Emmett Till, who was lynched by whites in 1955. As the *New York Times* reported, one protester insisted that "The subject matter is not Schutz'" (Kennedy 2017). Another protester felt similarly:

> [c]alling the painting "a mockery" and "an injustice to the black community," Mr. Bright adds that he believes the work perpetuates "the same kind of violence that was enacted" on Till "just to make a painting move."
>
> "I feel like she doesn't have the privilege to speak for black people as a whole or for Emmett Till's family," Mr. Bright says in the video. He also objects to the thought that the painting could be sold and make Ms. Schutz, whose work is highly sought after, a significant amount of money.

Here it seems, as with the Navajo trademark, that certain forms of culture are owned by some groups and stolen by others. "The subject matter is not Schutz'": this statement implies that the subject matter is owned by someone else. Similarly, only those who rightly own the intellectual property rights can profit off the form of culture at hand. Schutz's appropriation and profit are, apparently, theft. What is implied by this claim is that someone else owns the intellectual property rights to Emmett Till—not Till himself, of course, since he was murdered decades ago. The strategy of identification here is genealogical: only those properly within the African-American family tree can speak to or profit from Till's story.

Two things emerge, then, from the discourse on cultural appropriation. First, in order for it to function, the discourse assumes that cultures are monolithic, whole, and distinct from one another. Second, the discourse assumes that culture can be owned, and that some people rightly profit—and others unfairly profit—from the use or adaptation of such cultures. Despite the counter-hegemonic interests of those who level the charge of "cultural appropriation," the discourse ironically naturalizes the hegemonic logic of capitalism.

These two assumptions lead to some strange conclusions. For instance, despite the fact that none of the social critics discussed above seem to identify as Arab, I've little doubt that they use Arabic numerals (as opposed to, for instance, Roman numerals). Is the Navajo nation, then, stealing from or doing violence to all Arabs when cashing royalty checks from Urban Outfitters written using Arabic numerals? That would seem to follow from the background assumptions the criticisms of cultural appropriation rely upon, but I doubt few critics would accept such a conclusion. Despite their rhetorical power and appeal, without an elaboration or explanation of why some adaptations are condemnable "cultural appropriations" and others celebrated "creolizations," these criticisms remain theoretically vacuous.

I suspect that what lies behind the criticisms of cultural appropriation is a critique of asymmetrical power relations. According to the critic of the appropriation of yoga discussed above, "cultural appropriation involves power. Usually a systemic imbalance of power" (Barkataki 2016). We can accept that *all* culture is appropriated in some sense, and nevertheless still hope to draw attention to how some instances of appropriation—or syncretism—reinforce existing inequalities. However, the latter sort of analysis would differ from the criticisms reviewed above insofar as the emphasis would be on how culture—of whatever sort—is used in ways that reproduce unequal social relations, rather than on who owns the intellectual property rights to a reified, monolithic source tradition. For instance, when social actors practice yoga in California, are the interests of South Asian brahmins harmed? Are stereotypes about the "mystical East" reinforced in ways that disadvantage contemporary Indian-Americans? Does capital disproportionately accrue to corporations that deploy advertising campaigns that appeal to customers' sense of the exotic? Do Indian-American purveyors of yoga benefit from the circulation of Orientalist stereotypes? These critical questions about asymmetrical power relations can be asked without scholars committing themselves to the problematic assumptions that cultures are discrete or that they can be owned.

In addition, insofar as the *allegation of* "cultural appropriation" or "syncretism"—or whatever else we want to call the ubiquitous practice of ongoing adoption and adaptation of culture—can serve both hegemonic *and* counter-hegemonic interests, perhaps the allegation itself could become an object of scholarly analysis. When social actors allege that this form of adaptation is syncretic or appropriative, whose interests are served and whose are thwarted? Are African-Americans aided or harmed by the public objection that Schutz has appropriated Emmett Till's imagery? Who benefits from the charge that Oberlin's food service sells inauthentic food? And if, in response to the charge, the cafeteria served "more authentic" food, who would benefit? The purported "owners" of the source culture? The food service industry? The cafeteria's patrons?

All that is to say: the allegations of syncretism and cultural appropriation themselves are identity claims with social consequences, and attention to those consequences might be equally of interest to scholars as the allegations themselves.

Returning to Simmons' chapter, I might press her to explicitly theorize the material consequences of scholarly claims about syncretism. Her chapter concludes with the following claim:

> Nostalgically talking about what makes the space and its people unique and special, scholars get swept up in the naïve fantasy that their own designations name real things "out there." In so doing, they do not recuperate the marginalized but perpetuate the hegemonic—the very inverse of their articulated aims. (p. 93)

That is, scholars who, e.g., praise hybrid combinations of Caribbean and North American culture risk, with their praise, reinforcing essentialist and colonialist dichotomies between Euro-American cultures and its "others." While I don't disagree, it might nevertheless be useful to consider questions about the material consequences of such scholarship. Do scholars have an influence on the public sufficient to sway white Americans' stereotypes of the Caribbean? Are consumers of this sort of scholarly literature likely to develop sentiments of antipathy toward Caribbean "others"? Can scholarly stereotypes compete with the stereotypes deployed in the *Pirates of the Caribbean* film franchise? Who actually reads this scholarly literature, how might it influence their behavior, and would there be any appreciable effect on the interests of Caribbean-Americans?

References

Barkataki, Susanna. 2016. "Is My Yoga Cultural Appropriation? What to Do About It." *Huffington Post* (9 February). https://www.huffingtonpost.com/susanna-barkataki/is-my-yoga-cultural-appro_b_9191342.html

Friedersdorf, Conor. 2015. "A Food Fight at Oberlin College." *The Atlantic* (21 December). https://www.theatlantic.com/politics/archive/2015/12/the-food-fight-at-oberlin-college/421401/

Kennedy, Randy. 2017. "White Artist's Painting of Emmett Till at Whitney Biennial Draws Protests." *The New York Times* (21 March). https://www.nytimes.com/2017/03/21/arts/design/painting-of-emmett-till-at-whitney-biennial-draws-protests.html?mcubz=0&_r=0

Woolf, Nicky. 2016. "Urban Outfitters Settles with Navajo Nation after Illegally Using Tribe's Name." *The Guardian* (18 November). https://www.theguardian.com/us-news/2016/nov/18/urban-outfitters-navajo-nation-settlement

Craig Martin is Professor of Religious Studies at St Thomas Aquinas College. His research concerns theory and method in the study of religion and culture, specifically focusing on discourse analysis and ideology critique. His recent books include *Capitalizing Religion: Ideology and the Opiate of the Bourgeoisie* (Bloomsbury 2014) and *A Critical Introduction to the Study of Religion*, Second Edition (Routledge 2017).

6. Reply to Craig Martin

"The Other Is Not": Mediating Specialness and Specificity

K. Merinda Simmons

This reply to Craig Martin's "When Is It OK to Borrow?" returns to the discussion of power dynamics involved in narrative acts that describe particular histories of race and experience. Those dynamics are likewise at work in classifying whether various depictions and narratives are nuanced introspections or, following up on Martin's response, cultural appropriations. The question of what kind of priority is given to various identifications—and who gets engage in such ranking—should be considered in relation to Martin's helpful challenge to think in terms of the "material consequences of such scholarly claims about syncretism." In taking up this question, I argue that the problem is not with appropriation so much as it with the authenticity claims contained therein.

In one of the early seasons[1] of *Star Trek: The Next Generation*, viewers learn more about the android Data's character—at once robotic and idiosyncratic—in a scene that has stuck with me ever since. He and the *Enterprise*'s new Chief Medical Officer, Dr Pulaski (who would serve between stints of the more popular Beverly Crusher), have the following brief exchange after she pronounces his name with a short 'a' vowel ("DAT-ah" rather than "DAY-ta") and he corrects her:

---

1   The episode, called "The Child," is the first in the second season, to be exact.

Data, look at this.
Data.
What?
My name. It is pronounced, "Data."
Oh?
You called me "Data."
(laughing and finally turning to look at him) *What's the*
    difference?
One is my name. The other is not.

Of course the takeaway is not really about pronunciation or semantics but about the endearing frankness that audiences would come to
associate with one of the most compelling and enduring characters in
the *Star Trek* franchise (in my not-so-humble opinion). It also, however, illuminates deeper themes having to do with context, specificity,
self-identification, and the political/rhetorical power of naming. Since
this conversation is, broadly speaking, about the construction and
maintenance of insiders and outsiders, the irony of beginning with a
specific cultural reference important to those of "us" who blurred the
line between Gen-Xers and Millennials—and more so for the even
smaller sociocultural subgroup identified as "trekkies"—is not lost
on me. With the irony also comes appropriateness, though, as I will
claim in what follows.

I do not read Data's correcting Dr Pulanski as his appealing to
essence or a stable underpinning of the naming process. On the contrary, his emphasis on specificity and particularity—"One is my name.
The other is not."—forecloses such illusions. One connotation and
pronunciation of data does not collapse into the proper name Data.
There is, perhaps, an important distinction to make between specialness and specificity. My original chapter focused on what happens, as
I see it, when a case for specialness gets made in the name of specificity. In conflating the two ideas, the scholars I read in the piece lose
sight of the latter when emphasizing the former. That said, if I were
writing the chapter for the first time now, I would likely take greater
pains to nuance a cohort marked "scholars" that currently might read
as more of a monolith than I would like.

So I appreciate this chance to think again about the kinds of power
dynamics involved in narrative acts that describe particular histories

of race and experience. Those dynamics are likewise at work in classifying whether various depictions and narratives are nuanced introspections or, following up on Craig Martin's useful response, cultural appropriations. Martin is quite right to point out that, often, the same logic is at work structurally in critiques of cultural appropriation as is in celebrations of cultural hybridity—as he summarizes it, "some individual or group borrows from an authentic form of culture, creatively mixing and matching with elements from another culture" (see p. 97 in this volume). All the same, I am not willing to suggest (and I likewise do not read Martin to be suggesting) that two claims with similar structural logic have the same effect. Additionally, I would be dissatisfied here to say simply that how a claim is made or received depends on the interests or positionality of those making/receiving it and to leave the discussion there. Where to go, in that case? Martin moves the conversation forward by helpfully casting the discourse on cultural appropriation in terms of its reliance on capitalist ideology. He notes that "despite its apparent critique of colonialism and hegemonic powers," appropriation rhetoric "reli[es] on certain capitalist assumptions about ownership of culture and identity, assumptions that rely on the idea that culture is a form of intellectual property" (p. 100). In thinking about ownership and property—power and consumption—we should consider the ubiquity of something akin to rhetorical ownership, when it gives rise to scholarly analysis and when it gets left alone (despite our erstwhile emphasis on the curiosity of things mundane that order social worlds).

In other words, while the pronunciation of Data's name might seem an unassuming point of information, his correcting Dr Pulaski engages some of the thornier bits of social exchange. The joke is ultimately on the medical officer who assumes an android cannot "own" a sense of self, and the tables of naming power turn in the process. The reason the joke works so well is its appeal to Data as a specific character—the writers manage to personalize *him* (no one would dare call that synthetic life form "it") through his dispassionate correction of the oblivious Dr Pulaski. This specificity, however, cannot be confused with an appeal to authenticity or something particularly special about androids in general. Therein lies the distinction that I find very much worth making when considering what our discourses of cultural hybridity and/or appropriation—and our critiques thereof—are all about.

Martin's examples of the cafeteria options at Oberlin College and the Navajo name in Urban Outfitters products provide accessible moments of how such discourses—of authentic culture, as well as of the appropriation thereof—function in everyday consumer culture. However, there is not an easy one-to-one ratio we should use to quantify or read such moments in the name of savvy cultural criticism. So, while Martin is certainly right in his claim that "Arguably, depending on our interests, we could tell this story [of the Navajo Nation's fraught relationship with the Urban Outfitters chain] in one of two ways," I am not comfortable suggesting that the two ways[2] carry the same narrative weight. Neither am I interested in suggesting a "right" way to use or not use cultural markers. Instead, I find it more helpful to think in terms of what a productive emphasis on specificity, locality, and experience *can* look like. The connective thread that allows scholars like Martin and me to find similarities between discourses on appropriation and the dominant cultural codes they critique is their shared reliance on authenticity claims. There are all sorts of good reasons something called appropriation can be good or bad, expansive or reductive—the process itself and the discourses thereof should be no more essentialized than the cultures to which they refer, after all. However, when relying on authenticity, such discourses lose context specificity and, with it, any substance their users might wish to achieve.

We consistently and with ease assume that different social contexts entertain (or even demand) different codes of address, for example. I am "Dr Simmons" to my students, but my young child would not

---

2   As Martin describes it, "On the one hand, perhaps the Navajo Nation is syncretically and subversively adopting capitalist discourses for their own, counter-hegemonic ends? Or, on the other hand, perhaps the Navajo Nation is guilty of cultural appropriation, wrongfully adapting Euro-American elements of capitalist culture for their own purposes, passing it off as if it were their own, but without full attribution?" (p. 101).

recognize that name. Nicknames offered by my friends or partner, meanwhile, are not accessible to my students or new acquaintances. This is just typical relational discourse—we trade in different rhetorical currencies depending upon variant contexts, and doing so feels normal, even obvious. Despite playing such language games without much conscious effort, the dynamics of power and intimacy become quickly apparent if one scratches the surface to explore just how such codes operate. Or, in a more overtly "political" vein of identity and activism, we might think of how a category like "vagina" was redeployed in Eve Ensler's *The Vagina Monologues* (1996), whose performers inverted a label used to demean women and identified it as a source of voice and empowerment. Published just two years after Ensler's play premiered, Inga Muscio's book *Cunt: A Declaration of Independence* (1998) similarly calls for a reconfiguration of the associative stereotypes accompanying a word historically used as a pejorative slur. Critiques of both texts from progressive feminists that see them couched too much in the politics of second-wave feminism (privileging the experiences of white, cis-gendered women of relative means) are well placed. Nonetheless, they are both important examples of how the perimeters of intellectual property get redrawn in different spaces where intimacy and insider status is forged around rhetorical and cultural codes that have historically been used to ostracize the group in question.

There are myriad examples of such revisions, of course. What I find particularly worth paying attention to in relation to the conversation happening here is what conditions are in play to allow hegemonic groups to feel entitled to have access to these various spaces whose boundaries have been redrawn. That desire for and presumption of access are their own signifiers of the kinds of power Martin asks us to think about. The perpetual controversies surrounding the use of the n-word and the perennial irritation by white people over not being able to use it "ironically"—especially in contexts where there is white consumerism, like hip-hop—are cases in point. When historically dominant groups fail (or refuse) to see historically marginalized groups as simply employing the same linguistic and relational codes of power and intimacy, what we see are the effects of structural power and entitlement at work.[3] Solange makes the point effectively in her song "F.U.B.U.":[4]

> *Don't feel bad if you can't sing along*
> *Just be glad you got the whole wide world*
> *This us*
> *This shit is from us*
> *Some shit you can't touch*

People code-switch constantly, and there are all sorts of moments in which we are perfectly comfortable suggesting that this or that word, name, event, etc., "belongs" to a certain group. Likewise, forbidding others from gaining access to those same things is a longstanding mode of consolidating and perpetuating insider status and the power afforded to it. A scholarly discussion of these dynamics, then, would stop short if it pointed out simply that this happens universally, that competing groups employ the same strategies. An important addition to that discussion, to my mind, is one similar to the call for scholarly self-reflexivity that has become a common refrain among social theorists.

Dana Schutz's painting "Open Casket," whose controversy Martin discusses as well, is a perfect example of how such a call might work. Martin's hunch is that "what lies behind the criticisms of cultural appropriation is a critique of asymmetrical power relations" (p. 103), and I would agree that that is certainly part of what is operating in the debates and protests over Schutz's status as a white painter representing African-American subjects.[5] I would add to this, however,

3   Ta-Nehisi Coates made this point succinctly during a Q&A session at one of the events on his book tour of *We Were Eight Years in Power*: https://www.youtube.com/watch?v=QO15S3WC9pg
4   From her 2016 album *A Seat at the Table*.
5   Just a few of the resources outlining the intricacies of the controversy are as follows: https://www.nytimes.com/2017/04/04/learning/subjects-off-limit-artists-dana-schutz-henry-taylor.html
https://www.newyorker.com/magazine/2017/04/10/why-dana-schutz-painted-emmett-till
https://www.nytimes.com/2017/03/21/arts/design/painting-of-emmett-till-at-whitney-biennial-draws-protests.html

that another really important aspect is what I see, in this case, to be Schutz's failure to take adequate stock of those asymmetries and her role in them. Being self-reflexive about her own whiteness, how such a label works to perpetuate the structural discrimination against African-Americans, and how she is complicit in those same structures even when her politics decry them would go a long way toward productively complicating what otherwise can get read as a "BLACK DEATH SPECTACLE," to use the description of Parker Bright, who wrote that phrase on the back of a t-shirt that he then wore while standing in front of Schutz's painting. There has been much back-and-forth, with good points raised on both sides of the issue (perhaps the most eloquent defense of Schutz's painting coming from Zadie Smith's review in *Harper's* that bears the provocative subtitle, "Who owns black pain?").[6] A telling response came from Dana Schutz herself, however, who said, "I don't know what it is like to be black in America, but I do know what it is like to be a mother. Emmett was Mamie Till's only son. The thought of anything happening to your child is beyond comprehension."[7] In this statement, Schutz distances herself from the racial dimensions of the subject matter and instead presents her proximity to maternal subjectivity which, it is worth noting, is not rendered in the painting. Whence the prioritizing of racial identification in the work and of a maternal identification in its defense? What of Schutz's ability to engage racial identification when she chooses and cast it aside when it suits?

While the questions of whether personal experience is deemed necessary (and, if so, how much) in order to identify with a particular subject are certainly useful fodder for important discussions on this topic, the questions of what kind of priority is given to various identifications—and who gets engage in such ranking—should be considered in relation to Martin's helpful challenge to think in terms of the "material consequences of scholarly claims about syncretism" (p. 104). To my mind, the problem is not with appropriation (inasmuch as appropriation seems an unavoidable part of the constant

---

6   https://harpers.org/archive/2017/07/getting-in-and-out/

7   https://www.theguardian.com/artanddesign/2017/mar/21/whitney-biennial-emmett-till-painting-dana-schutz

code-switching that we do all the time in order to present the semblance of a stable self) so much as it is with the authenticity claims
contained therein.

Words and cultural codes do not contain meaning without context,
of course. That is why my students do not call me the nicknames my
friends have given me. These relationships are different, as are the
way we identify inside those spaces. So in acknowledging our status as consumers, we should ask ourselves: What spaces do we want
access to? And why? If we understand that we code-switch in normal
course depending on the specific relationality to local spaces, whence
the expectation to move into spaces to which there is little historical
and/or personal proximity? What groups tend to have that expectation? What kinds of power predicate that expectation? To what extent
are particular modes of capital and consumption relied upon in the
act of expecting?

In a terrific episode of their *Still Processing* podcast, *New York
Times* writers and culture critics Jenna Wortham and Wesley Morris
take up the "Open Casket" painting, as well as Jordan Peele's film
Get Out (2017). Wortham makes an important point about the shifting contextual registers of something called "blackness," noting that
British writer Zadie Smith's essay defending Schutz is paired with
a photograph by Deanna Lawson—a black photographer living in
Baltimore whose work was also part of the Whitney Biennial. For
Wortham, Smith's discussion of black experiences and representations conflate the vastly different identifications of racial otherness in
the U.S. and the U.K. To invoke Data, one is a particular context. The
other is not. This call for cognizance and more direct discussion of
that mode of specificity is one I find well worth heeding. Meanwhile,
as Wortham and Morris also mention, the conversation surrounding
the Whitney Biennial has largely focused on Schutz and what she
should or should not have access to, rather than the work of black
artists like Lawson or Henry Taylor, whose painting "The Times,
They Ain't Changin Fast Enough" represented the death of Philando
Castille at the hands of police.

The point is not simply that these artists are all using similar subject
matter to explore themes of racialized pain and exploitation. Nor is
it that competing opinions and representations utilize similar starting

points. Certainly this is the case, as is true across virtually every ave-nue of social life. After all, Dr Pulaski's mistake when addressing Data is that she thought she was talking about him when, in fact, she was revealing her own preconceptions. When Data offers his own self-identification in reply, the effect is so compelling because of its specificity—one difficult to argue with. Of course, it is also compel-ling because I am a *Star Trek: TNG* fan. Thus, Martin's good ques-tions about the material consequences of such discussions are more adequately approached when we take up the ways in which invisible norms work, the very real extent to which artists, writers, scholars —appropriators all—demonstrate their awareness (or lack thereof) about their own biases, codes, and insider statuses that necessarily get projected in their renderings.

K. Merinda Simmons is Associate Professor of Religious Studies and Graduate Director of the Religion in Culture MA program at the University of Alabama. Her books include *Changing the Subject: Writing Women across the African Diaspora* (Ohio State University Press, 2014), *The Trouble with Post-Blackness* (co-edited with Houston A. Baker, Jr., Columbia University Press, 2015) and *Race and Displacement* (co-edited with Maha Marouan, University of Alabama Press, 2013). She is working on a monograph tentatively entitled *Sourcing Slave Religion: Theorizing Experience in the American South*, as well as two co-authored books: *Race and New Modernisms* (with Andy Crank, Bloomsbury) and *Gender: A Critical Primer* (with Craig Martin, Equinox). She is the editor of the book series *Concepts in the Study of Religion: Critical Primers*.

SITE III:
ACTS OF COMPARISON

7. Writing Women out of Women's Movements

The Discursive Boundaries of Feminism

Leslie Dorrough Smith

Over the past several decades, various attempts have been made by feminist scholars to describe the activism of many international women's groups as "feminist" even though such groups often heavily resemble many American conservative women's groups that have often been labeled by the same scholars as "anti-feminist." Using the work of Chandra Talpade Mohanty and Uma Narayan as a frame of reference, I discuss how some scholars of "global feminism" use certain rhetorical techniques to make this identity labeling possible in order to fit a series of specific political interests, even though such techniques may depend on a philosophical double standard to achieve the appearance of consistency.

One of the most significant developments in feminist activism over the past several decades has been the recognition that feminism is not—to put it simply—a single thing. The 1960s and '70s saw a number of Western feminists rally around the notion that the world's women represent a unified sisterhood allied against patriarchy, but this sentiment was far from ubiquitous. Within the next couple of decades serious questions began to arise among feminist scholars and activists alike regarding which women feminism actually represented.

The problem was that many women from across the globe either could not relate to, disagreed with, or were being patently harmed by the ideals that the largely white, privileged, Western feminist movement espoused. For instance, while many American feminists poured much of their energies into positioning women as major players within labor forces fueled by capitalist economies, many women from other cultures and regions were faced with challenges to their physical survival that the spread of this very capitalism had wrought (including the loss of small-scale industries, the break-up of families pursuing rapidly disappearing employment, and ecological decimation, among others).

In response, scholarship on global women's activism began to focus more on the presence of multicultural, postcolonial, and third-world feminisms.[1] This series of umbrella terms refers to an array of worldwide women's movements that have represented the interests of many poor women, women of color, and women living in the third world. As a result of this diversification of perspectives, terms like "woman," "feminism," "oppression," and "equity" were subjected to serious interrogation, for it soon became clear that there is no single set of issues around which women organize, nor a single type of experience that women count as limiting, oppressive, or discriminatory. This latter point is one of particular importance, for some female activists worldwide have not only consciously embraced aspects of their culture's traditional gender roles, but have also rejected calling themselves "feminists" even as they pushed for social reforms that, in a different context, might have borne that label.

For those not familiar with the history of Western feminism's evolution, what this has meant, practically speaking, is that many who already identified as a part of (primarily Western) feminist movements have had to acknowledge that the campaigns undertaken by women worldwide are much more diverse than older feminist scholarship had previously described. In turn, more recent scholarship has documented how various manifestations of global feminism have often stood at odds with the platforms that Western feminists have traditionally espoused.

---

1   Although a multitude of scholars helped this movement come to life, major names include figures like Gloria Anzaldua, Cherrie Moraga, Elizabeth Spelman, Maria Lugones, Uma Narayan, Chandra Talpade Mohanty, bell hooks, Patricia Hill Collins, and Audre Lorde (and the list goes on).

Despite this, there still remains one sector of female activists who are rarely mentioned in conversations on global women's movements and who are instead discussed in separate, compartmentalized fashion: right-wing and otherwise conservative women. It may seem common sense that right-wing women would *not* be included in a discussion of global feminist activism, since many of them are openly anti-feminist. But as I will shortly discuss, concern about (and even opposition to) the values and platforms of Western feminism are often just as common among the members of what scholars call "global feminist movements" as they are among right-wing activist women. Nevertheless, these two groups tend to be treated in scholarship as if they are separate species even though their commonalities are often substantial.

With this methodological tangle in mind, my interest in this chapter is to consider what rhetorical moves are at play in the popular construction of the categories "global women's movements," "global feminisms," and (by implication) "right-wing women" within certain selections of feminist scholarship. I am inspired to address this topic, in part, by re-examining the observations made by Uma Narayan and Chandra Talpade Mohanty in their separate, but duly prominent, writings on the category "third-world women." In the passages of their work that I will shortly discuss, both Narayan and Mohanty focus on the manner in which third-world women and their cultures are approached by those who study them. My intention is to take the structure of their arguments and ask whether similar critiques might be applied to the manner in which liberal feminist scholars currently tend to approach both global women's and feminist movements through the unspoken "other," the conservative woman.

Because discussions on the processes of identity construction are often easily confused for moralistic judgments on how a group should portray itself, let me reiterate what I am *not* attempting to do: my interest in pursuing this topic should not be read as a campaign for the greater visibility of right-wing women in scholarship, an ethical indictment of tendencies in global feminist scholarship, or a treatise in support of the agendas of conservative women's movements. And even though I am suggesting that the specific pieces of scholarship I cite are indicative of larger trends in feminist thought, I am not reducing every instance of scholarship on global feminist activism to the selections I feature here.

Instead, what I am presuming of this body of work is much the same thing that I would presume when studying any social group, which is that the tensions, contradictions, and inconsistencies that underlie these most basic categories and terms are not a special flaw of or hypocrisy endemic to the feminists who create feminist scholarship. Instead, they are simply a normal part of the rhetorical tug of war that must take place in order for any group to craft an identity that is strong and yet inclusive enough to weather ongoing political contestation.

Selective Distinction

My interest in this topic is traceable to my own research on gender and American right-wing women's movements. Several such movements tend not to have extensive international ties in great part because concepts of American exceptionalism are so fundamental to their ideology. This is why it is noteworthy when, from time to time, they invoke the right-wing activism of women from other countries as a marker of the promise (and progress) of the spread of global conservatism.

Ironically, though, much of the international activism praised by American conservative women is often the same sort of activism appearing in volumes about global feminism, even if differently interpreted. For instance, both groups may praise grassroots female activism against prostitution, although the rationale of the former may include beliefs about the harms of institutionalizing non-monogamous sex in addition to the social, economic, and psychological damage associated with sexual exploitation that the latter may emphasize.

As someone interested in the ways that rhetoric is used to create specific social perceptions and realities, I find it difficult to bypass the contradictions in this phenomenon without giving them further examination. The scholarship on global feminist and women's movements certainly acknowledges that the women of the world embrace a variety of perspectives and fight for a number of different things in the name of liberation, but very little of it actually interrogates the unspoken lines that designate which women will be called "feminist" and which will be called "conservative" or "right-wing." Further complicating the naming process, scholarly portrayals of right-wing women's movements have long been crafted by left-leaning or left-wing scholars. The result is that conservative activism has often been portrayed as "static and ubiquitous," as Kirsten Marie Delegard describes it, crafting a wooden, homogenized conservative woman as a foil against which more progressive women are measured (Delegard 2012: 14).

Before directly engaging the scholarship itself, I want to take a moment to consider the dynamics involved in the politics of naming as they are discussed in the works of Uma Narayan and Chandra Talpade Mohanty, whose insights into the politics of Western feminism have been influential forces in shaping multicultural feminist scholarship. Although they address this directly to varying degrees, Narayan and Mohanty's separate works introduce the possibility that certain sectors of feminist scholarship may actually depend on creating notions of difference and opposition that can, themselves, generate oppressive circumstances.

In her well-known work *Dislocating Cultures: Identities, Traditions, and Third World Feminism*, Narayan begins by disclosing the challenges faced by third-world feminists who interrogate the patriarchal practices of their own cultures. She observes that traditional cultures attempt to shield themselves from cultural critique by claiming that their practices, however oppressive, bear some sort of special essence the loss of which will irreparably damage the culture if they are stopped. Third-world feminist scholars who seek to evaluate their own cultures through a feminist lens are thus often chastised for their critiques and are frequently accused of having become "Westernized," an epithet that suggests a sort of disloyalty to one's nation or people (Narayan 1997).

The context in which such critiques take place lends more complexity to the issue, for the women living in such cultures frequently reject feminism even though they are often deeply dissatisfied with their cultures for the very reasons that feminists highlight, Narayan observes. This irony is played out when such women are willing to engage in political activism, but do so by using the overt rationale that social changes will make them better wives, mothers, or otherwise reinforce some sort of traditional identity frame. The result is that they rhetorically lend support to the patriarchal status quo while at the same time attempting to free themselves of some its parameters (19).

Situations such as these are often the legacy of the injuries endured at the hands of colonization, Narayan notes, for the initial division between "Western" and "native" cultures was wrought as a critical precondition of colonization, wherein colonizers forged dramatic, symbolic lines between themselves and the colonized "others" in order to prove the illegitimacy of the latter (15). This rhetoric, she writes, depended on the valorization of certain ideals and principles that could never be realized if the power imbalance between the colonizers and the colonized was to persist, as in many colonialist's claims that they embodied liberty and justice while simultaneously enslaving those they colonized. The tendency to preserve even the oppressive aspects of one's culture is thus contextualized by Narayan as a rather natural defense mechanism created in response to colonialism's legacy.

What Narayan is ultimately showing, then, is that the stark identity distinctions wrought during times of social oppression can morph across generations into categories that, although fueled by different political concerns, nevertheless remain just as powerful and potentially oppressive. In this case, accusations of Westernization by third-world inhabitants against the scholars who study them, while grounded in a history of colonization and oppression, can nevertheless continue to function in the service of the once-colonized culture's patriarchal status quo (19–20). Narayan invokes Partha Chatterjee's remark that anti-Western and anti-feminist sentiment in the name of cultural preservation is nothing other than "ideological justification for the selective appropriation of Western modernity," for while feminism may be on trial in these charges, other instances of the infiltration of Western culture (including technology, media, etc.) are often quite welcomed (28). The issue, then, is not whether Westernization is desirable, but which "Westernizations" are accepted because they do not pose any significant threat to existing power structures (22–4).

If the politics of which Narayan speaks are about the selective use of a term for specific ends, then Mohanty's insights further demonstrate the power of rhetoric to create terms that not only define subjects, but also allow those who dominate the rhetoric the ability to control their own identity construction. Mohanty's famous essay, "Under Western Eyes: Feminist Scholarship and Colonialist Discourses," calls to task Western feminist scholars for constructing a "composite, singular, Third-World woman" whose identity—whether accurate or not—is portrayed in such a way that it feeds into the ideological needs of Western feminism (2003: 42). Mohanty's analysis has won considerable attention for the role that it has played in highlighting how feminist scholarship can be implicated in creating the very social barriers that feminists purport to tear down.

In an argument that echoes Said's Orientalist model, Mohanty notes that the predominant Western characterization of third-world women tells more about Western feminists than it does about any accurate reality that most third-world women collectively experience. Because Western scholars have tended to study third-world women in ways that homogenize and reinforce certain stereotypes about them (that they are poor and defenseless, among others), the end result is that the superiority of Western culture is asserted (42, 19).

In this sense, Mohanty argues that Western scholars have often portrayed third-world women in ways that are "arbitrarily constructed" and yet remain imbued with "the authorizing signature of Western humanist discourse" (21–2). Because of the power relationships established in this move, Mohanty is careful to note that her analysis is not applicable only to the Western study of third-world women, but "holds for any discourse that sets up its own authorial subjects as the implicit referent, i.e., the yardstick by which to encode and represent cultural Others. It is in this move that power is exercised in discourse" (21).

This latter point is one of some significance, for if we take Mohanty at her word that the technique of which she writes might be present in any number of power relations, then Narayan and Mohanty's arguments provide a foundation for considering the larger implications of the politics of labeling in feminist scholarship. More specifically, if we take the time to see the possible conflicts, contradictions, and gray areas in scholarship that characterize how the tendencies among "global feminists" are described, can we see a larger strategy at work?

High-Stakes Definitions

We can explore how this contestation in labels takes place through a basic examination of how scholars approach and describe global women's and feminist movements. In volumes devoted to this topic, many introductions start off by attempting to delineate the boundaries of feminism so that the reader can more clearly see how women across the globe are concerned about similar things. Indeed, there are many different types of activism that such research covers, including everything from campaigns against domestic violence, sexual harassment, female genital mutilation, and rape, and in favor of expanded voting rights, reproductive control, educational access, wage equity, financial independence, and landownership rights, to name just a few prominent examples.

The common assumption that permeates much of this scholarship is that most women's movements are also feminist in nature, something seen in great part by the tendency of several scholars to avoid specifically defining the term "feminist" even though it is used frequently as an adjective. Only occasionally in this literature do scholars outline the possibility of a distinction between a women's movement and a feminist one, as in Myra Marx Ferree's remark that the term "women's movement" refers to the gender constituency of those being organized, while the term "feminist movement" indicates activism that challenges women's subordination to patriarchy (Ferree 2006: 6). Because fundamentalist religion is one arena where women are often encouraged to engage in anti-feminist activism, it is also not uncommon to find scholars who take care to distinguish women who use religious arguments to advance an otherwise progressive agenda from their religiously traditional (and anti-feminist) counterparts (Arenfeldt and Golley 2012: 29).

On the whole, then, a vigorous conversation on where the line between "conservative" and "feminist" women's movements lies is often noticeably absent, as is a treatment of what sort of behaviors or attitudes a global women's movement would have to adopt in order to be considered anti-feminist. From an analytical perspective this is something of critical importance, for rarely (if ever) are women who are portrayed as explicitly conservative included in these volumes.

For Ferree's part, she (together with Alli Tripp) notes that feminism is "the broad goal of challenging and changing gender relations that subordinate women to men and that thereby also differentially advantage some women and men relative to others," but says that there are many ways to arrive at this goal (Ferree and Tripp 2006: vii). As Ferree and Tripp demonstrate, it is a common theme in scholarship on global feminisms to assert that feminist movements do not need to automatically forefront gender as an explicit cause at all times, as they may have other important concerns that are seemingly or actually disconnected from gender issues (Ferree 2006: 7–8). For instance, Bonnie G. Smith defines feminist activism as a "variety of activism on behalf of social, political, economic, and personal justice" (Smith 2000: 7). What constitutes "justice" does not receive elaboration, but Smith goes on to acknowledge the hotly contested nature of the term in her remark that "there is and has been no single global feminism, no single issue, no single way of pursuing women's ends" (9).

This is, it seems, an important framing technique that frequently appears in many studies: the women's activism featured in the research may not look stereotypically "feminist" in the sense of having a central focus on the abolition of patriarchy, but anything that might deconstruct androcentric or patriarchal power structures— indirectly or otherwise—may well be considered an example of feminism (Bull, Diamond, and Marsh 2000: 4).

If feminism is not limited to socio-structural, anti-patriarchal campaigns and can even include movements that indirectly or inadvertently fight oppressive structures, then much of the research on global women's and feminist movements also strongly forwards the idea that female activists need not call themselves feminists to be regarded as such. Many scholars note that the women they study are hesitant, if not outright resistant, to identify themselves by that label. While the reasons for their rejection are diverse (including the lack of a translatable term "feminism" in the spoken language of several of the activists in question), most female activists familiar with the term refuse it because of its associations with radicalism, anti-femininity, immorality, and hatred of men (Bridger 2000: 118; Lewis 2012: 45; Ferree and Pudrovska 2006: 260).

What this means, then, is that scholars who study global feminist activism do so without firm criteria in hand as to what constitutes such a movement, and this, by all accounts, is by design, since it is difficult for rigid criteria to reflect a multitude of perspectives. Subsequently, the label "feminist" can be deployed to describe most any and every sort of female activism that one chooses so long as one can link the activism to some iteration of female liberation. The refusal by many women's movements to adopt the term "feminism" is often treated as a problem of semantics, for it is presumed by the nature of their activism that their sympathies are otherwise allied with the larger aims of dismantling patriarchy.

The tension surrounding the "semantics issue" is particularly highlighted in instances where women who display quite conservative behavior and attitudes—sometimes blatantly supporting patriarchal institutions—are recontextualized as simply a different sort of feminist. For instance, Leslie Lewis has referred to a group of religiously observant Egyptian women as a "feminist movement" on the basis of their advocacy for women's and children's legal, social, and religious rights, this despite the fact that the women themselves desire no association with the name and otherwise support traditional gender arrangements (Lewis 2012: 45). Doris T. Chang describes how the Taiwanese women's movement is concerned with gender equity at the same time that it essentializes femininity and heterosexual gender complementarity, which she describes as an example of "relational feminism."[2] Similarly, Sue Bridger argues that several female Russian activists idealize the heterosexual, nuclear, consumerist family structure (which many Western feminists have worked so diligently to displace from the pedestal of normalcy) because it represents an economic and cultural stability that most Russians have not experienced in their lifetimes; this is nevertheless referenced by Bridger as a fledgling feminism that simply does not yet recognize what it is

---

2   This is Karen Offen's term. See Chang (2009: 8–9).

(Bridger 2000: 119, 128). Consider also Pernille Arenfeldt and Nawar Al-Hassan Golley's claim that even though many Islamist women are openly in favor of patriarchy, their increasing political activism continues to expand their roles, not contract them. This suggests that their political involvement represents something more liberatory than constraining, and thus warrants their inclusion in a volume on feminist movements (Arenfeldt and Golley 2012: 29).

While it is common for scholars to describe the people they study in ways that the people themselves may not find agreeable, what is ironic here is that many feminists often regard feminism as a tool precisely for women to describe their experiences and views in their own voices. However, what is arguably happening in these examples is that these women's very real objections to the Western feminist (if not liberalist) project are not acknowledged as a legitimate protest, but are translated into a problem of semantics, categorization, or unfortunate historical circumstance that will be remedied once the world's women "properly" understand that feminism is their ally. This is particularly paradoxical since the greater visibility of third-world feminisms is due in great part to frustration over the manner in which Western feminists were misrepresenting and appropriating third-world women, an act so memorably described by Mohanty as a symbolic re-colonization of those who had been previously (physically) colonized (2003: 18–19).

Mohanty's point appears to be one clear reason why so many feminist scholars take pains to remove many of the Western-influenced definitional parameters from feminism as well as significantly broaden its list of appropriate strategies. But an overt disenchantment with Western feminism's boundaries also appears in certain works that consider global women's activism (Shaheed 2010: 93–4).[3] For instance, consider Nancy Naples' comment that she prefers the term "transnational feminism" instead of "global feminism" in order to displace the privilege behind Western notions of individualism and modernity associated with the latter (2002: 6). There is also Lila Abu

3   Shaheed notes that the fight against gender inequity and the desire to create opportunities for women's empowerment were around long before there was a modernist liberal project in existence.

Lughod's critique of Western attempts to translate the Arab women's hijab into a form of female oppression, an idea used by the Bush administration to further strengthen the case to initiate American military strikes in Afghanistan. Although Abu Lughod is speaking only tangentially about Afghan women's movements, her critique is pointed at Western interpretations of the hijab as a form of constraint and oppression. In its own cultural context, she notes, the hijab holds quite the opposite meaning, one overlooked—if not ignored—by many Western commentators:

> Can we only free Afghan women to be like us or might we have to recognize that even after "liberation" from the Taliban, they might want different things than we would want for them? ... We may want justice for women, but can we accept that there might be different ideas about justice and that different women might want, or choose, different futures from what we envision as best ... ? (Abu Lughod 2002: 787–8)

This is actually one of the more pointed questions to consider in the context of the literature on global women's and feminist movements: if Western liberalist standards need not be the context through which the value of female activism is read, then what other standards should be operative? While I will shortly take up the issue of what role context might play in the politics of categorization, I am interested in considering the implications of the words of Sue Bridger, who cautions Western feminists about certain boundaries they should respect when groups of historically oppressed women do not wish to associate themselves with feminism:

> If many of them do not embrace the language and concepts of feminism, or find theoretical debate sterile and diversionary in a situation of such urgency and severity, this reflects both the depth of the crisis they face and the intractability of the theoretical legacy they inherit. In these circumstances, the greatest support western women can give is simply to listen, to try to understand, and only then to act in partnership. The current longevity of feminism in the West conveys no automatic right to preach orthodoxies and prescribe solutions which may be entirely inappropriate in a country where conditions

are chaotic, insecurity is endemic and there is no rule of law.
(Bridger 2000: 130)

This emphasis on empathy and partnership is certainly important to the relationships that help global feminist activism succeed. But embedded within this statement are important limits that deserve attention: if we take this statement at face value, does this mean that Western feminists *do* have "the automatic right to preach orthodoxies and prescribe solutions" in places where things *are* relatively ordered, secure, and law-abiding? Does this also mean that, when and if Russia is no longer in crisis, one can expect that Russian feminism *should* develop an interest in the language, concepts, and theories of Western feminism, and/or that any culture whose cultural attitudes can be called "intractable" is exempted from incisive feminist critique? Such questions are of critical importance since the context of the culture in question is often used as a justification for the tenor of the analyses that feminists produce, and thus it is issues precisely like these that fuel my own queries on the construction of feminist identity within global movements.

Moving Targets

Up to this point, I have established that much of the research on global women's movements is built around the goal of giving a voice to women whose political activism (either directly or indirectly) achieves greater gender equity and/or is geared towards the alleviation of gender-based social problems. There are mixed opinions on what activist women might do to render themselves anti-feminist (and thus ineligible as subjects in studies on global feminist movements), if the topic is addressed at all. Many authors discuss support for religious fundamentalism and traditionalism, more generally, as forces that valorize patriarchy and thus might oust one from inclusion, while others just as quickly note that in certain contexts, the discourses of even conservative religion and patriarchy can achieve liberatory ends. Despite this lack of consensus, what almost all scholars can agree on is that the members of global women's movements do not need to call themselves feminists or even necessarily mimic the forms of Western feminism to be included more broadly under the global feminist umbrella, so long as their advocacy can be construed to widen the realms of agency that women have at their disposal. Yet when we compare these statements to activist women's groups that are characterized as right-wing or conservative, a rather significant wrinkle arises. The problem, as earlier mentioned, is that the activism that has caused feminist scholars to label certain global women's movements as "feminist" is quite similar, if not sometimes identical, to the activism that has caused the same scholars to render other women's groups "right-wing" or "conservative." It seems rather standard in volumes on right-wing women to acknowledge that right-wing movements are quite diverse, and yet the scholarly focus has long relied on portraying such movements in rather one-sided fashion as reactive counterforces instead of legitimate movements in their own right (Blee and Deutsch 2012: 3). This means that when the similarities with what are considered more progressive movements are noted, this indistinct area between "feminist" and "right-wing" is often treated more as an inconvenient overlap rather than an actual commonality.

These presumptions are illustrated in Paola Bacchetta and Margaret Power's volume on right-wing women, wherein they concur that there is no singular set of propositions that makes a right-wing movement "right," nor is it uncommon for right-wing movements to share commonalities with more leftist groups, something they find "troubling, albeit unavoidable" (2013: 4, 7). Nevertheless, most scholarly treatments of right-wing women presume that their activism lies in diametrical opposition to feminist movements, as in the pair's observation of the following:

> [...] feminist scholars have preferred, understandably, to prioritize research on women whose perspectives they share because these have been silenced. However, we feel that feminist projects will benefit from understanding right-wing women precisely because in many cases they constitute major obstacles to feminism. (Bacchetta and Power 2013: 1)

Yet in the absence of firm criteria by which to demarcate a right-wing women's group, Bacchetta and Power do offer a series of patterns that they believe characterize right-wing women's movements, which include tendencies to: "otherize" or set apart a people or group who they oppose; villainize these "others" in order to create a social activist base that also opposes them; and perform these previous acts in the service of the heterosexual family and motherhood, which are often symbolically established as unquestionable institutions that deserve defense at all costs (1–18).

The problem with these criteria, of course, is that they also describe the salient characteristics of many of the movements treated under the global feminist umbrella (not to mention the tendency of Western feminists to "otherize" conservatives, even if they do so in support of a different set of principles). These similarities are often reconciled by using the trope of context, wherein the scholar argues that even though conservative politics might stem from a similar set of cultural events, one need not interpret its significance identically. For instance, Bridger's desire to explain the conservative tendencies among the nascent Russian feminist movement referenced earlier is the same rationale used by Kathleen M. Fallon and Julie Moreau to account for the existence of sub-Saharan African right-wing women's movements. All conclude that these women are behaving in conservative ways because they are the victims of oppressive and sometimes fascist political and social systems, meaning that conservatism, to use the words of Fallon and Moreau, "may not reflect women's political will," even though it is a reflection of their present response to the circumstances under which they live (2012: 78).

When asking how we explain the behaviors of activists within movements, can we simply say that context is everything—in other words, that the conditions under which women's activism takes place are a critical point of assessment in determining whether something actually widens the role of women or simply transforms them into brainwashed political puppets? There does seem to be something plausible if not outright logical to this argument. After all, it is quite impractical to expect that women living under extremely restrictive or fascist conditions are going to successfully challenge patriarchal institutions in dramatic ways if only because the necessary physical, economic, and cultural resources to make such radical shifts happen are often unavailable.

It might also be the case that women may have an interest in siding with conservative movements as an act of political obedience and subsequently a method of self-protection (Fallon and Moreau 2012). In this scenario, one can clearly see how activism that broadens the circle of women's empowerment in extremely limiting circumstances could be construed as something liberal, radical, or otherwise progressive, even if such efforts might be considered rather conservative in another setting. Similarly, it is not hard to understand why the relative freedoms that American and other Western conservative women often experience may render their activism unquestionably anti-feminist or right-wing, even when such activism may work to assist women in restrictive circumstances or to otherwise broaden certain women's political impact.

But there are further critical issues to probe here for, arguably, every political decision is one subject to, and resulting from, one's cultural context, and yet only certain contexts are treated by feminist scholars as repressive enough to excuse the conservative tendencies within them to the degree that they might be read as a form of feminism. So while the aforementioned Islamist women's movement that openly supports patriarchy (but works to realize other rights to improve women's lives) may be generally regarded as feminist and is included in a study on global women's movements, one would be hard-pressed to find an activist American evangelical movement that embraces similar philosophical inclinations discussed in the same scholarly genre. From a popular liberal feminist perspective, the former group would likely be seen as some sort of authentic and inherently positive form of diversity, while the latter might be seen as backward and dangerous.

These labels should give us some pause, for if one goal of the global feminist movement has been to undermine the hegemony of Western liberalism as the measure of cultural value, and if Western feminist scholars have recognized the limits of this ideological framework as it applies to the women of the world, then we must question why it is still held as the measure of progress for some Western women's activist groups. What this indicates is the presence of an active double standard, one that still normalizes Western liberalism in all its iterations. If one culture is deemed particularly repressive by scholars, rendering almost any sort of female activism within it "feminist," then this repression is judged and thus known by its comparison with Western liberalism. On the other hand, if a Western female activist group engages in what feminists call "conservative" activism, the critiques from feminists that they will encounter are, again, Western ones, likely to depend on false consciousness arguments (wherein women's conservative claims are dismissed as a misapprehension of reality due to oppressive social circumstances).

This methodological dilemma is a very real one for feminist scholars, for it begins to erode Smith's aforementioned affirmation of feminist diversity (that there is "no single way of pursuing women's ends"), instead demonstrating that Western feminism has clear (if shifting) limits (2000: 9). Additionally, it also uncovers the continuing selective use of false consciousness arguments, even though such arguments have fallen out of favor in many circles for the manner in which they rob women of their agency.

Indeed, there is much scholarship on right-wing women that clearly demonstrates how many conservative women are fully aware of the patriarchal impact of their alliances, are sometimes dismayed by the sexism they witness therein, and yet at other times fully support patriarchal and evenly openly sexist structures (Bacchetta and Power 2013: 3; Blee and Deutsch 2012: 18). In the field of religious studies, in particular, scholars R. Marie Griffith and Brenda Brasher were among the first to suggest that conservative evangelical women's movements could simultaneously endorse certain patriarchal ideas and provide empowerment opportunities for those women (Griffith 2000; Brasher 1997). Similarly, in her recent study of the role of conservative women in the formation of nationwide crisis pregnancy centers, Kimberly Kelly has shown that rather than blindly supporting every facet of the patriarchal structures in which they live, such outlets, even though they fall on the conservative end of the spectrum, give women a public voice and political power as well a sense of expertise and authority (Kelly 2012).

The recognition that certain conservative women are working with great amounts of agency in patriarchal subcultures thus seriously challenges the idea that women's conservatism is the natural result of the context of political oppression just as much as it interrogates the longstanding feminist claim that feminist work is about giving voice to all women's needs, experiences, and desires. Clearly, there are women whose voices and opinions feminists do not want to legitimize. How some of their ideas can nevertheless be transformed into examples of global feminism thus remains an interesting exercise in the politics of classification.

As if this situation weren't methodologically tricky enough, these identity politics become even more complicated when we notice that several of the groups that liberal feminists call "right-wing" call themselves "feminists." Consider the following three examples of what has been called "conservative feminism," and how such groups' platforms trouble both of the words that make up that label. More explicitly, these American women's movements introduce the problem of what standards are used to designate a legitimate form of female empowerment. If the boundaries of feminism are wide, and if each of the movements below calls itself "feminist" and has worked towards clear empowerment opportunities for women, then by what underlying criteria do many liberal feminists reject their "feminist" self-labeling (when compared with the inclusion of many of the global "feminist" groups mentioned above)?

- First, consider Concerned Women for America (CWA), a right-wing Christian group that unequivocally valorizes the nuclear, patriarchal family as well as conservative social and fiscal politics. It is explicitly anti-gay rights and anti-abortion. In the past, it has also been highly critical of feminism, calling it a radical position that is not representative of the values and desires of most American women. Despite this, over the past few years CWA has begun to describe itself as the embodiment of "true," or conservative, feminism. CWA claims that, for more than the past century, organizations of conservative women have been responsible for some of the nation's most important social reforms. Calling these women the "original" feminists, CWA locates itself as a continuation of this "feminist legacy" (Smith 2014: 96). In terms of promoting female activism, CWA has given thousands of American women an outlet into grassroots politics and has established prominent campaigns against sex trafficking and pornography, among other issues, in the name of improving women's lives.

• Feminists for Life (FFL) is another group that has caused particular ire amongst mainstream feminists because of its claim that the basic philosophical premise of feminism is inconsistent with pro-abortion advocacy. Its argument is not only that "women deserve better than abortion" (the group's official motto), but that when seen from the perspective of the fetus, abortion is both unjust and violent.[4] Like CWA, FFL contends that the early American feminists were explicitly anti-abortion, and that by continuing their activism it subsequently reflects feminism's true legacy.[5] FFL contends that the very fact that abortions occur is a sign that American society has failed to address the root causes and social conditions that make parenting difficult, and thus the group's activism focuses on fighting poverty (including the expansion of Medicaid and other government programs to include more coverage for families), increasing legal and social support for parents, and providing parenting skills education networks.[6] Interestingly, the group's activism does not include pregnancy prevention education (i.e., sex education/"safe sex" education), and this (among other things) is one part of the feminist critique against them.

• In a final example of a movement that many feminists would likely label "conservative" but which still calls itself "feminist," consider the recent wave of "Jesus Feminists," the evangelical movement taking its name from the 2013 book (authored by Sarah Bessey) that attempts to deconstruct Christian patriarchy

---

4   "Our Mission and Organization," Feminists for Life website, www.feministsforlife.org, accessed 17 July 2014.

5   "Herstory," Feminists for Life website, http://www.feministsforlife.org/herstory/m, accessed 17 July 2014.

6   "Resources for Pregnant Women, Parents, and Birth Mothers," Feminists for Life website, http://www.feministsforlife.org/you-have-better-choices/, accessed 17 July 2014.

through scriptural and historical arguments that render a pro-woman, pro-equity Jesus. This movement is unique in that it claims to reject all of the patriarchal elements of evangelical theology and yet simultaneously asserts that submission to the person of Jesus is the central act fundamental to creating social equity. Bessey has been criticized for failing to criti-cally consider how the complexities of feminist theory (not to mention the diverse needs, desires, and cultures of the world's women) intersect with the particular message of love and fair-ness to which her book might be reduced, as well as for giv-ing little critical consideration to what her book might mean for non-Christians. Nevertheless, what Bessey argues for is a clearly more progressive and positive view of feminism than many conservative Christians have attempted thus far.

These scenarios lay bare many of the politics on which the term "global feminism" hangs: the very fact that the boundaries of fem-inism can be described as almost limitless at one point but clearly exclusionary in others; that certain sorts of women's empowerment are interpreted as compelling and potentially positive while almost identical others are perceived as constraining; that virtually indistin-guishable behaviors and ideological claims receive much different treatments—all of these things reflect the reality that, when it comes to the Western deployment of the term "feminism," there are clearly unspoken boundaries in place, boundaries constrained by the pres-ence of composite ideals depicting both the feminist and the right-wing woman.

The Politics of Normalcy

I want to return for a moment to the previous conversation on Narayan and Mohanty's arguments on the politics of naming, for within their logic lies insight into the manner in which such political strategies operate within the sector of feminist scholarship that I am considering here. Whereas Narayan's critique isolates the political power embed-ded in the possibility of a shifting self-portrayal, Mohanty's analysis provides focus on the construction of the "other" who exists as a foil from which these multiple self-portrayals are crafted.

If, as Narayan suggests, charges of "Westernization" are used selectively by those who wish to maintain the parameters of traditional power structures, and if the term was (and is) based on a careful rhetorical creation of difference and value in order to justify the identity politics at play, then it seems that a similar dynamic is going on in the scholarship produced by many feminist scholars who study global feminist and women's movements in order to justify otherwise conservative behaviors. As I have shown, I suspect that terms like "conservatism" and "feminism" function much like "Westernization" in the sense that they are used very selectively to describe the behaviors of certain groups in one context, but are conveniently ignored in another.

With this in mind, can we take the applicability of Mohanty's warnings about oversimplified subjects seriously by asking whether concepts such as "liberal," "conservative," "progressive," and "right-wing" have been very specifically construed in some feminist scholarship so as to reinforce impressions of the diversity and inclusivity of global feminist activism? Conversely, can we use the same argumentation to demonstrate the construction of a composite "right-wing woman" whose uncomplicated persona permits Western feminists not only to demonize her with greater ease, but also to more delicately nuance (and thereby sanction) the otherwise right-leaning behaviors of other women worldwide?

While I suspect some will be tempted to view this as a problem that can be solved with more robust definitions and more detailed criteria, I tend to side with Judith Butler's observation that such tensions are inevitable, for when "the category of women is invoked as describing the constituency for which feminism speaks, an internal debate invariably begins over what the descriptive content of that term will be" (Butler 1992: 15). Thus rather than depict this present essay as one that grapples with the accuracy of descriptors and the sufficiency of categories, I tend to see this examination on the selective use of the term "feminism" as a rather normal part of the rhetorical processes involved in political contests. What I hope to have revealed is that the rhetorical constitution of "global women's movements," "feminist movements," and "right-wing women" (among other terms discussed here) do not label concrete things as much as they are themselves fluctuating attempts to achieve the present goals of many Western feminists, which include delegitimizing their more formidable conservative activists while at the same time preserving ties with international women's groups in the name of creating and supporting a pluralistic feminism.

This is why the current controversy over conservative women using the term "feminist" as a self-description has paradoxical overtones, particularly in light of Power's remark that there is no definitive answer on what to do when conservative women call themselves feminists, and that perhaps a more fruitful question is what they intend to accomplish by using the term (Power 2004: 148). The irony is that the use of every term is politically strategic, and yet few other groups already included under the wide umbrella of feminist activism are held to the same burden of proof.

This is not to say that I do not understand the frustration when one's political acts are rhetorically thwarted (for this, in my mind, is what the conflict over right-wing women's self-proclaimed feminism is really about). It does recognize, though, that the categories through which we organize the world around us are political ones, even (and especially?) those that we use to describe political processes themselves. One should not be particularly surprised, then, when one's "opponent" might, in a slightly different analytical context, also appear to be one's "sister," for in the discussions generated by the activism of dynamic social movements, conflict, shift, and contradiction are elements of political necessity.

References

Abu Lughod, Lila. 2002. "Do Muslim Women Really Need Saving? Anthropological Reflections on Cultural Relativism and Its Others." *American Anthropologist* 104(3): 783–90.
https://doi.org/10.1525/aa.2002.104.3.783
Arenfeldt, Pernille and Nawar Al-Hassan Golley. 2012. "Arab Women's Movements: Developments, Priorities, and Challenges." In Pernille Arenfeldt and Nawar Al-Hassan Golley, eds., *Mapping Arab Movements:*

A Century of Transformations From Within. Cairo: The American University in Cairo Press.

Bacchetta, Paola and Margaret Power. 2013. "Introduction." In Paola Bacchetta and Margaret Power, eds., *Right Wing Women: From Conservatives to Extremists Around the World*, 1–18. New York: Routledge.

Bessey, Sarah. 2013. *Jesus Feminist: An Invitation to Revisit the Bible's View of Women*. New York: Howard Books.

Blee, Kathleen M. and Sandra McGee Deutsch. 2012. "Introduction." In *Women of the Right: Comparisons and Interplay Across Borders*. University Park, PA: Pennsylvania State Press.

Brasher, Brenda. 1997. *Godly Women: Fundamentalism and Female Power*. New Brunswick: Rutgers University Press.

Bridger, Sue. 2000. "'Something Unnatural': Attitudes to Feminism in Russia." In Anna Bull, Hanna Diamond, and Rosalind Marsh, eds., *Feminisms and Women's Movements in Contemporary Europe*. New York: St. Martin's Press.

Bull, Anna, Hanna Diamond, and Rosalind Marsh. 2000. "Introduction." In Anna Bull, Hanna Diamond, and Rosalind Marsh, eds., *Feminisms and Women's Movements in Contemporary Europe*. New York: St. Martin's Press. https://doi.org/10.1515/9781400823550.3

Butler, Judith. 1992. "Contingent Foundations: Feminism and the Question of 'Postmodernism.'" In Joan W. Scott and Judith Butler, eds., *Feminists Theorize the Political*, 3–21. New York: Routledge.

Chang, Doris T. 2009. *Women's Movements in Twentieth-Century Taiwan*. Urbana: University of Illinois.

Delegard, Kirsten Marie. 2012. *Battling Miss Bolsheviki: The Origins of Female Conservatism in the United States*. Philadelphia: University of Pennsylvania Press. https://doi.org/10.9783/9780812207163

Fallon, Kathleen M. and Julie Moreau. 2012. "Righting Africa? Contextualizing Notions of Women's Right-Wing Activism in Sub-Saharan Africa." In *Women of the Right: Comparisons and Interplay Across Borders*, 68–80. University Park, PA: Pennsylvania State Press.

Feminists for Life. 2014. "Herstory," http://www.feministsforlife.org/herstory/m; "Our Mission and Organization," www.feministsforlife.org; "Resources for Pregnant Women, Parents, and Birth Mothers," http://www.feministsforlife.org/you-have-better-choices/.

Ferree, Myra Marx. 2006. "Globalization and Feminism: Opportunities and Obstacles for Activism in the Global Arena." In Myra Marx Ferree and Alli Mari Tripp, eds., *Global Feminism: Transnational Women's Activism, Organizing, and Human Rights*, 3–23. New York: NYU Press.

Ferree, Myra Marx and Alli Mari Tripp. 2006. "Preface." In Myra Marx Ferree and Alli Mari Tripp, eds., *Global Feminism: Transnational Women's Activism, Organizing, and Human Rights*, vii–ix. New York: NYU Press.

Ferree, Myra Marx and Tetyana Pudrovska. 2006. "Transnational Feminist NGOs on the Web: Networks and Identities in the Global North and South." In Myra Marx Ferree and Alli Mari Tripp, eds., *Global Feminism: Transnational Women's Activism, Organizing, and Human Rights*, 247–73. New York: NYU Press.

Griffith, R. Marie. 2000. *God's Daughters: Evangelical Women and the Power of Submission*. Berkeley: University of California Press.

Kelly, Kimberly. 2012. "In the Name of the Mother: Renegotiating Conservative Women's Authority in the Crisis Pregnancy Center Movement." *Signs* 38(1): 203–29. https://doi.org/10.1086/665807

Lewis, Leslie. 2012. "Convergences and Divergences: Egyptian Women's Activism." In Pernille Arenfeldt and Nawar Al-Hassan Golley, eds., *Mapping Arab Movements: A Century of Transformations From Within*. Cairo: The American University in Cairo Press. https://doi.org/10.5743/cairo/9789774164989.003.0003

Mohanty, Chandra Talpade. 2003. "Under Western Eyes: Feminist Scholarship and Colonialist Discourses." In *Feminism without Borders: Decolonizing Theory, Practicing Solidarity*, 17–42. Durham: Duke University Press. https://doi.org/10.1215/9780822384649-002

Naples, Nancy A. 2002. "Changing the Terms: Community Activism, Globalization, and the Dilemmas of Transnational Feminist Praxis." In Nancy Naples and Manisa Desai, eds., *Women's Activism and Globalization: Linking Local Struggles and Transnational Politics*, 3–14. New York: Routledge.

Narayan, Uma. 1997. *Dislocating Cultures: Identities, Traditions, and Third World Feminism.* New York: Routledge.

Power, Margaret. 2004. "More Than Mere Pawns: Right-Wing Women in Chile." *Journal of Women's History* 16(3): 138–51. https://doi.org/10.1353/jowh.2004.0069

Shaheed, Fahida. 2010. "The Women's Movement in Pakistan: Challenges and Achievements." In Amrita Basu, ed. *Women's Movements in the Global Era: The Power of Local Feminisms*, 89–118. Boulder, CO: Westview Press.

Smith, Bonnie G. 2000. "Introduction." In Bonnie G. Smith, ed., *Global Feminisms Since 1945*, 1–10. New York: Routledge.

Smith, Leslie Dorrough. 2014. *Righteous Rhetoric: Sex, Speech, and the Politics of Concerned Women for America*. New York: Oxford University Press. https://doi.org/10.1093/acprof:oso/9780199337507.001.0001

Leslie Dorrough Smith is Associate Professor of Religious Studies and Director of the Women's and Gender Studies Program at Avila University. She is author of *Righteous Rhetoric: Sex, Speech, and the Politics of Concerned Women for America* (Oxford University Press, 2014) as well as a forthcoming book (also with Oxford) about political sex scandals and American religion. Her research focuses on the interplay between gender, sex, reproduction, and the politics of American evangelical groups and conservatives more broadly.

8. Response to Leslie Dorrough Smith

Transgressions

Russell T. McCutcheon

Using the recent scholarly controversy of suggesting that our approach to understanding transgender identities may have implications for studies of what some call transracial identities, this chapter invites Leslie Dorrough Smith to consider the wider implications of the sorts of comparisons that are necessary for scholars to carry out their work—comparisons exemplified in her chapter.

In offering this response I should register, from the outset, that I am mindful of a variety of identity issues that, at least to some readers, might make someone like myself ineligible to engage Dorrough Smith on such topics as women and the manner in which the variety of feminisms is policed. Case in point: I recently co-wrote a response (Kavka and McCutcheon 2017) to an article published in a major journal on the ramification of colonialism on how people in some parts of the Arab world once saw, and then came to see, homosexuality (Mahomed and Esack 2017). While the response made clear our appreciation for the descriptive portions of the article—i.e., those documenting changing attitudes and attempting to link those changes to the effects of colonialism—we were highly critical of the normative portion, in which the authors switched gears and advocated what they contended were *better ways* in which homosexuality can be seen in the Muslim world. Somewhat like Dorrough Smith's key aside, early on in her chapter, concerning Bonnie G. Smith's failure to elaborate as to just what her idea of justice is, Kavka and I contended that these authors anchored their paper on a notion of justice that, in a footnote near the opening, readers learn is too complex to discuss in such a brief scholarly paper. Along with other aspects of the article, we saw this admission as a significant failure of critical scholarship and iden- tified it as such in our reply (which was reviewed by the journal's editorial team, rather rigorously in my opinion, before they agreed to publish it)—only to have one reader, in a social media post that was brought to our attention soon after the response was published (a thread to which we both eventually contributed comments), call into question our legitimacy as respondents. This policing, resulting from what this reader freely acknowledged to be "a quick perusal" of our reply, seems to have been based on whatever degree of acquaintance she happened to have with us—either as persons or as scholars. (I should say, perhaps, that I have never met this scholar nor am I famil- iar at all with her own work.) The post left the clear impression that the journal's editor would receive a letter of complaint for the man- ner in which, as it was phrased, cis-male, white, senior, U.S.-based scholars had apparently shut down (i.e., policed) the scholarship on homosexuality to which they had replied so critically; what's more, this reader was thanked, in one of the comments that was later added to the social media post, for "raising the alarm" concerning our, I gather, inappropriate response.[1]

Having thus had my own brush with how what some might term strategic essentialism (an identification strategy, associated with the early work of Gayatri Chakravorty Spivak, that we might add to the helpful list of identification techniques that Martin offers in his Introduction to this volume) can be used by those who perceive their position to be marginalized, as a tool to identify and then criticize people and positions with which they disagree—a strategy that gen- eralizes and homogenizes in ways that many scholars today find to be very problematic, at least when those seen to be in positions of

---

1   Upon learning, seemingly through the comment thread that resulted from her post (or perhaps private messages), that we were a little more com- plicated than this reader at first assumed, the initial identity-based argument of this reader was then fine-tuned as an argument concerning the privilege of our social locations.

authority engage in it—I admit that I am both somewhat wary while also rather enthused to discuss her chapter, in public and in some detail, with Dorrough Smith. The wariness comes from a weariness with the culture of quick perusals that we seem to now inhabit in some parts of academia, for my name and the topic of the chapter to which I am here replying may be sufficient for some readers to form a quick opinion that allows them to read no more. But this also constitutes the grounds for some enthusiasm, especially given my familiarity with how Dorrough Smith herself approaches what some might see to be controversial topics (her chapter, here, being but one example of the care she puts into her analysis);[2] for precisely because of the environment in which we now do our work—where some have blurred the line between a carefully reasoned argument that we publish only once peers have scrutinized it and a possibly impulsive social media comment that, lacking any filters, we post online—the challenge to press each other as part of our collaborative scholarly work is all the more relevant. So, as recently noted by Rogers Brubaker, I too am hopeful that "writing as an outsider may offer certain advantages" (2016: xi)—advantages long apparent in the field in which Dorrough Smith and I were both trained, in fact, since the premise of the academic study of religion, at least as we both practice it, is that non-participants with a comparative viewpoint might see something that those enmeshed in the practices overlook because they are taken for granted. For, as I recently heard the TV news correspondent Chris Cuomo say on CNN concerning the problems experienced by those living through Florida's Hurricane Irma—those without power and thus without news alerts and weather forecasts—"the closer you are to that experience the less you know about it."[3]

2   At this point, in the interest in full disclosure, I should add that I had the good fortune to supervise her 1999 MA thesis, at what was then Southwest Missouri State University (now Missouri State), entitled *Divine Order, Divine Myth: The Necessity of Gender Paradigms in the Study of Protestant Fundamentalist Thought*; since that time it has been my honor to have developed a long-term working relationship with her as a colleague.

3   To press this notion of insider and outsider further, though, for scholars who see as their job the redescription and thereby analysis of local claims, rather than their mere description and thus repetition, the distinction between

But apart from signaling my awareness of the thorny domain that I may be entering, I open my response with this aside concerning identity politics because I wish to invite Dorrough Smith to reflect on this as well, for while this is the focus of her chapter, her very approach to this topic may, at least for some readers, also constitute an improper boundary transgression of its own. For, given what has transpired since her chapter was first written—I think here of the manner in which more traditional notions of gender have been critiqued and then expanded over the past few years, at least in public and political discourse in the U.S. (where both Dorrough Smith and I live and work), let alone the sometimes swift and vehement reactions such critiques have elicited—I wonder what Dorrough Smith now makes not just of the plurality of feminisms and how invested and politically engaged actors manage that competitive economy (i.e., contesting labels, by means of what Martin describes as ad hoc classifications, and portraying this or that group of women as feminist or not) but also of the plurality of ways in which this very idea of "woman" is now coming to be defined and thereby the manner in which some human beings are admitted (or denied entry to) to this identity. (I think here of how some on the seemingly political left have, despite seeming to show empathy for and solidarity with trans identifiers, been outed as exclusivist for nonetheless assuming that transwomen are not somehow authentically female.) For, to quote her words, much like Dorrough Smith's opening characterization of feminism, so too "woman," apparently, "is not—to put it simply—a single thing." Or, to paraphrase Dorrough Smith, but as applied not

---

insider and outside ultimately falls apart (i.e., exists only at the level of data gathering) since the local practice is seen, by such scholars, as an example of a wider topic, something no doubt instantiated in its own way, either here or there, but which serves, for the scholar (i.e., the social theorist), as a variant on a wider theme. If this is one's approach, then no local or insider perspective is understood as unique; for while they may, of course, differ from others in a variety of ways, they are examined in the light of each other inasmuch as they are all thought to illustrate a common principle or process. This is simply another way of saying that the so-called outsider or comparativist's perspective is, in fact, the perspective from which gains in knowledge are made.

just to feminism as a movement, there now seems to be no single set of traits by which people are identified *as* women.

Apart from the seeming, or perhaps unconscious, ease with which I see the designator "women" used throughout the chapter—employed as if it names an agreed upon group which only happens to have internal contests concerning which of its members, and thus which of their political interests or organizing methods, count as feminist—what mainly prompts my query concerns not only the prevalence of trans identities that people today more easily, or freely, seem to ascribe to others or claim for themselves but a methodological move Dorrough Smith makes in order to set up the chapter. For her interest in how some scholars study what many would characterize as politically conservative groups (e.g., Concerned Women for America, Feminists for Life, or Jesus Feminists)—an approach that further marginalizes them inasmuch as they are hardly seen *as* feminist, given the way that their concerns are understood to deviate from other groups normally classed *as* feminist—is accentuated when compared to how differently some groups with rather similar concerns or techniques are studied by those same scholars. To set up this comparison Dorrough Smith cites a model: Uma Narayan's and Chandra Talpade Mohanty's own work on how so-called first-world feminists have studied third-world women. "My intention," Dorrough Smith writes, "is to take the structure of their arguments and ask whether similar critiques might be applied to the manner in which liberal feminist scholars currently tend to approach both global women's and feminist movements through the unspoken 'other,' the conservative woman." For, as she goes on to argue (see p. 130 in this volume):

> the activism that has caused feminist scholars to label certain global women's movements as "feminist" is quite similar, if not sometimes identical, to the activism that has caused the same scholars to render other women's groups "right-wing" or "conservative." It seems rather standard in volumes on right-wing women to acknowledge that right-wing movements are quite diverse, and yet the scholarly focus has long relied on portraying such movements in a rather one-sided fashion as reactive counterforces instead of legitimate movements in their own right … . This means that when the similarities with what are

considered more progressive movements are noted, this indistinct area between "feminist" and "right-wing" is often treated more as an inconvenient overlap than an actual commonality.

But in seeking methodological parity by applying the structure of the one comparison (a case involving national, ethnic, regional, and class distinctions) in a different setting (one involving a comparison of differently politically aligned social actors in the same country) I wonder if Dorrough Smith has herself transgressed an unspoken boundary. For while the goal of the first comparison may, in the eyes of those who make it, be judged credible (inasmuch as it is aimed at taking far more seriously, and thereby engaging, to whatever degree, a group whose members are judged usually to be overlooked, i.e., the no less hard-working, valuable, and oppressed women who happen to live outside the developed, liberal-democratic, or so-called Western world), assuming that a similar juxtaposition can then be made in which differences of social interest are now relativized, such that people with divergent political commitments can be examined in a comparable fashion, may be met with a rather more ungenerous reading. Simply put, while it may be in the interest of liberal feminist democrats (in the strictly lowercase sense) to acknowledge and thereby grapple with their privilege when it comes to their relations with distant third-world interlocutors, those interests may be undermined if their privilege is called into question when it comes to how they perceive their nearby and thus far more familiar contemporaries —i.e., those who differ with liberal feminists on what the latter see to be key, perhaps even non-negotiable social issues (such as, to pick but one, choice when it comes to reproductive rights). To put it in the form of a question: is there a type of dubious maternalism present when some so easily entertain the breadth of feminisms only when it comes to seeing oneself in relation to the third world as opposed to seeing oneself in the light of a political divide that cuts through one's own world?

This comparison of comparisons, i.e., Dorrough Smith using the structure of one comparison to set up her own, is of interest to me inasmuch as it resembles a related comparative move recently made by the author of a peer-reviewed article published in the noted feminist philosophy journal *Hypatia* (named after the 4th century CE mathematician and philosopher, Hypatia of Alexandria) in which the author, Rebecca Tuvel (an Assistant Professor at Rhodes College, in the U.S.) used recent discussions around transgender issues (with the notable example of the widely positive reactions to the onetime Olympian Bruce Jenner's very public transition to the transwoman Caitlyn Jenner)[4] as the basis for asking questions about how people react to cases where what we now term transracial identities are claimed (such as what may be the equally well-known case of Rachel Dolezal, a U.S. civil rights activist and onetime Africana studies instructor who was outed by her own parents, in 2015, as Caucasian despite having lived much of her recent life as African-American).[5]

As the abstract for Tuvel's paper reads:

> Former NAACP chapter head Rachel Dolezal's attempted transition from the white to the black race occasioned heated controversy. Her story gained notoriety at the same time that Caitlyn Jenner graced the cover of *Vanity Fair*, signaling a growing acceptance of transgender identity. Yet criticisms of Dolezal for misrepresenting her birth race indicate a widespread social perception that it is neither possible nor acceptable to change one's race in the way it might be to change one's sex. Considerations that support transgenderism seem to apply equally to transracialism. Although Dolezal herself may or may not represent a genuine case of a transracial person, her story and the public reaction to it serve helpful illustrative purposes. (2017: 263)

What makes this essay particularly interesting, though, is that despite longstanding arguments concerning the social construction of such identities as race, not to mention such other identifications as gender, consumer, class, or nationality, the swift and heated reaction that met Tuvel's essay—petitions and claims that it had done "epistemic

---

4   Using the former name could be characterized as "deadnaming" Jenner, by using the person's pre-transition name and thus identity.

5   That Dolezal's news hit within days of Jenner's widely seen *Vanity Fair* cover/photoshoot likely helped to set up the comparison for many. See what Brubaker describes as "the most detailed account of Dolezal's background" in Sunderland (2015).

violence" to those who read it—suggests that, at least today in the U.S., a specific notion of race is so central to a variety of key debates that, at least for some, it cannot be called into question or understood as an historical designation (i.e., a contingent identification).[6] To rephrase, what might seem to some readers (if not to Tuvel herself and the editors who initially made the decision to publish the article) as a relatively straightforward and uncontroversial comparison of Jenner's case to that of Dolezal—or better yet, a comparison of the public reception of one to the public reception of the other (for while the transgender Jenner has largely been heralded by many on the left, the transracial Dolezal has been both parodied and vilified)—to yet others it clearly crossed an unspoken line, regardless their thoughts on the ad hoc nature of identity.

And so, when seen in the light of the swift reaction her paper evoked, Tuvel's conclusion—

> [Sally] Haslanger writes, "rather than worrying, 'what is gender, really?' or 'what is race, really?' I think we should begin by asking (both in the theoretical and political sense) what, if anything, we want them to be" (Haslanger 2012: 246). I have taken it as my task in this article to argue that a just society should reconsider what we owe individuals who claim a strongly felt sense of identification with another race, and accordingly what we want race to be. I hope to have shown that, insofar as similar arguments that render transgenderism acceptable extend to transracialism, we have reason to allow racial self-identification, coupled with racial social treatment, to play a greater role in the determination of race than has previously been recognized.

6 As an aside, to argue that any identity is historically or situationally contingent, invented, or socially constructed is not, as some who counter this position have claimed (in order to dismiss such an approach as insufficient), to argue that it is illusory, fake, or somehow unreal. Rather, though changeable or ad hoc, it can nonetheless be understood to have practical effects—sometimes of what participants see as tremendous consequence. To pick but one quick example, though we all know that the custom of stopping at red lights is an historical accident (i.e., it could have been otherwise but is, instead, normalized through repetition and policing), choosing not to stop, while certainly an option, can lead to a accident with a fatal outcome.

> I conclude that society should accept such an individual's deci-
> sion to change race the same way it should accept an individu-
> al's decision to change sex. (2017: 274–5)

—prompts us to ask questions about the possible limits of the comparative method itself (i.e., how we drew conclusions concerning sameness, such that those "similar arguments that render transgenderism
acceptable," might be, as Tuvel does, "extend[ed] to transracialism").
These are questions about the interests that drive (and the implications of) juxtaposition, questions that prompt us to consider what
(appealing to Jonathan Z. Smith's work on the comparative method)
we might characterize as the usually unspoken third party that attends
a comparison of any two items: the comparativist's "with respect to"
that provides the intellectual conditions or controlled setting in which
we are able to place just these two things alongside one another in
just that way (see Smith 1990: 50–1). For what to one seems to be
an innocuous relationship that permits us to make interesting conclusions about otherwise unforeseen similarities can—as was all too
apparent in the case of the *Hypatia* article—prompt in another a variety of reactions, from displeasure to horror, at the thought of similarity being proposed.

Before proceeding, it may be worthwhile quickly to offer a brief
aside, so that the usual self-evidency or supposed innocence of the
comparative method can be reconsidered. For as I have noted in my
introductory classes many times over the years, if any two things can
be legitimately claimed to be similar (after all, you and I both have
mass) *while also being legitimately claimed to be different* (for you
are there and yet I am here), then it should make plain that much rides
on which "in terms of which" is selected and employed to drive any
given comparison. While many practical examples could be drawn
upon to illustrate this, consider one that is timely and which makes
the point rather provocatively: with the Fall 2016 election of Donald
Trump to the Presidency of the U.S. a number of commentators on
the far political left quickly noted that Hitler too was elected democratically (i.e., though he lost the Presidency in 1932, his party's large
share of the vote, and its strong turnout in subsequent elections, made
him von Hindenburg's almost inevitable selection for Chancellor in

1933); yet to those on the right such a comparison was seen as outlandish and inspired by irrational fear-mongering since, for them, the differences between early 1930s Germany and the U.S. in the early 21st century, let alone differences between Trump's platform and that of Hitler, overwhelmed any attempt to establish commonality. This nicely makes the point, I'd argue, that the key to understanding the comparative method is not to focus on the items being placed alongside each other (as if they just naturally ought to find a home there) but, instead, on the interests that enable just that particular placement to occur in just this way, to just that effect. And so, when seen in this way, comparison can be understood to be a strategic, rhetorical act.

Returning to my reply: I do not wish to go into any further details of the Tuvel/*Hypatia* affair here; suffice it to say that (so far) it involved a reactionary open letter (that gained well over 100 signatures within just days) that asked for the article's retraction as well as the journal's associate editors' responding apology for printing the piece (though the editor has, at present, done just the opposite of apologizing for the article);[7] interested readers are advised to see any one of the many online commentaries that followed its development, in early 2017, for a wide variety of responses on the episode.[8] (See also the already cited Brubaker 2016: notably 22 ff.) Instead, having no doubt that Dorrough Smith is more than familiar with the case, as likely are many readers, I'd like to invite her to entertain the comparison that *I'm* making (between her chapter and Tuvel's article) so as to reflect on the nature of the comparison that *she* is making—i.e., borrowing the structure of a first-world/third-world comparison in order to make another—and thereby to comment on the reception of her own work, in the academy, on right-wing U.S. evangelical women. For, as scholars of religion, we are continually told to "take religion seriously," but I have suspected all along that what remains unarticulated (perhaps strategically) in this common methodological command is the

---

7 For the editor's statement, see http://dailynous.com/2017/05/06/hypatias-editor-board-president-defend-publication-tuvel-article/ (accessed 20 May 2017).

8 For those unacquainted with this episode, a good place to start might be: http://www.chronicle.com/article/A-Journal-Article-Provoked-a/240021 (accessed 20 May 2017).

distinction between those we somehow know that we ought to take seriously (which is a code word for "understand empathetically") and those who so differ from us, on matters for which we cannot entertain making any compromise or seeing as in any way relative or comparable, that we cannot do anything but try to explain them and their world (i.e., trying to answer the question "Why would anyone ever believe such and such … ?" rather than simply entertaining, maybe even appreciating, what it is like to live in their world). For I suspect that studying politically right social actors in the U.S. today and seeing them as socially formative social actors who are little different from their far left counterparts—despite each group working toward rather different ends, of course—has been met with some push-back, though perhaps not as explicit as that experienced by Tuvel.

So, in response, I guess I'm asking Dorrough Smith to update her chapter in light of some recent transgressions that have caught our collective attention, from "toilet bills" in some U.S. state legislatures (making it illegal to use a public restroom other than the one that matches the gender on one's birth certificate) and the very public case of Caitlyn Jenner herself, coupled with the realization, today, that seemingly self-evident, traditional biological identifiers no longer mark the limits of the group known as "women," to the transgressive act of scholars comparing what some might claim to be the wrong things. (That the election of Donald Trump as President of the United States has also taken place since her chapter was first written, and the fact that 53% of white women voted for him, provides yet another item to take into account, perhaps.)⁹ For despite wanting to agree with Dorrough Smith's claim that (and I paraphrase it here), when studying political right-wing women, we should be able to examine them and their social networking efforts and effects in much the same way as when studying any social group, it seems to me that the scholars who do this sort of work sometimes see their scholarship as a form of intervention or advocacy, and thus they either have difficulty or principled reasons for not distinguishing description from prescription—as evidenced in that *JAAR* article, discussed in my opening and

9   See https://www.nytimes.com/2016/12/01/us/politics/white-women-helped-elect-donald-trump.html (accessed 19 May 2017).

to which Kavka and I critically responded in a co-written reply. Thus, contrary to Dorrough Smith's and, I admit, contrary to my own hopes and best efforts, there may be reasons woven into the very nature of our academic enterprise that preclude a level playing field when it comes to the methods that we use to study certain others; for, despite the egalitarian rhetoric on the left, some of those others may be of greater consequence to us than the rest, inasmuch as we may have invested them with the significance of being the necessary device by which we are able to think and act ourselves into cohesive, collective agency. If so, then a feminism that set out, as Dorrough Smith phrases it, "to undermine the hegemony of Western liberalism as the measure of cultural value," may turn out to be contributing to that very system in unwitting yet inevitable ways.

References

Brubaker, Rogers. 2016. *Trans: Gender and Race in the Age of Unsettled Identities*. Princeton, NY: Princeton University Press.

Haslanger, Sally. 2012. *Resisting Reality: Social Construction and Social Critique*. New York: Oxford University Press. https://doi.org/10.1093/acprof:oso/9780199892631.001.0001

Kavka, Martin and Russell T. McCutcheon. 2017. "Justice, That Fraught Idea: A Response to 'The Normal and Abnormal'." *Journal of the American Academy of Religion* 85(1): 244–54. https://doi.org/10.1093/jaarel/lfw085

Mahomed, Nadeem and Farid Esack. 2017. "The Normal and Abnormal: On The Politics of Being Muslim and Relating to Same-Sex Sexuality." *Journal of the American Academy of Religion* 85(1): 224–43.

Smith, Jonathan Z. 1990. *Drudgery Divine: On the Comparison of Early Christianities and the Religions of Late Antiquity*. Chicago: University of Chicago Press.

Sunderland, Mitchell. 2015. "In Rachel Dolezal's Skin." *Broadly*. https://broadly.vice.com/en_us/article/rachel-dolezal-profile-interview (accessed 20 May 2017).

Tuvel, Rebecca. 2017. "In Defense of Transracialism." *Hypatia* 32(2): 263–78. https://doi.org/10.1111/hypa.12327

Russell T. McCutcheon is Chair of the Department of Religious Studies at the University of Alabama. Author or editor of a variety of books and resources, his interests involve theories of religion, the politics of classification systems, and social theory of identity formation.

9. Reply to Russell McCutcheon

Navigating the Politics of Comparison

Leslie Dorrough Smith

In the main chapter of this section, I argued that many Western feminist scholars are often quite willing to overlook the conservative political interests of many international women's groups by calling such groups "feminist" so as to create the sense of a diverse and multicultural feminist movement. Mine is not a popular conclusion to reach, I note, since making such a statement reveals a clear double standard that is still present in some feminist activism. In response, Russell McCutcheon pondered whether my unpopular argument was like another controversial piece of scholarship from scholar Rebecca Tuvel, who infamously claimed that if a transgender identity is possible, then we must logically acknowledge the possibility of a transracial identity as well. In the present chapter, I consider the nature of McCutcheon's comparison between my conclusion and Tuvel's, and maintain that their similarities reveal the enduring life of certain unspoken biases in scholarship today.

It is my pleasure to respond to Russell McCutcheon's query about the politics (and subsequent limits) of comparison. As I read him, what McCutcheon has invited me to do is respond to the politics that surround the comparative act that grounds my previous chapter, which itself involved examining and critiquing yet another act of comparison. While I hope the reader won't be intimidated by the thought of having to wade through three layers of comparison (and likely more by the time I am done!), I offer a bit of a life-preserver in simply saying that I believe McCutcheon is asking for some reflection on how our politics influence the comparative analyses we are willing to both make and acknowledge, particularly when those issues that we discuss are personally volatile and intimate.

With that in mind, I think it's helpful to think through what counts as a sound comparison, which begins by understanding just what comparison accomplishes; without this foundation we cannot know whether our arguments stand. In an incisive volume devoted entirely to analyzing the act of comparison, Aaron Hughes asserts that "comparison ... is the artificial act that brings two (or more) phenomena together *temporarily* and for the sake of some desired *end* (2017: ix). In other words, comparisons are not natural acts per se, for as comparers, we are the ones who choose to juxtapose two or more things in order to reach a particular, desired conclusion that their purported similarity or difference enables.

The merit of our comparison is measured by whether the claims to similarity or difference that purportedly justify the relationship between these otherwise discrete items are understood as valid by the observer. Put much more simply, a "good" comparison is one that people generally say is "logical," "objective," or otherwise "sound." That's a very satisfying answer so long as we presume those adjectives are stable, but humans are a notoriously fickle bunch, and what they count as good and bad logic (and from that, objectivity) shifts with their political inclinations. That's not to say that we should consider the rules of logic as most of us observe them today to be completely moot in this discussion, but, rather, that we should always keep in mind that those rules are reconstituted continuously as cultural interests dictate.

When Hughes refers to the artificial nature of the comparative act, he is thus highlighting the separate nature of the data that makes comparison possible, but is also noting that not everything that bears a similarity or difference with something else will make a useful comparison. This is so because comparisons are, if anything else, strategic—they are intended to communicate a particular thing ("some desired *end*") about a particular similarity or difference wrought between otherwise separate things. While, from a cognitive perspective, comparison may be something that we naturally do, that does not mean that the conclusions we reach in our comparisons are inevitable or self-evident to others. Consider how, for instance, the widespread nutritional information that compares the sugar and calories in certain fruits to that in a candy bar is shocking to so many: the commonality that they share (equal amounts of sugar) is so often overlooked because of the abiding belief that fruit is inherently healthy while candy is not. Comparisons are thus often useful because they reveal an alternative set of qualities about something that is usually characterized quite differently.

Presuming a shared foundation of reasonability, then, one can easily strike a poor comparison, Hughes notes, if one fails to give proper attention to context—that is, to the parameters in which the comparer claims that a commonality exists. Apart from obvious instances where two or more things simply lack a similarity, bad comparisons can also occur when a certain universality or essentialism is generated from a similarity that, historically and logically, could only reasonably lead the analyst to a more nuanced, localized conclusion (Hughes 2017: 77). For instance, claiming that that particular piece of fruit and the candy bar are nutritionally *identical* is a bad comparative move, since the similarity of their sugar content does not necessarily speak to their other nutritional qualities. Hughes elaborates that a solid comparison will outline the contextual parameters in which it remains accurate (such as the time frame, cultural milieu, and duration of the shared similarity), as well as point out the purpose in making the comparison. To diminish these things or fail to treat them altogether, he notes, is one way in which scholars, whether intentionally or not, create a sense of a timeless and/or essential connection between things that do not otherwise share such a sweeping relationship (2017: 10).

Analytically speaking, then, it is possible to identify a bad comparison as a proposed similarity or distinction for which there is poor evidence within the established contextual parameters, or as a case where the parameters themselves are skewed beyond what evidence can support. Despite this rather straightforward framework, McCutcheon rightly notes that charges of poor comparison are generated all the time by scholars who find distasteful the otherwise sound analytical conclusions drawn by others, and it is this event that is the focal point of my inquiry.

The question thus becomes how one grapples with charges that one's seemingly logical and comparatively sound analysis is lacking because it does not accommodate the political views of certain groups who frame their own critiques within the language of privilege, identity politics, subjectivity, and yes, even logic. This is an incredibly important thing to consider, as those of us who study power relationships (such as those that generate debates about race, sexual orientation, and gender, to name just a few) know that many privileged groups will make arguments against recognizing the rights and experiences of the underprivileged that would otherwise sound reasonable if the world were a perfectly fair place. I cannot fairly say that a child educated in a poor urban underfunded school has the same shot at attending an Ivy League college as, say, another child who has been educated her entire life in private college preparatory schools. Even though one could say that these students could be compared with each other when it comes to things like hours devoted to study and overall GPA, the context characterizing each educational experience is so starkly different that the comparison's failure in terms of contextual similarity could easily render the analytical point meaningless.

Thus any argument that fails to take into account the demonstrable dynamics, conditions, and parameters that define social life is an argument that fails to mesh with the dominant cultural understanding of reality, and under those terms, also fails to have any logical traction, even if there are individual components of argumentation that appear rational. This is argumentative terrain that is familiar to many of us who study social life, for critiquing privilege is something that, for many, is a scholarly pastime. Indeed, the category of privilege is often the animating concept used to halt the validity of a comparison in its tracks. But rather than a foul flag that we can throw down anytime we do not like the conclusion others reach, taking privilege seriously means being able to verbalize why and how this particular issue of narrowed perspective (which is often the result of increased social power) undermines the logic that a person employs. In other words, privilege is not a random and wild-card rebuttal; it refers to demonstrable instances of epistemic limitation that result from differential access to avenues of social power.

This is vital to remember because there is no single identity category that permits omniscient license, and yet scholars will often lob charges of privilege at each other without actually making clear how the logic at hand exhibits the skewed perspectives that characterize privilege other than to simply assert that it does. I must admit that my own previous chapter would undoubtedly strike some as biased if they believed that there is an obvious disconnect between conservative first-world female activists and female activists from the third world. Because I assume this difference is neither innate nor natural, I have previously been accused of supporting conservative activists when I make such arguments, even though my own position is intended to redescribe the relationship between discrete groups, and not to be political at all (with "political" understood in the narrowest sense).

In that previous chapter, I ask why those third-world women who fight against things such as sex-trafficking even as they also advocate for traditional family structures are understood to be "feminists" by many feminist scholars, whereas American conservative women who do the same are considered "anti-feminist." The standard answer to this, if we could boil it down to just one, is that the lives of third-world women are constrained in ways that first-world women do not experience, and thus the former group's frequent allegiance to patriarchal structures can be explained by pointing to their limited cultural agency. The idea here is that if they had more rights and cultural capital, third-world women would throw off the patriarchal elements that many continue to maintain. Some might thus claim I have made a bad comparison, if not a completely first-world, culturally insensitive one, for if different cultural contexts cause people to behave in different ways, then juxtaposing the two is problematic. I can easily imagine being accused of exercising the same sort of privilege that I highlighted in the earlier example about schoolchildren and their Ivy League futures.

But it is terribly important to keep in mind that my dataset here is not activist women, but the scholars who are themselves trying to find a way to explain their comparative and thus classificatory choices in light of the fact that there is little data to support it. If the privilege argument is the most dominant way to justify this categorization, then we must recognize that it is precisely the privilege of first-world conservative women that throws this conclusion into peril, for as the evidence shows, having more privilege and power doesn't necessarily make a woman deny patriarchal structures. The retorts that feminist scholars often use to explain privileged, patriarchal women are also quite unsatisfying to many others in the feminist scholarly community, for claims of false consciousness (what is perhaps the most common explanation) have long been subject to suspicion, as has the trope of the culturally imprisoned third-world woman that makes the other side of the comparison possible.

In short, it's very difficult to find a good explanation for this classificatory double standard by appealing to facts alone, and this is why I conclude that the rationale behind this inconsistent naming process by which certain groups are granted or denied the label "feminist" is rooted in political desires for a global, diverse feminist community rather than demonstrable cultural patterns that exhibit these qualities. The trouble is, however, that we often pass off our political desires as methodologically sound analysis, which depends on the fantasy that the techniques of rational inquiry will inevitably support our political positions (or at the very least, not deny them).

I experienced the pitfalls of this critique firsthand in some of my previous work, wherein I analyzed the rhetorical tactics of a large and powerful conservative Christian women's group while also clearly concluding that such tactics are rather mundane (Smith 2014). As a major analytical point, I noted that scholars are notoriously uneven in the ways that they analyze evangelicals as compared to the ways that they treat other, more popular religious groups, and I provided clear and sound data to back this claim. Despite this conclusion, reviews of my book and related research almost always leave out the part about scholarly inconsistencies, focusing instead on the more traditional data that I provide about such groups themselves, data that can be easily used to reaffirm scholarly biases against right-wing groups. As I make very clear, my rationale for making this methodological argument was not to lend support to right-wing groups (far from it), but to showcase for scholars how easily our own political assumptions can sully what we otherwise believe is objective analysis.

With this in mind, the comparison that McCutcheon mentioned between my work and that of Rebecca Tuvel is, indeed, apropos. Tuvel is the scholar who recently wrote a very controversial and highly publicized article entitled "In Defense of Transracialism," which engages the legitimacy of the notion that one can identify with a different racial category than the one(s) assigned by one's family and society. In the article, Tuvel compares the case of Rachel Dolezal (the now infamous self-identified black woman born to a white family, and who was at one point the president of her local chapter of the NAACP), with that of Caitlyn Jenner, who has recently become the poster child for transgender visibility and acceptance.

While I will not recount every detail of her argument, Tuvel generally claims that if transgender identity has been legitimized on the basis that gender is a social construct that society has erroneously attached to certain biological features, then transracial identity must be considered a legitimate identity as well, for like gender, race is a social construct erroneously attached to certain biological features (2017).[1] Along the way, she addresses the most common arguments against transracial identity (including that it is an expression of white privilege, and that race is a genealogical reality apart from its cultural meanings, etc.), demonstrating that, on the whole, these arguments closely mirror the essentialist critiques of transgender identity that have generally been overturned in progressive circles. While she clearly does not equate transgender and transracial identities, she does demonstrate that they both rest on similar logic, and thus asks the reader to consider their willingness to accept one but not the other.

---

1 For those not familiar with this argument, it hinges on the observation that "gender" refers to modes of behavior and identification that, although popularly attached to people with certain kinds of bodies, are nevertheless socially constructed, something we can demonstrate due to gender's changing nature across time and place. In other words, if gender were something innate in one's chromosomal makeup, then all people born with the same chromosomes across the globe would presumably behave in similar ways, a notion for which we do not have evidence. Race, too, is another example of a construct generated from assumptions about particular types of bodies— namely, that certain skin colors and other physical characteristics will, by definition, result in a group of people who share some fundamental "core." Since there is no evidence of this, either, I therefore call these arguments erroneous.

The article Tuvel wrote was accepted by *Hypatia*, one of the field's preeminent peer-reviewed journals. Upon its publication, however, incredible controversy ensued, including calls for the article's retraction due to the purported harm that Tuvel perpetrated against people of color (Singal 2017). Most of her critics argued that even partial endorsement of Dolezal's transracial claim was tantamount to supporting a counterfeit who was using her white privilege to appropriate an oppressed group's identity for her own whims, thus leading to the erasure of the dignity, culture, and experiences of that group.[2] (Significantly, this is the same as one of the arguments—now strongly rejected—that some feminists have used against transwomen: they have used male privilege to "become" women, thereby erasing the experiences of "real" women).

What is perhaps most interesting to me in this larger discussion of comparison is that while several critics cite Tuvel's insensitivity to the oppression experienced by people of color, this critique is not explained in ways that logically undercut her central argument. In one of the most insightful commentaries that I've seen on the matter, scholar Ani Dutta acknowledges that while there might be flaws with Tuvel's article, they are flaws more widely associated with racist biases currently endemic to philosophy and are not unique to Tuvel (2017). Moreover, Dutta notes, many of the supposedly offensive remarks that Tuvel offers in her essay have been made by other social activists who have experienced little to no critique in their wake (2017). In other words, comparing Tuvel's words against those of more accepted voices reveals that the problem isn't likely her argument, but her own identity (white, cis-gender), which makes her more vulnerable to pushback even though her actual commentary is not substantively different.

Much of the critique against Tuvel is thus attributable, at least in part, to oversimplifications regarding identity and privilege that have been fodder for bad comparisons (as discussed above). As Dutta

2   A copy of the now famous open letter to *Hypatia*, which contains most of the major critiques of the article, is available at:
https://docs.google.com/forms/d/1efp9C0MHch_6Kfgtlm0PZ76nirWt-cEsqWHcvgidl2mU/viewform?ts=59066d20&edit_requested=true

notes, "… 'privilege' and 'identity' (social or personal) aren't linearly correlated in any case, and thus, one can neither adjudicate identity claims based on privilege, nor dismiss mentions or critiques of gender privilege as being transmisogynist in and of themselves" (2017). Instead of presuming that society is organized according to the categories that suit our politics, social life is infinitely complex, even if it is ruled by rather predictable forces.

It is navigating these very forces that brings Dutta to what I believe is the crux of the argument, which is that the discomfort that so many feel regarding the idea of transracial identity is tied to how identity arguments have been used in realms of race and gender more broadly. Put very simply, Dutta argues that we have grown accustomed to thinking of gender as an individual experience while race has been described more as a collective one, and these are frames that have been deployed because of their utility. Indeed, transgender rights activists have often used anti-essentialist claims to maintain that, due to its social construction (and thus invented nature), the parameters of gender lie with any one individual's self-understanding; anti-racism advocates, on the other hand, have generally found more social traction with collective arguments that emphasize a shared identity resulting from systemic oppression.

Dutta's position is thus that the visceral response that many have had to Rachel Dolezal (and by extension, to Tuvel) may very well be a reflection of certain epistemological norms within activist circles motivated by political interests rather than a verifiable ontological claim (i.e., that Dolezal "really is/not" black) or a failure in Tuvel's analysis. To be very clear, this does not mean that the politics that surround these issues are irrelevant—after all, Dutta is clear in being predominantly concerned with how people use Tuvel's argument in social networks of power, which is to be expected from someone in a field that is devoted to advocacy. Moreover, because social life is inherently political, there is no way that we can avoid politics as such. But what Dutta is asserting (in a circumstance that often does not typically lend itself to such clarity) is that we have grown accustomed to substituting our own politics for logical analysis, and that we should be forthright about the motivation behind our claims while simultaneously not disguising them as something they are not (2017).

So what does it mean when rational inquiry (here aided by comparison) leads one to a conclusion that transgresses the politics of the scholars who make up the surrounding community? It means that choosing to develop and stand by methodologically sound analysis (as earlier described) is never an apolitical enterprise, but that virtually all scholars, at some point, will have to make choices about what sorts of standards guide their work. I am not so naïve to argue that logical analysis should be our primary concern because it is stable, while political concerns and ethics take the backburner because they are shifting, for all three are the products of endlessly changing social forces. Perhaps obviously, I am also not saying that the political and ethical frameworks through which social life proceeds are unimportant —far from it. Yet it does seem that what brings together our very capacity for analytical engagement at all is a collective agreement that, despite what may be differing politics and perspectives, there are rational terms that guide our inquiry. If we diminish this capacity, then it seems that we chip away at the ability to meaningfully communicate at all.

References

Dutta, Ani. 2017. "On Tuvel, Adichie, Dolezal and the Privilege-Identity Distinction." https://www.facebook.com/notes/ani-dutta/on-tuvel-adichie-dolezal-and-the-privilege-identity-distinction/10155234495464437/ (accessed 14 January 2018).

Hughes, Aaron. 2017. *Comparison: A Critical Primer*. Sheffield, UK: Equinox Publishing.

Singal, Jesse. 2017. "This is What a Modern Day Witch-Hunt Looks Like." *New York Magazine*. http://nymag.com/daily/intelligencer/2017/05/transracialism-article-controversy.html (accessed 14 January 2018).

Smith, Leslie Dorrough. 2014. *Righteous Rhetoric: Sex, Speech, and the Politics of Concerned Women for America*. New York: Oxford University Press.

Tuvel, Rebecca. 2017. "In Defense of Transracialism." *Hypatia*, 32(2): 263–78. https://doi.org/10.1111/hypa.12327

Leslie Dorrough Smith is Associate Professor of Religious Studies and Director of the Women's and Gender Studies Program at Avila University. She is author of *Righteous Rhetoric: Sex, Speech, and the Politics of Concerned Women for America* (Oxford University Press, 2014) as well as a forthcoming book (also with Oxford) about political sex scandals and American religion. Her research focuses on the interplay between gender, sex, reproduction, and the politics of American evangelical groups and conservatives more broadly.

Afterword

Strategic Acts I and II

Russell T. McCutcheon

[T]he history of religions is destined to play an important role in contemporary cultural life. This is not only because an understanding of exotic and archaic religions will significantly assist in a cultural dialogue with the representatives of such religions. It is more especially because, by attempting to understand the existential situations expressed by the documents he is studying, the historian of religions will inevitably attain to a deeper knowledge of man. It is on the basis of such a knowledge that a new humanism, on a world-wide scale, could develop. We may even ask if the History of Religions cannot make a contribution of prime importance to its formation. For, on the one hand, the historical and comparative study of religions embraces all the cultural forms so far known, both the ethnological cultures and those that have played a major role in history; on the other hand, by studying the religious expressions of a culture, the scholar approaches it from within, and not merely in its sociological, economic, and political contexts. In the last analysis, the historian of religions is destined to elucidate a large number of situations unfamiliar to the man of the West. It is through an understanding of such unfamiliar, "exotic" situations that cultural provincialism is transcended. (Eliade 1961: 2–3)

So wrote the famed Romanian ex-pat and noted University of Chicago scholar of religion, Mircea Eliade (1907–86), more than half a century ago, in the opening article to the still important peer-review journal, *History of Religions* (an essay that was reprinted a few years later as the opening chapter to his own essay collection, *The Quest* [1969]); it was a time when, as we now know, the academic study of religion was poised to be invented in public universities all across the United States and Canada—a field that was by then long established in Europe (since the late 19th century, in fact) but one which, despite a brief appearance in North America in the early years of the 20th century, has had a more tenuous position on this side of the Atlantic. And, arguably, it was Eliade's confidence for the scope, impact, and thus bright future of the field that helped not just Chicago's grads to find work in those newly opened departments (not to overlook the largely unsung role of his number two at Chicago, Joseph Kitagawa [1915–92], well known among grads for helping them to land positions), but also helped to open those very departments by inspiring the rhetoric employed by countless professors in their conversations with administrators, colleagues, and granting agencies, all in order to gain the faculty lines, office space, and (the usually small) budgets necessary for a group of scholars to invent an academic field.

For in conceiving of religion as an affective and deeply meaningful dimension of the human, the history of religions, as they still call it at Chicago (their translation of the field's name in Germany, *Religionswissenschaft*), could provide the basis for another renaissance—a new humanism, as Eliade called it—by training scholars to carefully and properly decode and organize the timeless expressions of the sacred all throughout culture and history, thereby providing a window onto what he often termed the lost existential situations of past peoples. It was a field destined for greatness.

And so began what I'll call Act I in the study of religion's story, at least where all of the authors in this book work. (I'll read the early 20th century's various false starts for the field on this continent as mere prologue.) That those included in this volume either were trained by or now work in North American departments dedicated to the study of religion—though not all work in public universities, of course—testifies to the strategic success of predecessors who, like Eliade, argued for the unique and virtually boundless contributions to be made by scholars trained to identify the special and, as they once phrased it, irreducible dimension of religious beliefs, objects, actions, and symbols. For though historians and sociologists, psychologists and anthropologists had already been long studying religion and teaching courses in publicly-funded universities on things religious (e.g., myths, rituals, church history, etc.), there was something invaluable to be gained—or so the argument went—by seeing religion not simply as something historical or something anthropological but, instead, by seeing it as such scholars thought the devotees themselves saw it: *as something inherently and essentially religious*. As insightful as so-called reductionist studies might seem (such as those claiming religion to be a merely secondary effect of such prior things as rigged economies or maladjusted psyches), what such work missed—again, as the argument went—was what many termed the irreducibly unique dimension of the sacred. And administrators (many of whom surely identified themselves as religious, suggesting that they were more than likely predisposed to be sympathetic to such claims), along with a variety of private funding agencies that helped to provide some of the resources to get the field going (many of which were themselves openly theological or at least politically liberal, such as The Danforth Foundation, which was active between 1927 and 2011, whose mission was "promoting the well-being of mankind"), all agreed—and, voila, the study of religion (understood as the cross-cultural study of a diverse number of external, empirical items that provided the opportunity to infer the existence of an internal, non-empirical, and universally shared quality that was said to animate them all) was born in North America. Its grand ambition, as exemplified in that opening quotation from Eliade, was seen as non-sectarian, inasmuch as it wasn't read as promoting any one denomination or what was quickly coming to be termed a religious tradition, so it seemed to meet the demands of a religiously neutral approach, what was then significantly called teaching *about* religion as opposed to teaching religion.

But if we fast-forward to today, which will soon be 60 years and several academic generations later, and consider the preceding chapters that readers have hopefully worked through prior to arriving here, at the Afterword, it should be evident that there's considerable distance between Eliade's early hopes for the field's future and what the scholars of religion collected in this volume have ended up doing in their careers; for religion has gone from being seen as uniquely privileged to utterly mundane and (as nicely evident in the Appendix to the volume) comparable in a myriad of perhaps unanticipated ways to who knows how many other equally commonplace elements of day-to-day life. And this is a gap in approaches that is worth mulling over, I think, for what this set of essays offers to readers is a model for the future of the field that could not be more different than the one that Eliade and his followers provided (and thus one that is quite different from how the field is practiced in most Departments today). For while he claimed religion to be the pristine *expression* (not an insignificant term) of an eternal and deeply meaningful experience, set apart from all others, the one presupposed in this book is that, whatever we may call religion (and yes, *we* are the ones deciding, based on countless different sets of criteria, what will or will not count *as* religious), both the thing so designated as well as this very act of designation itself, are routine aspects of specifically situated cultural practices. So much so that studying both religion and the act of naming something *as* religion provide opportunities for these authors to examine many of the ordinary, day-to-day procedures that they find happening virtually everywhere in that domain that we have come to know as culture—identification techniques so routine that we may often overlook them, as if our world was pre-arranged by classifying, ranking, and thereby organizing itself. And it is precisely because Eliade et al., in one camp, and my colleagues, in another, are suggesting alternative courses for the field to chart, it seemed sensible to end the volume by inviting readers to reflect explicitly on the gains that may come not from continually perpetuating the origins myths of our field (and thereby grounding the legitimacy of our work in the utter uniqueness of our object of study) but, rather, by opting for what I'll just call a second, socially theoretical act in our field's still unfolding narrative.

For the main chapters in this volume (not to mention the further examples included in the Appendix, the latter of which are all pithy and thus easily read case studies in this volume's alternative proposal) are likely best seen each as providing an instance of how to think through a certain sort of problem (something that is productively complicated by each main chapter's collegial back and forth between author and respondent)—a problem, contrary to what Eliade and others might argue, that is hardly unique to the domain on which each of the three main chapters focuses; thus, it is something more than likely also apparent at any number of other social sites, all of which are well outside what we usually call religion. For, as noted above, all of these sites constitute places where social actors are involved with the mundane but still interesting acts of signifying their world, thereby creating contingent identities for themselves and others (sometimes tactically planned, as in the conservative women's reaction to liberal feminism, and sometimes unforeseen because happenstance, such as the invention of the Nones from out of a few questions on a pollster's survey). This is accomplished by establishing, among the many possibly random items that populate their environment, relationships of similarity and difference that strike actors as advantageous for the various projects they are tackling. So instead of seeing the scholar of religion as a careful and gifted interpreter (or hermeneut, as Elaide phrased it), capable of cracking the sacred's mysterious and camouflaged symbolic code as it is manifested first here or there (to only slightly paraphrase Eliade's own often-used language), this volume works under the assumption that it is our *method*, and not our object of study, that sets us apart from other scholars of religion, inasmuch as we share a wide (and widely applicable) interest in examining all acts of signification and, when it comes to social life, identification. But inasmuch as it sets us apart from those who continue to work with Eliade's model (and, whether they read him still or not, the model he represented is still prominent), this set of general interests in social theory prompts us to think that what we have to offer may be relevant to readers well beyond those in the study of religion, those who are game to rethink their own approach; it therefore unites us with those working in other fields who are willing to take seriously that what we, as scholars, have on our hands when studying human beings is simply people doing things—people who act with intention but who do so in multiple structured, historical settings that overlap, complement, and even contradict each other (often in unanticipated ways).

The problem, then, is not to intuit the meaning of the sacred but, rather, to study how social life proceeds in such circumstances, examining the techniques actors use to advance interests, form coalitions, contest alternatives, and authorize their own inevitably historical and sometimes chance claims and practices—as well as to understand how their intentions and so-called feelings may themselves be historical phenomena, called into existence in those very structured settings in which people live and work as opposed to being seen as originary, interior sources for their public actions. It is therefore a model that takes agency seriously but which understands that very agency to be the product of, and to be exercised within, contingent settings that are not of the agent's own making—a dialectical approach to agency and structure that differs dramatically from the one that helped to found our field. In fact, as already suggested, the earlier model, in which Eliade's so-called hierophanies (i.e., the term he coined for what he called manifestations of the sacred, much as the German Protestant theologian, Rudolf Otto [1869–1937], before him coined the still used word numinous for the quality he sought to study) pretty much acted of their own accord, manifesting themselves (as Eliade phrased it on not a few occasions) in discrete historic situations, only to be witnessed by us and thus properly recognized (or not) for what they truly were, is hardly a strawman that dates only from our field's founding, for it can indeed be found all throughout the field as it is practiced today.

I think here of no better example than Robert Orsi's (b. 1953) latest book, *History and Presence* (2016). Onetime President of the American Academy of Religion (in 2003—the AAR is the field's largest professional association for scholars of religion) and among those who helped to establish a now thriving subfield (inspired, in part, by the social history movement) devoted to the bottom-up study of religion in day-to-day life (variously known now as religion on the ground, lived religion, or material religion), Orsi's work on American Catholicism is widely influential, such that a doctoral student interested today in studying this area will more than likely be assumed to be working in his intellectual tradition. He is a well-known advocate for a model of the field that takes participant claims so seriously that describing, perhaps even appreciating, them seems the end goal of scholarship. Case in point, in an earlier essay that, at least to my ears, oddly described Otto as a "theorist of the holy" (Orsi 2011: 86 [a use of the signifier "theory" that, I would claim, is so broad as to make it utterly un-useful for any scholarly purposes]), Orsi anticipated his recent book's topic by noting that many approaches to the study of religion are incapable of entertaining

how Jesus is a real figure in a Pentecostal woman's everyday
experience, as real to her as the other people around her, as real
as her kitchen table and her arthritis. She does not "believe in"
Jesus. Jesus is present to her. Moreover, this woman's Jesus
has an existence that is greater than the sum of her intentions,
desires, needs, hopes, and fears, and that cannot be completely
accounted for with reference to her social circumstances. He has
a life of his own in her life. (2011: 85)

Inasmuch as such scholarship finds causality somewhere else, natu-
ralistic and explanatory studies, Orsi maintains, "fall short of the realness of the phenomena they purport to describe and explain in people's
experience" (2011: 84). I would maintain that what we see here, and
more extensively demonstrated in his 2016 book (not to mention in
the now much celebrated work of the anthropologist Tanya Luhrmann,
e.g., her book *When God Talks Back: Understanding the American
Evangelical Relationships with God* [2012]), is a largely unrecon-
structed Eliadean, even phenomenological approach, inasmuch as
historically situated human beings are conceived as *responding to*
but never as *creating* or *animating* the deeply meaningful symbols or
structures that surround and impinge upon them. It is a passive, reactive, and philosophically idealist model of the human that grounds
its legitimacy in the asserted special character of its object—a specialness, or should I say a realness, that, or so it is asserted, scholars'
usual methods of study are simply incapable of grasping.

Our object of study, at least according to the still playing first act
of the field, is therefore hardly mundane. But this is precisely the
position from which the foregoing essays diverge.

While I have rigorously critiqued Orsi's approach elsewhere (e.g.,
see an earlier essay reprinted as chapter 8 in Culture on the Edge's
first published set of essays [Miller 2015]), the chapters in this book
bring his work to mind once again, especially when reading this volume as providing a second act for how we practice the academic study
of religion today: seeing it as one among many cross-disciplinary
moments in a broader social theory of human practices, tackling at
this one site the implications for how mundane (but consequential)
acts of signification and identification interrelate, rather than seeing
our object of study as already set-apart and obviously significant,

and thus only to be studied by means of the so-called Queen of the Sciences (a title once reserved for theology but one which Eliade's new humanism surely aimed to apply to his version of the history of religions). In fact, as suggested earlier, and as so nicely exemplified in this volume's responses and replies, it is this very act of setting something apart *as* special, *as* unique, *as* inexplicable, etc., that now catches our attention—for we no longer assume distinction as a naturally occurring social fact merely expressed by objects—inasmuch as we begin to pay rather more careful notice of our own actions, our own distinctions, given that scholars in this alternative track recognize that systems of classification (i.e., naming, relating, and ranking)—the scholar's no less than anyone else's—play a primary role in determining what in the world we will talk about and come to know (not to mention ignore).

As I have long argued, based on my own doctoral training in a cross-disciplinary unit (that, since my time at the University of Toronto, has unfortunately been collapsed into the graduate wing of a Department of Religious Studies), it is such a shared approach, and thus shared curiosities, that unifies us as a field, and not our presumably unique object of study. This organizing principle for a field is borne out by the contributors to this very book, inasmuch as no two of us study the same thing—if by "thing" one means the supposed subject matter, such as the already-mentioned American evangelicals in Dorrough Smith's case or the Nones in the case of Ramey. But if we expand such a noun as *thing* or *subject* to include processes (such as how groups work to naturalize what can otherwise be demonstrated to be historically contingent situations, actions, or artifacts), and if we specify that the questions we ask and our method for studying them is what unites us, then this shift from object to approaches starts to get at what has unified this otherwise disparate group of people into the research initiative known as Culture on the Edge. For despite drastically different training and expertise—from Simmons, with a PhD in English literature, to Martin's interest in early modern political theory and Touna's background in classical Greek language and history—this group formed around shared curiosities concerning how groups that we usually take for granted came into being, how they are maintained despite daily challenges, how their demise occurs, and what new things might come after that; so this interest in developing a common approach to studying what we might call the natural history of identification is what unifies us, along with our shared frustration that so few in our field seem able to make this shift in how they approach their studies. For the myth of the self-evident signifier, one that expresses its own deep meaning, rather than being conjured into being by the reader, persists.

While it is still too early to report on its success, the shift indicative of what I'm proposing as our field's second act has at least breathed new life into the Department that has hosted Culture on the Edge since its inception, the Department of Religious Studies at the University of Alabama, in which four of our group's members now work (Ramey, Simmons, Touna, and myself). Given that I have written on our Department's reinvention before (see my own Afterword to Ramey 2015), I'll not repeat what I have said elsewhere; I only wish to observe that, beginning in 2001, a gradual but continued process of reinvention took place in what was then our small (three tenure-track and one tenured faculty members) and marginalized Department—a unit in which it was then profoundly evident that "covering the material," a goal of many curricula and syllabi, was simply not possible. Choice was therefore necessary, since our objects were sadly insufficient if "breadth" was our goal, and it seemed productive to choose from among our common questions and interests (rather than our ostensibly shared data—for there we found little or no overlap), rather than simply assembling a team capable of studying religion in all the places where it is now thought to manifest itself. (I think here of the AAR's annual program, in which the "Religion and ..." rubric is virtually unending in its application or the areas into which many doctoral programs divide up the fields in which their students must specialize.) From a colleague studying U.S. popular culture to another working on holocaust and genocide studies and another examining the history of medieval Tibet, it soon became apparent that, whether recognized by each of us or not, we indeed studied drastically different things but, in doing so, all shared an interest in how social identities came into being, were continually reinvented, and, eventually passed out of being (as I've before remarked, people no longer call themselves Prussians ...); we were therefore all scholars who happened to study religion but, unlike Eliade, *we did so as a means to another end.* To phrase it in terms of the work of another influential Chicago scholar of religion, Jonathan Z. Smith (1938–2017), the things that we studied were simply examples for wider processes that we could easily also see at other cultural and historical sites—sites where one could equally well pursue answers to these questions.

Since that initial (and admittedly gradual) realization of what actually united us—our questions and methods, and not our objects—each of the Department's new hires have attempted to add members to the team who could enhance this project by deploying this shared interest in a new site, whether a period in history or a region of the world— e.g., adding an Americanist but one who studied early U.S. reactions to Orientalist findings coming from what was then the newly colonized Indian subcontinent, along with a scholar of ancient religion who used it to study modern Greek identity and a scholar studying Pentecostal converts in Japan but as a place to examine responses to the pressures of global migration. For in each case the item in which the scholar specialized turned out to be but an instance of a far broader and mundane interest—a Petri dish, if you will, where an experiment in the techniques of social formation could be carried out. And, capitalizing on this newfound unity among the faculty—a group that, since 2001, has grown to 11—a new MA degree was devised and then launched (in the Fall of 2017), focusing explicitly on social theory of religion (as well as the digital skills that we hope will help set our graduates apart in an increasingly competitive academic and labor environment). It was out of this setting, with these specific interests, that Culture on the Edge was first conceived: as a site that had little explicitly to do with religion but to which a small group of scholars of religion, interested in using their tools to shed light on everyday, culture-wide processes, might contribute something that people both inside and outside the field would hopefully find worth reading.

So, in going over the preceding chapters, and the short (and hopefully engaging) pieces of the Appendix (all of which originally appeared on the group's extensive blog), my hope is that readers keep in mind that there is a choice here for *them* to make, concerning how they wish to use this term religion: whether they will continue to employ it passively, to name what are claimed to be deeply special moments that are said to transcend culture and history or, as we instead propose, to see it as one among many words that specific groups of people proactively use to name and rank items in their environment (calling this sacred as opposed to that being secular), all in order to make sense of their worlds in ways that, or so they likely hope, have some competitive advantage over the many other ways that yet other actors are busily signifying *their* worlds. We recommend the latter, of course, and if it is chosen then we contend that such an approach will not just open new opportunities for scholars of religion to carry out their studies—not because religion is now found where we hadn't expected to find it (i.e., the-religion-of-baseball approach), but because the tools to study signification here will be no less relevant there—but will also open new readerships for our work, people who come to realize that studying religion is but another site where we can study issues found all throughout human behavior. For now the tools that we use, to study how groups authenticate and authorize the worlds they themselves create, nurture, and even contest, may strike people with no special training in this one field as illustrative of basic things happening all across culture.

And this, in conclusion, is the utterly ironic part of it all: the wide relevance Eliade and others hoped to have as a result of our field's first act may finally be achieved in the second; for by relinquishing the uniqueness of our object of study—a specialness that, it seems to me, merely ghettoized our field from the start, inasmuch as our existence, as a academic pursuit, was tied to our privileged, yes, but also irreconcilable distance from all other intellectual pursuits—we may create new and fertile links to all other parts of the human sciences, since we will be using the study of things called religions as but useful examples and helpful, illustrative cases that call for comparison to the many other sorts of things that people do or that they leave behind when they're done with their doings. So while I would not be so bold or confident as to assert, as Eliade did, that the study of religion "is destined to play an important role in contemporary cultural life," I do hope that, in the reinvented second act, the field might come to be understood by readers well outside the study of religion as offering something helpful to anyone curious to understand this elaborate project that we call social life, the one in which we are all engaged.

References

Eliade, Mircea. 1961. "History of Religions and a New Humanism." *History of Religions* 1(1): 1–8. https://doi.org/10.1086/462437

Eliade, Mircea. 1969. *The Quest: History and Meaning in Religion*. Chicago: University of Chicago Press.

Orsi, Robert A. (ed.). 2011. *The Cambridge Companion to Religious Studies*. Cambridge, UK: Cambridge University Press. https://doi.org/10.1017/CCOL9780521883917

Orsi, Robert A. 2016. *History and Presence*. Cambridge, MA: Harvard University Press.

Luhrmann, Tanya. 2012. *When God Talks Back: Understanding the American Evangelical Relationships with God*. New York: Vintage.

Miller, Monica R. (ed.). 2015. *Claiming Identity in the Study of Religion: Social and Rhetorical Techniques Examined*. Sheffield, UK: Equinox Publishing.

Ramey, Steven W. (ed.). 2015. *Writing Religion: The Case for the Critical Study of Religion*. Tuscaloosa, AL: University of Alabama Press.

Russell T. McCutcheon is Chair of the Department of Religious Studies at the University of Alabama. Author or editor of a variety of books and resources, his interests involve theories of religion, the politics of classification systems, and social theory of identity formation.

APPENDIX

ACTS OF CLASSIFICATION

1.   Creatio Ex Nihilo: Pew Forum and the "Nones"[1]

Steven W. Ramey

New analysis suggests that almost 1 in 5 people in the United States have no religious affiliation! Media coverage has sensationalized the publication of this analysis from the Pew Forum on Religion and Public,[2] and various church and institutional leaders have presented explanations for the increase of the "Nones," as some call them, and suggestions of how to change the trend.

The difficulty is that the analysis from Pew, and in response to Pew, creates an illusion of commonality through the construction of this group ex nihilo. Those who chose "no religious affiliation" have a wide range of attitudes, practices, beliefs, etc. Some are atheist or agnostic (two broad categories in themselves) but reportedly 68% of them believe in some "higher power." Some pray (41%) and some do not. Some feel a connection to the environment (58%) and some do not. Some think government should shrink (52%) and some do not. What holds the group together is their response to one question, religious affiliation. The assumption/construction of commonality leads analysts to attribute generalizing characteristics to the group despite the data. *USA Today*, for example, reports a lack of political activity

1   Ed. Note: This is the first blog post that appeared on the Culture on the Edge site on 31 May 2013, https://edge.ua.edu/steven-ramey/creatio-ex-nihilo-pew-forum-and-the-nones/ (accessed 20 December 2017). It was originally posted on the *Bulletin for the Study of Religion* blog, http://bulletin.equinoxpub.com/2013/01/creatio-ex-nihilo-pew-forum-and-the-nones-2/ (accessed 20 December 2017).

2   http://www.pewforum.org/2012/10/09/nones-on-the-rise/ (accessed 20 December 2017).

among "Nones," as they do not participate in political organizations or vote as (dare I say it) religiously as white evangelicals.

The error of presumed commonality, however, is not limited to a group such as the "Nones." Assuming commonality for people identifying in similar ways on a survey creates faulty generalized assertions. A recent book by M. Steven Fish, *Are Muslims Distinctive?* (Oxford University Press, 2011) uses multinational surveys to query if those who identify as Muslim are more prone to violence, have different levels of religiosity, or have greater education. Despite careful statistical analysis and nuanced conclusions, the work assumes that identifying oneself as Muslim in a survey reflects a substantive commonality, despite differences in specific context (what constitutes illegal violence, political participation, etc., in different nations). The assumption that being Muslim trumps those significant differences is similar to constructing the "Nones." Rather than overreacting, recognize the Pew data as an example of constructing group labels ex nihilo. Otherwise, respond simply with a shrug.

2.   Discourse All the Way Down[3]

Craig Martin

In *Sex/Gender: Biology in a Social World* (Routledge, 2012),[4] Anne Fausto-Sterling provides us with an interesting metaphor with which to think about the nature/nurture debate. Sometimes the discussion is framed in terms of how much nature and nurture each contribute, as if they're taking turns filling a bucket. Imagine a 100 gallon bucket:

> Suppose two people (oh call one Mr. Nature and the other Ms. Nurture) are filling up that bucket with separate hoses. If Mr. Nature added 70 gallons and Ms. Nurture 30, then we could say that the 100 gallons is due 70 percent to nature and 30 percent to nurture. (113)

---

3   Ed. Note: Posted on 8 August 2013, https://edge.ua.edu/craig-martin/discourse-all-the-way-down/ (accessed 20 December 2017).

4   http://routledgetextbooks.com/textbooks/_author/fausto-sterling-9780415881463/ (accessed 20 December 2017).

However, this is not the only way we could frame the conversation.

> But suppose instead that Mr. Nature supplies the hose, while
> Ms. Nurture brings the bucket. Then what percentage is due to
> nature and what to nurture? The truth is, the question doesn't
> make any sense. (113)

Framing the metaphor in the latter way suggests that "nurture" contributes to the *entire* process, as does "nature." There's no way to create a pie chart reflecting each one's contribution.

Arguably, the discussion about the extent to which our world is just out there versus the extent to which it is socially constructed is similar. Some people seem to want to pin down how much of it is "real" and how much of it is discursive, as if material reality contributed 70 gallons to our bucket and discourse contributed 30. By contrast, I'd allege that reality is socially constructed all the way down, insofar as discourse contributes to the *entire* process for us. This does not mean the world is made up of words—as if an insult and a punch were the same thing—but rather that discourses operate at every level of our reality.

The usual objection, of course, is that things are there independently of discourse. Dogs may not have discourse, but that doesn't prevent them from seeing—and chasing—cats, right? But try the experiment suggested by Donald Davidson:[5] swap out the word for one less familiar to a monolingual English speaker, a speaker without feline breeding expertise: does the dog see—or *identify*—an American Polydactyl, an Arabian Mau, a macksa (Hungarian) or a 貓 (Chinese)? Could you identify an Arabian Mau in a feline police lineup? I couldn't. I don't know what the dog "sees," but I'm fairly certain that seeing or identifying an American Polydactyl requires the deployment of a set of concepts that the dog does not have. The same is true of "cat," which is also discursive. It seems that we forget that fact when using words or concepts that are so familiar to us as to have become naturalized.

5   Donald Davidson, "Rational Animals," *Dialectica* 36(4), 1982: 317–27.

Some seem to fear the idea that the world—at least the world *for us*—is discursive all the way down because it implies that words and concepts somehow get *between* us and the world. It's presumed that discourse is a lens through which we perceive the world. But discourse is not a lens that gets between us and the world. Concepts *sort* our world.

Discourse doesn't get between us and the world any more than the sorter in a silverware drawer gets between us and our forks and spoons. One could, of course, use a different sorter; perhaps we're holding a garage sale and we want one that separates out silver from stainless steel utensils. Using different categories we get a different drawer—a different world—but that doesn't mean that the categories prevent us access to the forks or the spoons, the stainless steel or the silver.

Imagine you are watching a picture on your computer screen, thousands of tiny dots called pixels compose the picture—can you spot them? If you successfully spot them, you've had to use concepts (for example, you see a "tree," or a "sunset")—you couldn't identify them without concepts—but those concepts did not get between you and the pixels. Those pixels are, for us, discursive all the way down.

3.   "And You Shall Call His Name Jesus"[6]

Monica R. Miller

What's in a name?[7] Well apparently a whole lot according to one judge in Eastern, Tennessee (Child Support Magistrate Lu Ann Ballew)[8] who ruled (while the parents were in court for not being able to agree on the child's last name) that the first name of a 7-month-old baby be changed from "Messiah" to "Martin," arguing that only *one* person is

6   Ed. Note: Posted on 20 August 2013, https://edge.ua.edu/monica-miller/and-you-shall-call-his-name-jesus/ (accessed 20 December 2017).

7   https://edge.ua.edu/russell-mccutcheon/whats-in-a-name/ (accessed 20 December 2017).

8   https://www.theguardian.com/world/2013/aug/12/tennessee-judge-messiah-martin (accessed 20 December 2017).

deserving of the name Messiah, and "that one person is Jesus Christ." The mother of the child, Jaleesa Martin, is appealing the decision.

Although "Messiah" topped the charts as one of the "fastest rising baby names in 2012," Ballew argued, "It [Messiah] could put him at odds with a lot of people and at this point he has had no choice in what his name is." She added that the name Messiah puts the child in geographical danger because Cocke County, where the child lives, is largely "Christian."

What's interesting about Ballew's argument is that in conjunction with reading her own religious anxieties and moral panic into the naming of this baby, she (using the signifier "choice") takes a rather curious approach to "naming" when she states that the child's identity vis-à-vis naming should not be interpellated before the child can choose for themself what it is that they want to be named (for theorists have long pointed out the quagmires associated with the tension between interpellation and "choice" and "non-choice"). She seemingly holds in tension a rather confessional, hegemonic and conservative view of naming; then strategically makes a postmodern move in her argument to secure her own projected anxieties onto the subjectivity of the child (thus, appearing to take the side of an innocent child, who can't yet freely "choose" in the world).

Theorists of identity might suggest that Ballew already misses the mark when she assumes that the interpellation of the child's identity hadn't already begun (before the "naming" of the child) with the pronouncement of the sex of the child at birth, and even before. On this point, Judith Butler writes: "Consider the medical interpellation which shifts an infant from an 'it' to a 'she' or a 'he,' and in that naming, the girl is 'girled,' brought into the domain of language and kinship through the interpellation of gender."[9]

On the grounds of "religious freedom,"[10] many are suggesting that the judge's Christianist impositions from the bench are skewed and incorrect—arguing that she is wrong in her position that there is only

9   Judith Butler, *Bodies That Matter: On the Discursive Limits of "Sex"* (New York: Routledge, 1993), 7.

10   http://www.latimes.com/local/lanow/la-me-ln-judge-messiah-name-change-20130813-story.html (accessed 20 December 2017).

"one" Messiah, and that there have been "many" Messiahs over the last 2,000 years.

This story nicely illustrates the manner in which meaning and human interests is/are often read into empty signs and signifiers of identity, like naming, while the details and events of this case point towards the sorts of "operational acts of identification" that Jean François-Bayart so poignantly demonstrates in his work.

Citing "Jesus" and obscuring her concerns over the "Christian" narrative somewhat under an empty concern over "choice" on behalf of the child (which she in part uses as her defense), Ballew assumes she gives choice/agency/identity back to the child by taking away the parents' right to choose a name for their child and then giving the child a new name (Martin) that has not been "freely" chosen either by the parents *or* by the child.

At stake here is not "identity" per se, but rather, a protectionist preservation of a particular narrative, made religious, of a particular social actor in a very particular historical moment, whose identity has been made unique, stable, transhistorical, unchanging, and universalized—of course in a very local sort of way.

On "Imagining Identity"[11] and the "invisible threads" that create stories and folktales of identity narratives, Craig Martin said it best when he suggested, "It is this myth we use to draw lines—or invisible threads—from the past to the present: this invisible thread that we call the 'Christian tradition' connects persons in the 1st century with persons in the 21st century."

4.   Making Distinctions[12]

Craig Martin

When I was in graduate school, one of my philosophy professors, when lecturing on Kant, said something like the following: "In

---

11   https://edge.ua.edu/craig-martin/imagining-identity/ (accessed December 20, 2017); also see the Introduction to this volume, p. 2.

12   Ed. Note: Posted on 20 January 2014, https://edge.ua.edu/craig-martin/making-distinctions/ (accessed 20 December 2017).

making this argument, Kant is sort of in a tight spot here—between a rock and a hard place. What does Kant do when backed into a corner? Like all philosophers, he *makes a distinction.*"

I don't remember what case the professor was talking about, but one can imagine: "Yes, that's true of hypothetical imperatives, but not categorical ones." Or, "Yes, this claim is contradictory, but only when we're talking about phenomena, not noumena."

Much of what we're doing here at Culture on the Edge is not theoretically earth-shattering. We're just tracking the distinctions people make—for instance, between religion and politics, between religion and spirituality, between pilgrimage and tourism—and the social work accomplished by such distinctions.

As I discuss in my book, *Capitalizing Religion* (Bloomsbury, 2014), a number of scholars distinguish between institutional religion and individual religion or spirituality; a number of them use the terms normatively, giving the latter a positive valuation. Interestingly, they are using practically the same distinction that Ronald Reagan employed to distinguish between communism and democracy. For Reagan, communism is affiliated with totalitarianism, repression, orthodoxy, tyranny, controlling political forces, the subordination of the rights of individuals to the collective, and it stifles human freedom and muzzles self-expression—reasons for which communism is declining—while democracy is affiliated with diversity, tolerance, freedom, choice, self-determination, human rights, and is "responsive to the needs of their people"—reasons for which democracy is growing. Democracy must be helped along, of course, and Reagan recommended that we cultivate as widely as possible the ideology of individual choice. For Reagan, cultivating such an ideology "is not cultural imperialism; it is providing the means for genuine self-determination and protection for diversity" (see Reagan's "Evil Empire" speech,[13] given to the British House of Commons in 1982). Similarly, Wade Clark Roof, Paul Heelas, and Linda Woodhead—all leading sociologists of religion—affiliate organized religion with obedience, deference to authority, collective

---

13 https://www.youtube.com/watch?v=uCu7-Ka_zbY (accessed 20 December 2017).

conformity, and iron cages, while by contrast they affiliate individual religion or spirituality with openness, freedom, options, individual choice, self-determination, autonomy, independence, and individual rights—reasons for which spirituality is a growing force. The fact that these scholars unwittingly and unreflexively mirror Reagan's normative vocabulary is revealing; these normative distinctions accomplish social work.

We all use distinctions. Which ones are central to your work, and what do they accomplish?

5.   Making Magic Work[14]

Monica R. Miller

An old[15] story has been making its rounds and sparking discussion online over the past few weeks and it was too good for me to pass up on giving it a little Culture on the Edge consideration.

> *I, for one, would like to see the so-called evidence this school has that a 15-year-old girl made a grown man sick by casting a magic spell.*
> —Joann Bell, Executive Director, ACLU, Oklahoma Chapter

The story went a little something like this: 15-year-old student, Brandi Blackbear, of Union Intermediate High School, was accused of "casting a magic spell" that left her teacher sick and hospitalized. She was suspended. A civil rights lawsuit was filed with the U.S. District Court in Tulsa, Oklahoma on behalf of the student, which indicated that the student was banned from donning and drawing Wiccan signs and symbols in school.

---

14   Ed. Note: Posted on 27 January 2014, https://edge.ua.edu/monica-miller/making-magic-work/ (accessed 20 December 2017).

15   https://www.aclu.org/news/aclu-oklahoma-files-federal-lawsuit-behalf-student-accused-hexing-teacher?redirect=religion-belief/aclu-oklahoma-files-federal-lawsuit-behalf-student-accused-hexing-teacher (accessed 20 December 2017).

It's hard to believe that the school took such a peculiar accusation
—which was likely to be laughable to most people reading the
story—so seriously. I began to wonder if this story was *real* or simply
satire gone viral. According to the story—the following "evidence"
was used to justify the suspension:

1. A seized notebook where Blackbear wrote and recorded horror
   stories
2. Knowledge that the student had read a library book about
   Wiccan beliefs (which led the assistant principal to suggest that
   Blackbear practices witchcraft)
3. The source of the teacher's illness was "unknown"
4. All of the above = concluding that the student was an immediate
   "threat" to the school" and "disrupted" the educational process.

The moves employed to mark this student as deviant (i.e., "suspi-
cious" behavior) and single-handedly responsible (i.e., casting a spell)
for her teacher's illness rely upon the manipulation and arrangement
of arbitrary data in attempting to produce a persuasive, plausible and
coherent effect.

Think for a moment about the abundance of analogous yet "less
obvious" examples in academic discourse (that often go unquestioned) where appeals to the mechanisms of similar domains—i.e.,
meaning/motivations—are epistemically treated like spells awaiting
magical enactment to be used as "evidence" for a wide variety of
claims and assertions. The authority granted to the spell-casting student by the teacher and assistant principle reminds us that: (1) the
"spell" said to be cast by the student was never self-evidently "there"
as a thing; rather, it was manufactured with the hopes of producing a
certain sort of *effect* based on a collection of disparate and arbitrary
data arranged in a certain sort of way by the classifier, and (2) more
often than not, hermeneutical attempts to *uncover* meaning (i.e., the
cause of the teacher's "unknown illness") don't so much as reveal a
"thing" (i.e., a successful *spell*). Instead, such efforts underscore the
social interests and techniques at work in making something like a
"spell" (or meaning) "work."

For, much like the strategies that enable identity-making, there
was no magic spell-casting hat that pre-existed the teacher's illness.

Rather, the teacher and the assistant principal in and through the very acts of marking, naming, and labeling constituted the spell—the illusion, as such.

We know all too well that magic and the "tricks" or "spells" that make the idea of magic possible are in fact *techniques*—rehearsed sleight-of-hand—and effects of the techniques executed properly and precisely. If anything, in the end, the school constructed and validated the spell that never was—getting *others* to believe in *their* magic.

6.   Which Past Do You Authorize?[16]

Vaia Touna

I'm testing a theory: if tomorrow's present is yesterday's future-not-imagined, then every present justifies its presence by clinging onto a past not considered previously, by which it will then imagine a different future, and so on. The problem that arises, then, is that since there are many presents—that is, competing interests in the present about possible futures—then there are, as well, many available pasts, to choose from. I think that this, somehow, explains why we anchor to the past, because it's the only thing we think we know, even though it is as obscure as the future. But since we "were" yesterday it stands to reason that yesterday was; and no doubt yesterday was, but what form, shape, and meaning we will give to yesterday is contingent upon our current interests and needs, and the possibilities are innumerable. Yes, you are right to think that just like anything else the past is in the eye of the beholder, though it is fairly complicated and one complication is: Who is behind the eye of the beholder?

Take for example a fresco that has been revealed in Italy. Before reading the story[17] which is entitled "Vatican unveils restored catacomb with frescoes showing 'female priests,'" just looking at the

16   Ed. Note: Posted on 3 February 2014, https://edge.ua.edu/vaia-touna/which-past-do-you-authorize/ (accessed 20 December 2017).

17   https://www.theguardian.com/world/2013/nov/20/vatican-unveils-frescoes-restored-female-priests-catacomb (accessed 20 December 2017).

picture I saw a group of people one of whom was at the center standing with hands raised as if in appeal to the divine. Of course I already knew from the headline that that was a fresco in a catacomb, therefore I was reading the fresco already in a preset setting. As my experience in religious matters derives from Greece and since there are no female priests there, and any kind of discussion around this matter is out of the question, I was also pre-set not to see a woman-as-priest and I therefore proceeded to read the article with curiosity (all this makes evident, from the start, how my present location as reader is playing a significant role).

The article offered two explanations of what the fresco depicts: One comes from the Association of Roman Catholic Women Priests which argues as you can very well imagine that the scenes show women priests. The other comes from the Vatican, according to which the woman in the fresco is "just a woman praying," though of course theirs is a reading of the past as well despite what Fabrizio Bisconti, the superintendent of the Vatican's sacred archaeology commission, said concerning others' alternative readings of the past: "These are readings of the past that are a bit sensationalistic but aren't trustworthy!" Now, neither of these readings is necessarily wrong or right, for that matter, and neither of them is necessarily about what the fresco really depicts. If I take seriously the opening of my syllogism "there are as many pasts as there are presents" then the two explanations are two out of many possible readings, prompted by two out of many competing interests in the present, creating two out of many equally possible pasts because of different agendas in the present.

Suffice it to say of course that which past is chosen, which is read as persuasive, legitimate, or just right, affects not only the identity of specific groups, but also what kind of identity will be authorized in the present and whether and what kind of future that identity can imagine and work toward. Therefore what such readings "really" depict is no longer of much interest, at least to me, but instead what is of interest is: How is it that one of the two readings prevails, and how that reading affects me the reader/observer who, even though I don't have anything at stake, is still part of the process of authentication and identification? After all I didn't see a woman either (but to the careful reader I hinted why I didn't "see" a woman priest!).

The answer to the above question, which I can barely touch upon in this post, lies I think in who has the power and means to authorize one reading, and thus one past, over the other. Though the article, which is itself a form of power/authority, doesn't really take a position and it seems that it leaves the reader to decide which of the two explanations is the "right" one, the fact that we, curiously enough, only learn the justification of one side, one authority (that of the Vatican), tells us much about which reading the news source sees as legitimate!

So, the question then about what happened in the past is better rephrased as: Which yesterday do you choose and authorize today?

7.   Just Really Old … Or Historical?[18]

K. Merinda Simmons

BBC news ran a feature this morning entitled "Temple of Mithras: How do you put London's Roman shrine back together?"[19] about a 60-year-old excavation of a Roman temple, the remains of which were found when an insurance firm was being built on the site where the 3rd-century shrine once stood. In the span of a couple of weeks, back in 1954, a whopping 400,000 people lined up to see the ruins before they were moved and placed on display.

But now that Bloomberg is building on that same site, the Temple of Mithras is going to be reconstructed there beneath the office block, and the questions of originality and authenticity speed to the fore. Namely, to the point of the BBC feature, "how do you put a Roman temple back together again?" Like the restrictions placed on renovations of homes deemed "historic," there are attempts at "getting it right" here, too (There's a telling post on the blog for "Old House" entitled "How to Find Out if Your Home is Just Really Old

18   Ed. Note: Posted on 24 September 2014, https://edge.ua.edu/k-merinda-simmons/just-really-oldor-historical/ (accessed 20 December 2017).

19   http://www.bbc.com/news/blogs-magazine-monitor-29309824 (accessed 20 December 2017).

or Historical").[20] The team reconstructing the site are working from the 1954 excavation records, along with "calling on people who saw the 1954 dig to help out and send colour photos, cinefilm or oral memories." Hardly exact science. But then again, how could it be? In another article about the move,[21] current site director Sophie Jackson is quoted as saying, "The only bit of the entire building that we can be absolutely certain is both original and in the right place is the doorstep." And besides, "ground level in Roman London is seven metres below today's city." So, *everything* in the present city is built on top of something else.

The question for wannabe-homeowners with a taste for all things vintage applies here, too: Namely, just how do people find out if a relic or site is "just really old" or "historical"? Those classifications, it would seem, once applied, garner vastly different degrees of value … and funding.

8.   Green Means Go?[22]

Russell T. McCutcheon

Debates over religion and science have long bothered me and the problems could not be any better illustrated than this 5 February 2015 tweet by the scientist and science popularizer Neil deGrasse Tyson:

> Had to wait in line to renew a Passport allowing me to visit members of my own species across artificially conceived borders.

For here we have a perfect example of the naïve realism that often animates the science side of these debates no less than the positions they critique.

20   http://www.oldhouseweb.com/blog/find-old-house-history/ (accessed 20 December 2017).

21   https://www.theguardian.com/uk/2012/jan/19/roman-temple-mithras (accessed 20 December 2017).

22   Ed. Note: Posted on 9 February 2015, https://edge.ua.edu/russell-mccutcheon/green-means-go/ (accessed 20 December 2017).

First off, I'm not clear on why artificial (code word for cultural, maybe even historical, presumably) gets such a bad rap; for as a friend on Facebook commented when I posted it there:

> Wonder why Tyson qualifies these particular borders as "artificial" as if most borders are not? Is "artificial" any less of an "authentic" border, any less (or more) deserving of observation, than some imagined non-artificial border?

After all, what we call red surely doesn't "really" mean stop—whatever that even signifies—but there can be some pretty profound implications of failing to observe our red/green convention when you're driving through town, no? From arrest and jail time to car crashes and fatalities, flouting the so-called artificially conceived rule system—i.e., it has a history, people invented it, it changes over time, and thus isn't carved into reality—has consequences, making it pretty real in my books.

Ten minutes later, Tyson followed up with the following:

> I wonder what Passports & Immigration & Border Patrols look like to real aliens—the kind from space. Might they ask, "WTF?"

What bothers me is the way that yet another classification system is implicitly authorized, without any persuasive argumentation whatsoever, by his dismissal of another—an authority move unbecoming of the rigorously rational, evidence-based discourse that we're continually told science is. For in the first Tweet we not only trivialize nationalism but we authorize a biological taxonomy that was no less invented by people, has a history of its own (dating from the 18th century)[23] and a variety of reasons for its continued use today, while in the second we for some reason portray hypothetical off-planet residents as the proper referents for an ancient Latin term[24] that only in

---

23 https://en.wikipedia.org/wiki/Linnaean_taxonomy (accessed 20 December 2017).

24 https://www.etymonline.com/word/alien (accessed 20 December 2017).

the last 100 years or so has taken on an interstellar connotation (for it's a term that, as a noun, once just meant stranger or foreigner, as in "People with a Green Card are resident aliens in the U.S.").

At least the last time I checked it wasn't self-evident that all life ought to be divided into kingdoms, phyla, and so on, and so on, all the way down to the species he talks about, and why the distinction between terrestrial and extraterrestrial is somehow more authoritative than any other same/strange distinction we commonly use to identify ourselves as distinguished from others utterly escapes me. That is, his preferred classification systems are no less, what?, artificial and self-interested than any other, regardless how useful they may strike many of us as being.

So just because 11,255 people retweeted it doesn't make it an uncontested fact.

Come to think of it, the supposedly really real thing that is science utterly depends on funding from the supposedly fake things like nation-states, along with their presumably arbitrary tax systems and their utterly unpredictable federal funding priorities. So the fake apparently makes the real possible.

And so although I go to the doctor when I'm ill, do indeed presume that a force called gravity accounts for the movement of masses relative to each other, and am glad I was vaccinated by my parents as a kid, it's Tweets like these that help me to imagine the frustration of yet others when they come across scientists who presume an unquestioned authority to their own naïvely realistic positions but who are utterly ungenerous when talking about the positions of others. Perhaps we're giving away the farm if we acknowledge that gravity is a theory, a bold prediction about the future behavior of objects based on a large volume of past observations under uniform conditions, or if we recognize that only if you grant the authority of our biological taxonomy is there a need to develop a theory of how something changes from one of its (correction, our) categories to another (i.e., the theory of evolution to account for changes in species)—after all, as Mary Douglas[25] taught us so long ago, without our imposed

---

25   Mary Douglas, *Purity and Danger: An Analysis of Concepts of Pollution and Taboo* (London and New York: Routledge, 1966).

taxonomies nothing is any more related to anything else and nothing can be classed as either an anomaly or ideal type (i.e., things become anomalies only inasmuch as our system fails to contain them). But it seems to me that doing anything other than making such admissions indicates that we're doing something other than the science we claim to be doing, something more akin to the ahistorical, normative moves made by that position from which scientists fight so hard to be distinguished.

9. Maps, Interpretations, and "The Territory"[26]

Vaia Touna

Over a year ago I wrote a post (see Appendix #6, p. 188 above), which has haunted me ever since I wrote it; starting with the idea that "every present justifies its presence by clinging onto a past not considered previously," I looked at two different readings of a fresco in the catacombs of Priscilla, in Rome, and concluded that these two readings of the past each authorize different interests in the present.

A few weeks ago I was recommended by a good friend to read Keith Jenkins's book *Why History?* (Routledge, 1999) in which he writes (and which finds me in agreement):

> Of course, the past per se is not imagined in the sense that "it" didn't actually occur. It did occur, and in exactly the way it did. But it is an imaginary with respect to the historical meanings and understandings, the significances and purposes it has been deemed to have for us, both as a whole and in its parts. For no matter how much we may have "imagined" that such meanings and significances—both general and particular—have been found by us in the past, in fact the current generation of interpreters, like previous ones, constitutes the only semantic authorities there are: it is we who do the dictating in history. Put simply, we are the source of whatever the past means for us. (14)

26   Ed. Note: Posted on 6 March 2015, https://edge.ua.edu/vaia-touna/maps-interpretations-and-the-territory/ (accessed 20 December 2017).

"The past" then, as I understand it, is subject to constant interpretations and often competing ones depending on situated readers and their interests, both consciously and unconsciously, in the sense that we understand the past through categories and concepts we have not necessarily invented but we nevertheless use—in other words: through language itself, which is always historically specific and which we can't escape.

Even though I do not wish to "give away the past," as Willi Braun wrote in his comment to my blog, "to those who cavalierly represent it as an authorizing precedent for whatever interest gets them excitedly out of bed in the morning," which as he says "is, ironically, a means of enabling precisely the ideological representations of the past that [I seem] implicitly to lament,"[27] I'm in agreement with J.Z Smith's famous line: "Map is not territory but map is all we possess." So I'd argue that interpretations are all we possess. In other words, even though interpretations of the past may not be "the actual past," they are all we possess and through the uses of our own anachronisms and classifications, we fabricate the past—we make use of the past as we understand it now.

We do care about the past, or what we perceive is the actual past, because it is through talking about the past that we can authenticate ourselves in the present and we therefore invest time and energy in its understanding, interpretation, and preservation. In that sense, I can't think that there will ever be a time when we will lose interest in the stuff of the past since out of that we make objects to fit our own discourses and therefore interests. And that is because it is through our contemporary interpretations of past material, whether texts or material artifacts, that we learn and make sense not only of the world we now inhabit but ourselves as well.

In other words, interpretations, like mapping of the territory, are acts of identification. So acts of interpretation are all we possess; actually, understood in this way, interpretations make the past—even more so when the past is so far away from us that there is no one

---

27 See comments section on https://edge.ua.edu/vaia-touna/which-past-do-you-authorize/ (accessed 20 December 20 2017).

present, and in authority, to contest our interpretations (though different interests, and thus different readings, in the present will no doubt do in their absence).

So, I suppose now the question is what we, as scholars, wish to study: "the actual past" (which often comes with phrases like studying history "on its own terms," and getting "back to the sources," etc.), thereby in this case trying to figure out which of those two readings of the catacombs fresco is correct, or those always modern acts of identification (i.e., interpretations, representations, anachronisms, discourses, and the like) and the politics behind those acts that constitute "the past" in the first place?

10. Look How Tall You Are![28]

Russell McCutcheon

The ease with which identity is presumed to be an inner trait projected outward is pretty easy to document, which makes critiquing it something less than a challenge. For example, I thought about writing a post on the animated film *Inside Out* (2015) and the popular folk understanding of identity (so nicely illustrated throughout the movie) as being an internal quality only subsequently expressed outwardly, such that the social interaction is the effect of a prior and private sentiment.

But that just seemed too easy. And, besides, the film seems kinda fun.

Despite this being the commonsense model we all probably have of ourselves, this blog has consistently tried to press an alternative model, one that argues for the self as being a social product through and through. It's counter-intuitive, sure, but there are plenty of mundane sites where you can experiment with reconceptualizing identity in this alternative way.

---

28 Ed. Note: Posted on 24 June 2015, https://edge.ua.edu/russell-mccutcheon/look-how-tall-you-are/ (accessed 20 December 2017).

Case in point: I bet lots of us had our heights measured and marked, from time to time, against a wall or doorpost as we were growing up. I certainly remember my parents doing this. What's useful about this example is how nicely we see the way a subject's identity is formed by the application, by others, of a grid or classification (or, we could also say, value) system (in my case, it was a yardstick—the metric system hadn't yet hit Canada's shores).

It's an instance of what Louis Althusser termed interpellation, no?

> In Marxist theory, interpellation is the process by which ideology, embodied in major social and political institutions, constitutes the nature of individual subjects' identities through the very process of institutions and discourses of "hailing" them in social interactions.[29]

For the child probably is not naturally rushing to measure his or her height; they most likely don't even know that they're growing and changing—it's so gradual, who can see it happening to themselves? But mom and dad know changes are coming, and they're the ones who are keen to know if their child is ahead or behind the curve (How early did they talk? When did they take their first steps? What grade did they get in math?). So the application, by others, of a grid not of our choosing (does the young child even know what an inch is, much less a decimeter?), results in a little pencil line, and a date written on the doorframe (not insignificantly in someone else's handwriting, by the way), against which we quite literally learn to measure ourselves at some future point in time. And sooner or later we find enough marks there that we can start telling a developmental narrative about ourselves, about then versus now, which anticipates a future that's not yet even happened.

29 https://en.wikipedia.org/wiki/Interpellation_%28philosophy%29 (accessed 20 December 2017).

11. The Harm of World Religions[30]

Steven W. Ramey

While discussions of "World Religions" often attempt to encourage appreciation of human diversity, these presentations have become the focus of scholarly critiques because of the harm that they cause. Such presentations appear to provide a clear way of describing the world (as illustrated in the map above),[31] but the assumptions behind them often serve to promote European dominance that people present as simple descriptions. A recent animated presentation[32] on *Business Insider* illustrating the spread of five major world religions becomes the object of a range of critiques.

The conclusion of the animation makes almost all of the world one of these five religions. When compared to some of the cited sources, similar to the map at the head of this post, areas that others list as "indigenous religions" become either one of the five major religions (as in all of Canada is Christian) or left blank (as in Siberia) within this animation. The selection of five religions reflects other assumptions, as Sikhism (according to cited sources) has more adherents than Judaism but is excluded, not to mention Shinto/Japanese religions, Chinese religions, and the aforementioned indigenous religions.

30   Ed. Note: Posted on 13 July 2015, https://edge.ua.edu/steven-ramey/the-harm-of-world-religions/ (accessed 20 December 2017). This has been among the most popular posts on the Culture on the Edge site with a total of 4,941 views by 14 January 2018.

31   This map, not reproduced here, divides the world's land masses into nine colors for the various religions according to their geographic distribution, using the following categories: Christianity, Islam, Hinduism, Buddhism, Judaism, Chinese religions, Korean religions, Shinto, Folk religions, and no religion. Available at https://commons.wikimedia.org/wiki/File:Major_religions_distribution.png (accessed 23 December 2017).

32   This animated map shows how religions spread around the world, as each religion spreads from a point of origin to cover increasingly more territory as time moves towards the present. It can also be found on YouTube: https://www.youtube.com/watch?v=AvFl6UBZLv4 (accessed 20 December 2017).

Jonathan Z. Smith in his "Religion, Religions, Religious"[33] essay had a useful insight on the selection of which religions to include:

> It is impossible to escape the conclusion that a world religion is simply a religion like ours, and that it is, above all, a tradition that has achieved sufficient power and numbers to enter our history to form it, interact with it, or thwart it. (191–2)

In other words, what counts as a world religion is more about the people making the list (their interests and perspectives) than a straightforward description of a separate reality.

I want to push these critiques further. What commonality is our basis for recognizing groups as part of a specific world religion/community? Is it self-identification, belief, practice, text, birth, or some combination of these? While the animation starts with Hinduism in the Indus Valley 4,500 years ago, what do the people of that valley have in common with people who identify as Hindu today? What about the Israelites and contemporary Judaism or the crucifixion of Jesus and Christianity?

The narrative that the animation follows applies the assumptions, interests, and labels of today back in time to construct the origins of each religion. Following a common understanding of the time of Jesus, at the time of his crucifixion his followers did not have the New Testament or even the Gospels, did not have the sacraments or creeds of today, and did not identify as Christian. Similarly, Abraham and David neither identified as Jews nor followed the same beliefs, practices, texts, etc., as Jews today. Those who composed Vedic hymns in the Indus region, commonly seen as the originators of Hinduism, similarly did identify as Hindu, did not have the same conception of the world, the same texts or practices of today. While we can trace connections from where we sit back to these points of origin, labeling these figures/events as points of origin for each religion has very little to do with the people and events at the point of origin. Rather, they

---

33   Jonathan Z. Smith, "Religion, Religions, Religious," in *Relating Religion: Essays in the Study of Religion* (Chicago and London: The University of Chicago Press, 2004), 179–96.

have everything to do with giving a legitimating history of communities today.

Such descriptions of world religions and their origins have serious implications. Besides marginalizing those communities who do not make it into the presentation, the simplified origins narratives reinforce those (often those already in power) who use the narrative of a singular origin to legitimize their own sense of acceptable practice and necessary reform while further marginalizing those who see the development of society and practices as more fluid and complex and resist the more narrow reforms based on a constructed origin. Such constructions, therefore, often have shaped communities (rather than describing them) and furthered physical and ideological conflicts that utilize these narratives and labels to mobilize support.

We cannot fully blame the creator of this animation. He did his homework, at least on one level, and cited a variety of academic sources. Scholars need to incorporate the best in academic research, including the complicated theoretical reflections, into public representations and introductory courses. Too many World Religion courses and textbooks simply retell this type of simple narrative as truth, despite knowing the problems with the narrative. Such presentations encourage its repetition and continue to influence the complicated negotiations and contestations that exist in our world.

12. Standing in Line at Chipotle (or, The Hefty Politics of Naming)[34]

Leslie Dorrough Smith

Several years ago, at Chipotle, I realized that one of the workers behind the counter was a student of mine, one to whom I'd spoken the week before about his poor performance and a particularly compulsive (and, for me, wildly distracting) propensity to text during class.

34   Ed. Note: Posted on 6 September 2016, https://edge.ua.edu/lesliedorrough-smith/standing-in-line-at-chipotle-or-the-hefty-politics-of-naming/ (accessed 20 December 2017).

As we were suspended in an awkward moment where he was asking me what kind of salsa I wanted, another question came out of his mouth as well: Did he still have to call me "Dr Smith" when he was at work?

My answer, as I remember it, was stumbling and incoherent, comprised of "uh" and the general surprise of not knowing what to say. On the one hand I didn't really care what he called me, for plenty of my students call me by my first name. On the other hand, though, Dr Smith was not mentally in the building, so to speak; I was not expecting anyone to call me by my professional title, so I was caught off guard when it came up in a weekend conversation about tacos and corn salsa. But before I could think much more about the significance of what he had asked and how I had responded, the chatter devolved into guacamole and credit cards, and the exchange was over just as fast as it happened.

I've hung on to that memory in great part because it pinpoints how seemingly tentative are the politics of authority at the same time that they endure far beyond our momentary awareness of them. In his well-known book on the subject, Bruce Lincoln points out that authority is more the *perception* of being in charge rather than actually holding that particular control, for if one is asked to prove one's authority, then it has already begun to erode.[35] In other words, the fact that a different scenario has entered the minds of those doing the asking indicates that they have begun to scrutinize the power status quo.

This was, after all, what was going on in that brief exchange. While I thought it somewhat impertinent to point out that his job didn't require knowing his customers' names, my name was not at issue as much as the disappearance of the political context that marked our previous relationship, one where I was not only "in charge," but had also asserted some of that authority in a way that had recently highlighted his shortcomings. His questioning of my name thus introduced the possibility that our politics might be reversed or at least neutralized in a setting that was more "his turf" than mine, and I suppose in so doing, potentially delegitimize the critiques he'd recently experienced.

35 Bruce Lincoln, *Authority: Construction and Corrosion* (Chicago: University of Chicago Press, 1995), 6.

And yet what stands out to me in all of this is the enduring power of interpellation, that term Althusser used to discuss the ways in which we almost subconsciously submit to the classificatory schema that society imposes upon us. In his famous example of a policeman yelling "Hey, you!" Althusser demonstrates that the moment we give ourselves over to the possibility that we are the "you" in question and start to turn around to face (and thereby accept) the label, we demonstrate how imminently social our identities are—how very much they are the products of forces far outside of our own creation. In this case, even though I failed to give a coherent answer to the student's question in that moment, I did not fail to be a professor. In other words, I could not ignore the fact that "Dr Smith" was with "Leslie" at Chipotle that day.

ACTS OF APPROPRIATION

13. That Ain't The Queen's English[36]

Russell T. McCutcheon

One of the premises of Culture on the Edge is that an implicit, untheorized norm is still presupposed, and its legitimacy is thereby reproduced rather than being historicized, despite many scholars' recent efforts to develop what they see to be more nuanced, historically sensitive, and situationally specific approaches to identity studies. For it is not uncommon to find seemingly anti-essentialist scholars now studying various identities in terms of their hybridity, seeing them as creoles, studying how diaspora movements have traveled and changed, and documenting the complexity of syncretism—developments understood as important improvements on what are now seen to be previous generations' far too simplistic studies of social life. After all, as important an early sociologist as Emile

36 Ed. Note: Posted on 5 June 2013, https://edge.ua.edu/russell-mccutcheon/the-queens-english/ (accessed 20 December 2017).

Durkheim seems merely to have understood "society" to be a homogeneous, undifferentiated unit.

But these now preferred terms—hybridity, diaspora, creole, syncretism—are the tips of no less troublesome icebergs inasmuch as their use presupposes an unexamined origin and thus norm against which the resulting moving mix can be judged *as* a mix (i.e., because *that* is the pure standard, then *this* is blended), as having moved (i.e., moved from where? From the homeland, of course), and thus, being the result of prior, stable, original component. But sadly, those supposed sources are themselves generally not also understood as the inevitably blended results of yet even more primordial elements which, yes, are themselves the blended results of ... . Well, you get the idea, for surely someone else was there before some people became a "we" and made some place "our" homeland, no?

Freezing the continual change of that limitless archive we simplify by calling it history, and doing so for our analytic purposes, is perfectly fine, of course—in fact, it's necessary if we're going to talk about anything *as* a discrete thing that can be talked about. "For my purposes, I shall consider American culture to be ..." is a perfectly respectable scholarly move, to stipulate one's starting point for one's own intellectual purposes, since we can't talk about everything all at once, can we? But when I read scholars writing about, say, early Christianity being a syncretistic movement (all in an effort, of course, to complicate antihistorical narratives[37] of how it supposedly was an utterly unique phenomenon that just sprang onto the stage of human history of its own accord) it seems taken for granted that the things considered to be its prior components, from which it borrowed—say, Judaism and Greco-Roman culture—were themselves already and always firmly in place, much like two distinct billiard balls colliding and producing a sound. Thus the effort to destabilize the origins tale we tell about one social formation (i.e., early Christianity) is premised on stabilizing two others.

But do a little digging and it won't be difficult to see that the billiard balls themselves were hardly solid objects, for they were not

---

37 http://www.renewamerica.com/columns/mwest/110318 (accessed 20 December 2017).

just internally diverse (the tricky compound "Greco-Roman" should have already told us as much) but, perhaps, this or that ancient material's delimitation *as* Jewish or *as* Greco-Roman is a modern effect, boundaries read backward in time based on what one today thinks of as rightly Jewish, as properly Greek, as legitimately Roman. While we may have no choice but to do this we *can* choose to recognize it is us who's doing it.

Case in point: generally, many of us would never refer to English as a creole, since creole languages—as everyone knows …—are those of "other" peoples, marginal peoples, those that developed from what are called pidgins: languages of necessity developed between different peoples who find themselves in need of communicating. It's with just such an understanding in mind that the editors of *The Creolization Reader* are able to know that "[t]here are about 84 recognized creole languages worldwide."[38] English, instead, is among the sources often drawn upon by others who develop their own creoles, right?[39] (This position makes sense, of course, given how the British spread their language, along with their navy and their political/economic system, worldwide.) But a simple visit to Wikipedia's page for Foreign Language Influence on English[40] makes evident that it's rather illusory to think of English as some sort of unified thing when we consider its derivation (its many current dialects make its modern diversity profoundly apparent as well—how do you pronounce "been"?).

But the very title of that Wikipedia page—Foreign Language Influence on English—makes the problem evident: only if we essentialize the language and take modern English (but which one?!) as the necessary, virtually Hegelian outcome of historical processes would we talk of how things that existed prior to it "influenced it," instead of concluding that what we today refer to as the English language

---

38   Robin Cohen and Paola Toninato (eds.), *The Crealization Reader: Studies in Mixed Identities and Cultures* (New York and London: Routledge, 2009), 5.

39   https://en.wikipedia.org/wiki/English-based_creole_languages (accessed 20 December 2017).

40   https://en.wikipedia.org/wiki/Foreign_language_influences_in_ English (accessed 20 December 2017).

(the subject of that third person pronoun "it" that was apparently busy borrowing from its neighbors) "resulted from" these earlier linguistic systems. But in phrasing it as Wikipedia does—not dissimilar to how I above too casually referred to early Christianity as if it was an already existing subject that "borrowed" from other linguistic objects of its time, as if it was already there at its own origin—in presuming that one would never refer to English itself as a creole language of practical necessity that arose, like any other, from a complex blending and mixing (some intentional and some accidental) from prior sources that were themselves the results of yet more blends (some intentional and some accidental) from even earlier sources, we nicely normalize the known and the familiar that some of us now take for granted, thereby employing it as a standard against which to judge the deviance, change, or marginality of other so-called derivative systems.

Simply put, what does qualifying a language as creole accomplish, other than normalizing those mixes that we wish to represent as if they were instead pure and timeless? For "creole language," let alone "syncretistic culture," strikes me as utterly redundant. Thus there are rather more than 84 creole languages worldwide, no?

Light years (and surely some very different politics) seem to span someone talking today about cultural hybridity and creolization, on the one hand, and, on the other, someone else preferring "the proper Queen's English"[41] to all others. But I'm not so sure they're all that different.

14. Habla Espanol?[42]

Leslie Dorrough Smith

I was at Chipotle this weekend, waiting to order my favorite fast food (crunchy chicken tacos with veggies, heavy on the corn salsa). The

---

41   https://www.urbandictionary.com/define.php?term=Queens%20 English (accessed December 20, 2017).

42   Ed. Note: Posted on 13 July 2013, https://edge.ua.edu/leslie-dorrough-smith/habla-espanol/ (accessed 20 December 2017).

white man behind me in line spoke fluent English to a child with him, but when it was his turn at the counter, he looked at the young female employee and began ordering in Spanish. The glitch in the plan was that, while he was talking to a woman with brown skin (who, according to popular identifiers, might have a better chance of being a Spanish-speaker than others), she was not a Spanish speaker at all; in fact, as she pointed out to him, she was Asian. After a few embarrassing laughs the burrito bowls and extra guac were ordered, and everyone scooted out the door.

What I witnessed there in the checkout line was another stunning example of the fluidity of identity's construction, or more fundamentally, the forces that create the differences that we call "identity." Like most of the examples that we discuss at the Culture on the Edge site, there are many levels on which this particular example might be analyzed; in this case, for instance, we could talk about the power of white privilege to homogenize "others," or the commercialization (and preceding construction) of certain ethnic personas.

But I suppose what really caught my attention here was how the man likely entered the restaurant expecting to speak Spanish because he already had a preconceived notion of Chipotle as a place with Spanish-speakers. Because he anticipated a certain sort of difference —and thus identity—he found it. This, of course, doesn't mean that an Asian woman wouldn't necessarily speak Spanish, but I think it's fair to say that because he saw at least some of what he expected (brown skin on a Chipotle employee), his perceptions of difference were provided enough data to align with his expectations, even when those perceptions were inaccurate.

Rather than being a rare event, it seems to me that this is the way that so many of the distinctions that we craft into identifiers work. It's incredibly easy to label something in a particular way when we are lacking the context to see it as anything else. I hang my head in a bit of embarrassment when I report that I have, on more than one occasion, mined my local thrift store for treasure, only to figure out that what I'm hauling up to the register is stuff that I donated to that same store just a couple of weeks before. Why do I not see my own cast-offs as the junk they once were? The answer is that, in this new context, I've mentally remarketed the thrift store as the place where exciting, affordable goodies are found, so that those ill-fitting pants don't strike me as "things I've already owned and didn't like enough to keep" but become transformed into "fun, cheap stuff!" In this sense, it's interesting to consider how our anticipation of a certain identity is perhaps more fundamental to the labeling process than concern over the "accuracy" of the identity we're crafting.

15. Frames of Identity[43]

Vaia Touna

I find myself back in Greece to do research and so, a few days ago, I had the chance to visit the Benaki Museum in Athens. What struck me as interesting—apart from the narratives that surround all such museum exhibits, that place them in a certain time and frame them in a way that justifies a nation's origins—was that some artifacts were marked with numbers that corresponded to explanations beside their display case that made no sense. For example, I could see a horse but the explanation talked about a vase that also had the same display number. It took me a while to realize that in the various display cases some of the artifacts were placed in orange frames. Once I realized this I immediately searched for an explanation at the information desk. The lady enthusiastically informed me that these were objects from the gift store of the museum that, celebrating 30 years of its opening, were now included in the displays.

My first reaction was that this was absolutely unacceptable. But then I started wondering what prompted this reaction—obviously my sense of fake versus real, authentic versus inauthentic, and original versus replica.

Of course the museum had successfully made sure that those distinctions would be evident to the spectators by the use of those orange markers—thereby highlighting the difference. But at the same time, by integrating the "replicas" with the "originals" the museum

43 Ed. Note: Posted 20 July 2013, https://edge.ua.edu/vaia-touna/ frames-of-identity/ (accessed 20 December 2017).

effectively reinforced the "nation's" enduring identity across time by signaling that what was produced a few years ago was also worth being displayed among items made thousands of years ago, thereby effectively linking modern Greece with its ancient heritage. What was different in one way was the same in another.

But, come to think of it, those apparently authentic, ancient items from 2,000 years ago were "touched," restored, and put back together again (we've all seen what most archeological remains look like when first discovered, no?) by modern Greeks as well, suggesting that, in a way, everything in that display case could be placed within an orange boundary. All of which raises questions for me not only about the way time moves—that is, as a linear line from past to present or, quoting a famous line (for those familiar with the *Dr Who* series), as a path that instead is "wibbly wobbly, timey wimey"[44]—but also about choices and systems of classification.

16. In Other Words ...[45]

K. Merinda Simmons

A little while back, Russell McCutcheon prompted our Culture on the Edge colleague Monica Miller and me to think about the notion of code-switching. People use the phrase to refer to everyday modes of discourse that come to be seen or understood as exceptional— specifically the phenomenon of talking or acting in particular ways depending on the group or context that surrounds someone. He gave us a clip from the movie *My Fair Lady*[46] as an example. The story is all about Eliza Doolittle's (successful, by the accounts of those around her) attempt to become a "lady" rather than—to quote Professor

---

44   Episode "Don't Blink" https://www.youtube.com/watch?v=q2n-NzNo_Xps (accessed 20 December 2017).

45   Ed. Note: Posted on 22 July 2013, https://edge.ua.edu/k-merinda-simmons/in-other-words/ (accessed 20 December 2017).

46   https://www.youtube.com/watch?v=uVmU3iANbgk (accessed 20 December 2017).

Higgins's early assessment—someone "so deliciously low." In order to trade her harsh cockney accent for that of a person in high British society, she goes through endless lessons attempting to change her speech, manner of dress, and behavior. For example, who can forget the famous "rain in Spain" breakthrough? It's practically on par cinematically with Patty Duke's spelling out w-a-t-e-r into miracle worker[47] Anne Bancroft's hand.

Eliza successfully code-switches. But why do we understand her to be the only one doing so? After all, Henry Higgins and Colonel Pickering certainly speak differently to Eliza than they do to each other, even if their accents remain steady. And come on—what about the dancing?

There was a similar question being asked in the recent post about costumes and ideology.[48] The dominant group (those with neckties) is thought to be untethered to ideology, leaving the presumption that "those in costume" *must* be anyone *other* than the men wearing neckties.

In various discourses of identity studies, scholars have talked about the privilege imbedded in what they identify as an "invisible norm." Masculinity studies emerged in part as a response to the assumption that, if we're talking about "gender," we must be talking about women (as they are *marked* by their otherness). Whiteness studies have a similar story. In *Playing in the Dark* (Harvard University Press, 1992), Toni Morrison draws our attention to whiteness as an invisible norm, describing her attempt to get us to look critically at whiteness as itself constructed by and contingent upon certain actions, certain scripts that people identifying as "white" follow: "My project is an effort to avert the critical gaze from the racial object to the racial subject; from the described and imagined to the describers and imaginers; from the serving to the served" (90).

In this move, the line between subject and object gets blurry pretty quickly. We can start looking at men wearing neckties in a new way,

---

47 https://www.youtube.com/watch?v=9yumsFUReDg (accessed 20 December 2017).

48 https://edge.ua.edu/russell-mccutcheon/seeing-the-ordinary-as-curious/ (accessed 20 December 2017).

taking notice of their own codes and social scripts instead of taking for granted their seemingly obvious or neutral role/place.

What does this have to do with code-switching? Well, the norm, or dominant set of behaviors or patterns—basically, what we're thought to be shifting *from* (or are trying to switch towards)—is thought somehow to be uncoded. That is, we don't see ourselves as performing a role or series of codes when in our "normal" or dominant context. Thus, moments of code-switching refer typically to performances within non-dominant spaces. This is where the problem comes in. If we start looking at that dominant context as its own manufactured space, though (as approaches like whiteness studies and masculinity studies have begun to do), "code-switching" only perpetuates the faulty idea that the dominant space is neutral and without a code of its own. It suggests we look at some variant outside the norm ... when the norm is all variance in the first place.

We've talked amongst our Culture on the Edge group about the word "creole"—specifically, how the term normalizes dominant linguistic and cultural codes by suggesting that only some languages or cultures are in fact "creole." We don't talk about English being a creole language after all ... but isn't it? Aren't all languages? In that sense, there is no culture not creolized, not heterogeneous or hybrid in some way.

So, to pose the question that Russell put to Monica and me, "Whose variation gets to count as variation?" A different emphasis with the same punch line might be phrased, "Whose variation *must* count as variation?" No matter what qualitative value or lack thereof might be given to the supposed code-switcher, there seems still to be a problem of how we maintain the very hegemonies that seemingly progressive scholars studying identity like to think they're disrupting.

What's more, even though the dominant seems without or beyond codification, it also provides the irreducible language/system to which other codes translate back. So, while the dominant enjoys invisible norm status, it nonetheless dictates a very specific and managed set of rules to aid in the translation or conversion of non-dominant codes. For example, when I taught writing/composition courses a few years back in an English department, I talked with my students about the rules that governed the system of Standard Written English.[49] This system was taken as a given and basically obvious format to which their writing had to conform, and students consistently acquiesced to the Modern Language Association (MLA) rules I taught them. Of course, the debates over whether or not sentences really can end in prepositions have been heated ones among grammarians. The rules are not at all thought to be stable or ends-in-themselves. Further, scholars of rhetoric and composition (not to mention politicians at times) continue to disagree over whether and how to incorporate other codes (Ebonics, Spanglish, web lingo, etc.) into the course content. Do we allow other modes of discourse to "count" in such settings? Should a student be able to write in her own dialect or linguistic system? By way of pacifying students, teachers often use the adage, "You've got to know the rules before you can break them." But that's just it—right there, we admit that there are rules (and again, very specific and hotly contested ones if we're talking rules of grammar) to the dominant system but nonetheless treat it as the obvious and neutral norm.

Depending on the brand of scholarship, code-switchers are often cast as making progressively subversive moves, strategically outmaneuvering the master narrative. I start thinking, for example, of Audre Lorde's famous saying, "The master's tools will never dismantle the master's house."[50] But actually, demonstration of proficient use of the proverbial master's tools has tended to be a prerequisite for any sort of social mobility (Frederick Douglass's pivotal reading instruction, or Toussaint L'Ouverture's literacy and use of ideological claims from French Revolution, just to name a couple of examples). So, scholars tend to see the non-dominant as crafty in the undoing or reappropriation of dominant codes, but such acts are invariably (perhaps necessarily?) cast in light of that dominant structure, thus reifying its seeming neutral and obvious privilege.

When we think that we're using "code-switching" as an innocuous or objective term used to describe certain actions, we forget that all

49 https://www.thoughtco.com/what-is-standard-english-1691016 (accessed 20 December 2017).

50 http://lists.econ.utah.edu/pipermail/margins-to-centre/2006-March/000794.html (accessed 20 December 2017).

descriptions are situated and decidedly *not* neutral. In this manner, code-switching as a category might be thought of as normative, even imperial. After all, what is interesting is not the thing itself but the describer's relation to the thing (or category, or what have you).

Or, as Eliza Doolittle suggests after having learnt the lessons and run the gauntlet, "The difference between a lady and a flower girl is not how she behaves, but how she is treated."

17. Whose Switch is a Switch?[51]

Monica R. Miller

Code-switching is often used to reference the actions (usually lin-guistic variations) of a particular person/group that is assumed to be breaking from their own "natural" practices to perform codes "not their own" for the purposes of fitting in, acquiring capital, and access-ing spaces that are thought to perceive the "native" practices of the switcher as illegitimate or illegible. This switching, or shifting as some call it, is often painted with a stroke of fluidity and described as taking knowhow, precision, performance, and rehearsal to achieve. While the durability or recapitulations of code-switching may come to be seen as natural over time—when it's no longer recognized or described as a switch—it's often thought to be something that is, and can be, (consciously) turned off and on like a light switch by the social actor.

In a previous post written by Merinda Simmons about code-switching (see Appendix #16, p. 208 above), the question of "whose variation gets to count as variation" was posed as a way to think about what practices—or things—become classified, seen, or understood as switching, and which ones are often left unnoticed and thus seem-ingly absent of code. Can discourse on code-switching perpetuate a notion that some (usually of the marginal group) switch more than others (such as those of the dominant group)? While it can certainly

---

51   Ed. Note: Posted on 23 July 2013, https://edge.ua.edu/monica-miller/whose-switch-is-a-switch/ (accessed December 20, 2017).

be argued that code-switching in and of itself arises as a push against, and critique of, what is deemed to be normative, could the logic of switching run the risk of giving normativity an appearance of naturalness, leaving it in place and without question?

Put differently, might talk of something being "hybrid" or "creole" for example normalize "dominant and linguistic cultural codes" through an assumption that some languages are mixed and others are not? Or, assuming that two or more homogenizing things meet up, intermix, and create something new, while not recognizing that the two things we set aside as "pure" are already in and of themselves mixed? In part 1 of this series (e.g., see Appendix #13, p. 201 above), we suggested that it's often the case that English is not considered a creole language ... but, after all, isn't it? Furthermore, whose English gets to count as English? Aren't all languages and cultures creole to some extent?

On a different note, we might consider how some switching practices presumably "pass" (are able to accomplish a particular goal) and others "fail" (are left unrecognized). If a switch fails, who is doing the misrecognizing? If it must be done "just right" in order to accomplish that which it sets out to do—are those seen as "unable" to switch lacking some sort of coded ability compared with the successful switcher? Where might switching end and *habitus* begin? If habitus is misrecognized for switching, does it (switching) then lose its supposed subversive edge? Perhaps, they're one in the same. That is, habitus helps us understand the ubiquity/ordinariness of code-switching because it helps us to think about even our conscious choices as being coded/structured.

NPR's blog *Code Switch*[52] suggests that, "When you're attuned to the phenomenon of code-switching, you start to see it everywhere, and you begin to see the way race, ethnicity and culture plays out all over the place"—encouraging a closer look at and consideration of an expanded understanding of how the everydayness of code-switching can help to explain the world.

---

52   https://www.npr.org/sections/codeswitch/2013/04/08/176064688/ how-code-switching-explains-the-world (accessed 20 December 2017)

Let's take for instance the cruel and unfortunate character assault that ensued as soon as 19-year-old Rachel Jeantel, the star witness for the prosecution in the trial of George Zimmerman for the murder of Trayvon Martin, opened her mouth to testify. Born and raised in Miami, Jeantel's first language is Creole (through her Haitian mother) and she also speaks Spanish and English. In most instances, someone who is trilingual is celebrated as "smart" and "exceptional"—but in this case—these qualities were not extended to Jeantel. When she began to testify in the courtroom, defense attorney Don West broke his cross-examining script by asking, "Are you claiming in any way that you don't understand English?" This was a curious question to put to someone who had been, all along, both understanding and responding to the questions asked in the English language. Unable to get over his own stereotypes of difference and linguistic purity, West pushed his question further by asking Jeantel if she had difficulty *understanding* English given that "Creole" was her first language. Of course, she replied, "No." West's violent interrogation and policing of the "sound" of Jeantel's English (enough to make it an issue) was further perpetuated through harsh public comments about her "poor English skills," competency, and education level. Pathological claims that led many to question the credibility of Jeantel's testimony. As you can imagine, and rightfully so, many commentators rushed to the defense of Jeantel, claiming that she does know and speak English— just a "distinct" sort of English as the result of combining and moving in and out of three linguistic abilities (Haitian Creole, Spanish, and English).

Although West singled Jeantel out for her linguistic "difference" based on sound, suggesting that it was different to the point of unintelligibility and misrecognition—he failed to see himself as speaking a hybrid language too, a language disciplined by the codes of power in the courtroom. Moreover, in our rush to defend Jeantel's dialect and distinctive linguistic hybridity, we too run the risk of propagating the ideas that English is not a product of variation and that there are certain ways to speak it "properly." The reality is that Jeantel—had the circumstances, context, and power arrangements been different than they were—could have easily asked West the same question—giving him back what he thought was a problem but was in reality a problem of his own making not uninfluenced by racialized difference.

One could suggest that Jeantel was already code-switching to the extent that the idiomatic rules of each language were operative while giving her testimony. But if code-switching is a script of ability/consciousness/awareness witnessed by a certain kind of affirmative *effect* and *outcome* where the switching largely goes so unnoticed as to appear natural—then how do we explain—or do justice to—"scripts" or "switches" that are illegible and become misrecognized as something else (like disrespect)? Jeantel did what she was supposed to do as a witness—the claims of illegibility rest upon the classifier and not the classified.

Might the everydayness of switching make it something not so exceptional after all? Take for instance the context of an office with a wide variety of workers from Presidents and CEOs to secretaries and interns. Might the secretary speak to the intern in the same manner in which he or she might speak to the President? Probably not if the secretary is privy to where power lies in the structure of the office, and thus, what codes are necessary to follow as protocol and which ones aren't. At a company dinner these codes and expectations are liable to change. More than likely the secretary's speaking to people in different ways would not initially be classified as code-switching—for he or she would just simply be seen as "doing his/her job."

Do students code-switch in the classroom when they show a certain kind of deference to the professor that is not extended to their peers, or are they just being students, staying in their place and respecting authority?

When we begin to see code-switching/shifting as something ordinary and always happening—rather than something exceptional and unique with an always subversive intent—we begin to see that the "invisible norm" of the dominant group is neither neutral nor unchained from ideology[53] (although certainly powerful enough to be able to navigate the social world as if their variations are *not* variations).

---

53 https://edge.ua.edu/russell-mccutcheon/seeing-the-ordinary-as-curious/ (accessed 20 December 2017).

If we maintain a discourse of code-switching as *deviation* from or *shifting towards* the norm through a hybrid like re/presentation *of* the norm that re/performs the (seen as natural) codes of the norm, does that not ultimately leave "the norm" in place *as* the norm while creating another master narrative of successful subversive switches by which other group members can then be judged? This type of thinking contributes to the illusion that Jeantel's variation was the one out of place while West's use of the English language was natural, proper, and without difference.

The dilemma of "Whose variation gets to count *as* variation?" necessitates, in the first place, an awareness that it's all variation, and second, a dissociation of variation with value, meaning, consciousness, and ability.

18. Double Standards[54]

Vaia Touna

My love for the ancient Greek theater certainly derives from my upbringing and schooling in Thessaloniki, the second largest city in Greece. For many Greeks seeing our ancient literary heritage being performed in outdoor theaters, especially during summer festivals, is certainly seen as being a step closer to our past. Today, the most well-known festival in Greece is the one that takes place every summer (since 1955) in one of our ancient theaters (known also for its great acoustics)[55]—the "sacred" (as you will hear it often referenced in Greece) theater of Epidaurus.

Every actress/actor in Greece therefore dreams of the day when she/he will be able to perform at the theater of Epidaurus, and participating in the Festival (known as the Athens & Epidaurus Festival) associated with the theater is the way to do so. Troupes have to apply

---

54   Ed. Note: Posted on 1 August 2013, https://edge.ua.edu/vaia-touna/double-standards/ (accessed 20 December 2017).

55   http://www.nature.com/news/2007/070319/full/news070319-16.html (accessed December 20, 2017).

to the Festival's committee, which consists of seven members, and which decides who will be able to perform each year. In the official website of the Festival[56] where one can find its history, there are references as to how the political situations in Greece since 1955 have affected the criteria and, thus, the selection of the Festival's various performances—often resulting in being more conservative rather than progressive. And this is how the Festival, today, describes its purpose:

> *The Challenge*
>
> A reversal of this state of affairs was clearly necessary—to pursue modernism once more, to systematically open up the Festival to cutting-edge international productions, and to promote young Greek artists who have something to say to contemporary audiences. To spread the events of this arts festival across the entire city, to seek out new and different audiences, and to cater for ever more arts lovers through the select events of a contemporary festival.
>
> A new identity—a festival that is inclusive, that reflects its host city, and that brings the livelier aspects of society back into play. This is the challenge to be met; work to this end began in earnest in 2006, and the wager has yet to be won.

Of course you can't be inclusive without being exclusive, so some criteria are needed to decide who will annually take part in the Festival; there is nothing wrong with that, for not everyone can perform during the Festival (which takes place on eight weekends in July and August). But what attracted my interest this summer—and made me think about the criteria of legitimacy and thus who gets to be authenticated in performing these plays in this specific theater—was that the application of one troupe in particular was declined. What is special about this troupe, which is performing Euripides' tragedy *Bacchae*, is that its leading actor is a very popular singer, Sakis Rouvas, who was sent twice to Eurovision—a very popular song contest in Europe—to represent Greece (a representation based on countrywide voting).

56 http://greekfestival.gr/en/content/page/history (accessed 20 December 2017).

It's of interest to note that the Eurovision song contest[57] is a specifically popular (as in "pop") song contest open to any European singer/group who wishes to participate, which takes place every May in the European country (since 1956) that won the previous year's contest. Every country has individual competitions of its own prior to that, and committees, or the public, or both, vote on which participant will represent their country each year. It's the same in Greece: singers and groups apply to the public television broadcaster (ERT), which is responsible for the contest in this country. The interesting thing is that since 1974 (when Greece joined the Eurovision contest) Rouvas has been the only singer to represent Greece twice in the contest (in 2004 and 2009) by direct appointment from the public television company (ERT), i.e., without competing against any other singers.

And although his participation in the Eurovision contest was highly acceptable to the Greek public, as noted above, this was not the case when he decided to perform in an ancient tragedy (which I saw in Thessaloniki). There have been various comments in the media—mostly critical—regarding a pop singer's participation in an ancient tragedy, concluding that it is unacceptable for him to perform in Epidaurus despite his being a young and widely popular artist and, more importantly perhaps, despite the need of the Festival (as described on its site) to "seek out new and different audiences." According to one journalist, the Festival declined the application of the troupe exactly because Rouvas was a performer: "The people of the Greek Festival [were] hesitant and feared that the presence of a pop star will 'irritate' the most conservative of both artists and viewers and so backed away."

What I find interesting in this whole episode, though, is not so much whether the committee was right or wrong to decide against the participation of Rouvas in the Epidaurus Festival, but, rather, the way criteria of legitimation (criteria that are themselves historical products, and thus constantly changing)[58] work. For I assume that there is

---

57   https://eurovision.tv/events/ (accessed 20 December 2017).

58   Since I wrote the blog post in 2013 the official site of the Athens & Epidaurus Festival has revised its history section, which reflects now, especially in the last two paragraphs, the Greek economic crisis and how that has affected the criteria used in who gets to perform in the festival:

in most Greeks a very clear idea/image of who should perform in that theater. Of course it needs further investigation but my hunch is (well it's more than a hunch) that a certain ideology is being translated into criteria of legitimation to create a certain identity, both of the festival but also of how "our" past should be portrayed and thus by whom—thereby making "us" today into a certain sort of Greece. In other words, there is nothing self-evidently natural about who ought to be able to represent the so-called classics; on the contrary, unnoticed criteria are always in operation and they create, promote and authenticate both the actor and the group judging him/her.

19. Pizza Hut: The Best Indian Food Around[59]

Leslie Dorrough Smith

I had the good fortune to be able to accompany a group of my students on a short-term study abroad trip to India last year. It's perhaps

---

It is of paramount importance to make sure that the Festival is actively engaged with the production of Greek culture, the goal being to re-introduce an aspect of Greekness that is divested of any stereotypical folklore elements. To that effect, the Epidaurus Lyceum, an international summer school of ancient Greek drama, will be launched in 2017. Young actors and drama students from all over the world are eligible to enrol.

In these times of social and cultural crisis, it is imperative that the Athens & Epidaurus Festival contributes to social cultivation, encouraging love for high art. At the same time, the Festival needs to actively support contemporary artists. Highlighting contemporary art and paving the road for audiences that are more critically engaged are both instrumental in enabling the operation of a progressive, cultural institution insofar as they promote a better society: a society of proactive thinkers rather than a society of helpless people at the mercy of market forces.

http://greekfestival.gr/en/content/page/history (accessed 20 December 2017).

59 Ed. Note: Posted on 7 March 2014, https://edge.ua.edu/leslie-dorrough-smith/pizza-hut-the-best-indian-food-around/ (accessed 20 December 2017).

no surprise that, while there, I consumed a lot of Indian food. On the surface, that last sentence may seem rather ridiculous if only because it seems so obvious—much like saying "While in India, I saw Indian things!" But an event on our trip forced me to reconsider just how simple that observation really is, and where the parameters surrounding "authentic" and "traditional" cultural labels really lie.

On one particular night, our Indian hosts offered us a very impressive, home-cooked meal featuring many traditional foods of that particular region. It was a lavish spread. As our group ate, our host's grandchildren—two pre-teen boys—happily bypassed the elaborate feast for their preferred food (which, their mother noted, they ate weekly): a barbecue chicken pizza from Pizza Hut. As we all ate, I made a passing comment to the boys about their preference for pizza over "real" Indian food, and they laughed a bit in polite dismissal before being sucked into the reality TV show that they were watching.

As I later considered my brief exchange with the boys, I had a vision of how ridiculous it would sound to ask a bunch of kids from the American south if the Pizza Hut that they were eating was some sort of snub or forfeiture of their traditional foods of collard greens and fried chicken, or if kids from Maine somehow feel a little less state pride knowing that their pizzas are replacing their consumption of lobster. Nevertheless, this was exactly the sort of question I had posed when I engaged the boys, for I had presumed that they had some sort of tie to the food I was eating (the traditional Indian meal), and that I had a more fundamental connection to the food that they were eating (the pizza).

It might seem that the main thing to observe from this culinary phenomenon is the shrinking of the world's cultures at the homogenizing hand of globalization, for clearly there are foods that once did not exist in India (Pizza Hut) that now are available worldwide. This, however, seems to be only one side of the story. If we apply that same standard of authenticity and age in our labeling of other phenomena, we may suddenly find ourselves enmeshed in very blurry, shifting barriers over which and whose practices constitute "legitimate" cultural exercises, based on perceptions of identity that are not only static, but also quite singular. As scholar Stephanie Coontz has noted in her research on the structure of American families, the nuclear, heterosexual, middle-class white family idealized in the 1950s was more a figment of the imagination than it was a realistic expectation for most Americans, if we look at the sheer number of Americans who lived that lifestyle.[60] Despite this, our expectations and ideals still revolve around various incarnations of Ward and June Cleaver, even though they represent "the way we never were," to quote Coontz's title.

I suspect that those boys would have been just as shocked to hear that their pizza and reality TV are "un-Indian" as I would be to hear that my weekly yoga class and foreign-made (but highly popular) vehicle are "un-American." Acknowledging the dynamism involved in claiming cultural authenticity, then, is not a rejection of the fact that things have distinction and come from somewhere, but it is an acknowledgment of something else: that our current interests often dictate how these things are situated in our own symbolic constellation more than any essence held by the "thing itself."

20. Conceiving the "We" in Pluralism[61]

Craig Martin

On the surface, pluralism in the college curriculum seems like an obvious social and political good. Why can't we all just get along? Well, pluralism suggests that we can, in fact, all get along. Perhaps we can get along once we realize that we are, at bottom, similar in essential ways. On the other hand, where fundamental differences within the group might nevertheless persist, we might attenuate social conflict with a deep, empathetic understanding of others. Thus can pluralism cultivate the virtue of tolerance or even acceptance toward

60   Stephanie Coontz, *The Way We Never Were: American Families And The Nostalgia Trap* (New York: Basic Books, 1992).

61   Ed. Note: Posted on 7 April 2014, https://edge.ua.edu/craig-martin/conceiving-the-we-in-pluralism/ (accessed 20 December 2017). This was among the most popular posts on the Culture on the Edge site with a total of 2,055 views by 14 January 2018.

others in modern societies with whom we must work and cooperate. What could be wrong with that?

From the perspective of the social theory here at Culture on the Edge, the "we" in the pluralist circle is likely not pre-existing but rather conceived and brought into being by such pluralist curriculums. Pluralism can perform an act of social partuition, transfiguring oppositional identities into a newly born "we." And, as with all discursive practices, we can ask a number of critical questions regarding this act of social magic.

The first critical question: Where are the lines around the "we" drawn? Who is excluded? All societies are, in fact, pluralist: every society encourages, permits, or tolerates a delimited range of identities, behaviors, social practices, etc. It is not that some societies are pluralist and others are not; rather, different societies have different pluralisms.

The second critical question: Who is permitted to draw the lines? Are the boundaries around who is permitted and who is excluded drawn democratically? Are they drawn by the nobility or an elite class? Are they drawn by legislators? Corporations?

The third critical question: Whose interests are served by drawing a circle around the "we" in this way rather than that way? Presumably those outside the "we" do not benefit, but—in addition—it is likely that not everyone *within* the "we" benefits. Do some of "us" benefit more than others?

Typically these questions are not raised in a pluralism curriculum. On the contrary, the "we" is taken for granted by the authors of the curriculum and students are invited to see similarities or engage empathetically with those the authors have already deemed part of the "us." There are, of course, constitutive exclusions, which are likely presented as so beyond the pale as beneath mention. Muslims are perhaps welcome to join the "we," except of course Al Qaeda, which everyone knows doesn't belong with us.

Because attention is not directed to these questions, this sort of curriculum naturalizes one particular "we"—neglecting the fact that there could be other "we's"—and mystifies—by making invisible —the process by which the circle was drawn in the first place. The conception and birth of the "we" is rarely, if ever, brought to the attention of the students, any more than a baby sees its own birth.

From this perspective, I suspect that many pluralism curriculums today are designed to domesticate social differences to prepare students for life in late capitalism: your differences are accepted and you are welcome to join the "we" as long as you're willing to accept the nation-state's monopoly on violence, willing to submit to an education process designed to make you a particular type of laborer, willing to go to work upon completion of the education process, and thereupon engage in the consumption of commodities. When it comes to "religion," any religion is okay as long as it doesn't interfere with any of these things. If your religion encourages dissent from the nation-state, forbids you access to mainstream education, interrupts your working habits, or prevents you from being fashionable, then perhaps your religion is fundamentalist and beyond the pale.

As an instructor interested in critical thinking, I see my job as drawing attention to the processes that naturalize or mystify the "we," rather than as further naturalizing or mystifying the "we." In sum, my job is to demystify pluralism rather than to promote it.

21. Staking a Claim[62]

K. Merinda Simmons

Check out NPR's latest bit from their *Code Switch* blog[63] on what's been termed "Columbusing," or claiming originality for something that's been around for a while, just in a context different from one's own.

On its face, the impulse here is a relatively useful one: the things we think are new and edgy tend to be ..., well, not. It can be pretty funny, too, thinking about all the latest fads that can be demystified

---

62   Ed. Note: Posted on 4 July 2014, https://edge.ua.edu/k-merinda-simmons/staking-a-claim/ (accessed 20 December 2017).

63   https://www.npr.org/sections/codeswitch/2014/07/06/328466757/columbusing-the-art-of-discovering-something-that-is-not-new?ft=1&f= (accessed 20 December 2017).

by pointing out that they've been around for another group of people for a long time. Besides, scholars in anthropology and religious studies have long suggested there's good work done in the process of making the strange familiar and the familiar strange. Maybe you've come across the oldie-but-goodie "Body Ritual among the Nacirema"[64] (1956) wherein Horace Miner describes modern (well, mid-20th-century, anyway) America as it might appear to a non-participant, rendering it all but unrecognizable to the American students reading it in my Introduction to Religious Studies course. What's become even more interesting still for me in teaching it is seeing even the revealed practices—what he's "really" talking about—start to become unfamiliar to my students as more time passes. For instance, when we find out that his description of women baking their heads in ovens is "actually" a description of seated hood[65] hairdryers, some of my students have no context for *that* either, being at least a couple generations removed from when those were used regularly. Just goes to show: there are always inevitably layers of familiarity and unfamiliarity, description and redescription, rendering the practice of seeking out original or authentic cultural artifacts a self-defeating one.

And there's what I find problematic about the Columbusing article, even in its good intentions toward walking a few steps outside our own shoes. Not far beneath that surface lesson lies yet another claim about a true or real origin—and, consequently, about who owns what. It's just that the claim is reinscribed in the service of a nominally progressive aim. The idea is that our ethnocentric narcissism would take a hit if we just understood that the increasingly popular color runs did not invent the idea of tossing colorful powder at passers-by. That tradition has been going on for ages in the centuries-old Hindu festival Holi. Our clever hand-pies are *actually* empanadas, and so on. Enter progressively minded writers who are here to help us realize what we are *really* doing, eating, and referring to. Thus, "Columbusing is when you 'discover' something that's existed forever," the article tells us.

64   Horace Miner, "Body Ritual Among the Nacirema," *American Anthropologist* 58(3), 1956: 503–7, http://www.sfu.ca/~palys/Miner-1956-BodyRitualAmongTheNacirema.pdf (accessed 20 December 2017).

65   https://www.huffingtonpost.com/2014/03/15/hair-dryer-photos_n_4961380.html (accessed 20 December 2017).

Therein lies the rub: the label "Columbusing" is used to mark instances of appropriation as special or unique, as if such cultural borrowing is not happening all the time already. It's a rather ordinary occurrence, in fact. What ritual, musical genre, or turn of phrase *hasn't* taken cues from something else? But that something else surely wasn't original either, and around and around we go. Learning social codes is all about performance and mimicry, and in that manner, there is not a pure or pristine original from which we create derivative forms. Instead, our quest for origins and ownership will only ever result in the discovery of further iterations, more copies—an endless game of telephone except without the original utterance (and even in that game, no idea appears "originally" in a vacuum) and so no clear way to identify one rendering or another as "borrowed" versus "stolen" versus "cleverly appropriated."

For instance, what should we make of an article (thanks to Russell McCutcheon for passing it my way) describing people dressed as monks while asking for money on the streets of New York City?[66]

Is this an instance of cultural theft? Borrowing? Appropriation? The difference between insensitive manipulation and savvy retooling is a line that is ever-shifting, and it has everything to do with those making the call—people with vested interests in either protecting or deconstructing the "original" form. After all, as the bit on Columbusing points out, pizza has become downright American! And some cover performances have outsold those of the original songs they copy. But in the instance of the folks asking for money in NYC, they are giving a bad name to "real Buddhists." So, we call something borrowed or stolen only in certain instances. Making sense of when this happens and why—as opposed to identifying something as a strategic appropriation—is what I find interesting.

The author of the Columbusing article suggests that, in order to ensure we do not wrongly stake the flag of originality on another culture's tradition (suggesting, again, a clear ownership of this or that tradition), we should ask ourselves a series of questions about

66 https://www.nytimes.com/2014/07/06/nyregion/panhandlers-dressed-as-monks-confound-new-yorkers.html?_r=0 (accessed 20 December 2017).

our intentions: "It is best to enter a new, ethnic experience with consideration, curiosity and respect." But therein lies another question of classification: what is the line between considerate curiosity and patronizing condescension? The answer, of course, depends on how much is at stake for you in declaring the origins of that slice of pizza ... .[67]

22. Almost Black?[68]

Monica R. Miller

Almost Black,[69] the story and book by "Jojo," er, Vijay, an "Indian American who got into medical school pretending to be an African American" has the internet abuzz and many in a rage. After shaving his head and trimming his "long Indian eyelashes," 17 years ago Vijay Chokal-Ingam, the "Indian-American frat boy" with a 3.1 GPA, transmuted into "Jojo," the African-American affirmative-action (which he refers to as state-sponsored racism) applicant to medical school.

"Why now?" many have asked. To this, Vijay responds[70] that "he's revealing his race ruse now because he heard that UCLA is considering strengthening its affirmative-action admissions policies." He argues, "... it's a myth that affirmative action benefits the underprivileged." Also, and perhaps most pressing, he has begun promotion for a memoir he is working on, *Almost Black*,[71] which chronicles his "social experiment." To add humor to the explicitly politically

67   https://en.wikipedia.org/wiki/History_of_pizza (accessed 20 December 2017).

68   Ed. Note: Posted on 13 April 2015, https://edge.ua.edu/monica-miller/almost-black/#more-8185 (accessed 20 December 2017).

69   http://almostblack.com (accessed 20 December 2017).

70   https://nypost.com/2015/04/05/mindy-kalings-brother-pretended-to-be-black-to-get-into-med-school/ (accessed 20 December 2017).

71   The memoir has since been published under the title *Almost Black: The True Story of How I Got into Medical School by Pretending to Be Black* (Pensauken, NJ: Bookbaby, 2016).

problematic, Vijay pats himself on his own back by affirming the public benefit of him *not* becoming a doctor.

There is a good bit of "obvious" grist for the mill to pick and pull apart here, but let's for a moment bracket the "politics" of this code-switching-gone-wrong (or right, depending on perspective) social experiment, and focus rather on the manner in which such "passing" happens so very often at the level of the seemingly "mundane." You know, the "stuff" that is so ordinary that we often forget it, too, is no doubt an appendage of the "operational acts of identification" that are strategic and socially, culturally, and politically interested. Although Vijay has something much more strategic in mind with capitalizing on the "results" of his social experiment, his story about why he "really" got into medical school is made possible by connecting and constructing exaggerated illusions of disparate data over and against an obvious case of missing data. For one, he never tries to apply *as* an Asian-American (thus, the comparative data is lost although he later receives his MBA from UCLA where he decides to apply as "himself"); two, he assumes that admissions standards are formulaic and self-evident (they are not); and lastly, he fails at his own "social experiment" once he assumes that he must "authentically" live that which he initially designated (i.e., self-identifying *as* black on his application). Perhaps I am wrong about this, but in my experience, I have never heard of an admissions counselor sneaking into dorms to "inspect" the identity of admitted applicants to ensure that the properties of their self-identifications "match" that of their prior designations. Maybe, after all, Vijay could have kept his "long Indian eyelashes" and spared his "Indian hair" (and identity) from the chopping block. With the "politics" of what Vijay is currently doing with his self-constructed data aside, the public upset to his social-experiment-gone-wrong-but-right reveals more about identification more broadly than the actual story itself.

The detractors lobbying that he "cheated the system" assume, a priori, that blackness is inherently pathological, at a deficit in its very definition, defined *as* deficit, and something that through its self-naming affords social privileges that are unwarranted and unsubstantiated. Are there not ways that Jojo's story might offer a moment to reflect on how we're understanding and defining something like blackness—with a pathologized "need" (i.e., those "worthy" of a handout) versus blackness as industriousness in the face of adversity whether real or imagined (i.e., those who refuse to accept the need for a handout). That is, in his act of defining himself as "black," does he not effectively *become* black, in his refusal to be refused admission into a site of social privilege? Perhaps these aren't the only options for blackness, but the identitarian sleight-of-hand, at the very least, offers a moment to calibrate (or recalibrate) what sort of operational acts are taking place in the deployment of blackness (whether by "black" folk or [presumably predominately] white admissions folk). And does not the "admissions" board or committee represent American normativity, and the prospects of if, when, and how black might ever come to constitute a component of American social normativity? Who decides what is normative? And by what criteria of evaluation are norms determined?

In addition to using his story to critique affirmative-action policies, Vijay also chronicles the "unintended consequences" of his social-experiment-gone-wrong: what happens when one is *perceived* or *read* as black. To this he adds, "Cops harassed me," "Store clerks accused me of shoplifting," and "Women were either scared of me or couldn't keep their hands off me." When the everyday realities of being signified *as* black met up with the rubber of a lopsided social system, it seems as if Jojo gained more than admission to medical school when the "experiment" got *too* real.

But rather than selling *that* story in his memoir, he has instead chosen to use his experience (from over 15 years ago) as a sensationalized universalized empirical appeal to challenge affirmative-action policies today in a transhistorical manner (that somehow what happened "then" happens exactly as is "now"). Unfortunately for Jojo, in an age when state-sanctioned violence continues to mark black humanity in America, that he survived to tell, sell, and market, his story, when Walter Scott, Trayvon Martin, and so many others did not, should welcome critical reflection as to *how* stories are told when we turn ourselves into data[72] and what purposes turning in on oneself serves (my colleague Russell McCutcheon's latest Culture on the

72   https://edge.ua.edu/russell-mccutcheon/profiling-bloody-mary/ (accessed 20 December 2017).

Edge post is a good example of how to effectively make this move). Jojo has done well to manufacture a crisis of his own making, and the public reaction *to* his story provides a market for his story to be bought, sold, and traded in a market obsessed with narratives about the promise and peril of identification, as such. In the end, it seems as if Vijay wanted the *assumed* social privileges of claiming marginality within a carefully managed setting of self-utility, from the inside-out without the "extras" that often come with *how* our identities are often read from the outside-in—those most notably situated somewhat outside of our full ability to control and manipulate the projected gazes and interpellations.

23. What Should You Be on Halloween?[73]

Steven W. Ramey

A culture is not a costume. That sentiment has become a common theme on social media and student newspapers (from James Madison University[74] and from Chapman University,[75] for example) with the approach of Halloween. The sentiment makes sense with people, primarily identified with a majority community, masquerading for fun as a stereotyped member of a minority. The history of using minority images for the entertainment and benefit of majorities is long and painful, including the blackface minstrel shows of a century ago. Such costumes reinforce the costumed person's majority status as he/she masquerades as something other, thus demonstrating differences in power.

However, accusations of cultural appropriation also can become assertions of power and control from some in minority groups. In the

73   Ed. Note: Posted on 29 October 2015, https://edge.ua.edu/steven-ramey/what-should-you-be-on-halloween/ (accessed 20 December 2017).

74   http://www.breezejmu.org/opinion/people-need-to-think-about-cultural-appropriation-when-choosing-halloween/article_111065dc-7b76-11e5-b982-476494d8c8ea.html (accessed 20 December 2017).

75   http://www.thepantheronline.com/features/culture-or-costume-cultural-appropriation-on-halloween (accessed 20 December 2017).

video entitled "White Party—A Lesson in Cultural Appropriation,"[76] the narrator describes cultural appropriation as "when you hijack a part of a culture without permission, not out of respect or tribute."
The assertion about permission illustrates the complexity of cultural control, as who has the authority to grant that permission? In the video, the narrator (at 2:00) heightens this difficulty as she asserts that having one person identified with a culture claim that they are not offended is insufficient to make a stereotyped theme party acceptable. Obviously, the person not offended cannot speak for everyone in her/ his cultural group.

Some people, however, put themselves in the position of determining what in a culture needs protection from appropriation. When Selena Gomez[77] wore a bindi, some who identify as Hindu accused her of cultural appropriation. The person who most vocally denounced her use of the bindi, Rajan Zed,[78] presents himself as a "Hindu statesman" and attempts to promote his conception of Hindu values. While some who identify as Hindu accepted Gomez wearing a bindi, Zed's complaint centered on the sexually suggestive style of Gomez's dancing. Thus, the accusation of improper cultural appropriation also served to reinforce Zed's vision of proper modesty and sexuality along with his authority. To reverse the video's question, if one person finds an act to be an improper appropriation of something that he identifies as part of his culture/ethnicity, does that automatically make it problematic cultural appropriation?

The issue of cultural appropriation extends to literature and artistic images. For example, *Sita Sings the Blues*[79] is an animated retelling of the Ramayana, commonly identified as one of the central epics in Hinduism. Filmmaker Nina Paley tells the story of Vishnu's incarnation as Rama from the perspective of Rama's wife Sita, emphasizing Sita's faithfulness to Rama and Rama's mistreatment of her. (Read

76   Posted on Youtube by Akilah Obviously, https://www.youtube.com/ watch?v=1px3fKn4G3U (accessed 20 December 2017).

77   http://articles.latimes.com/2013/apr/16/entertainment/la-et-mg-selena-gomez-bindi-mtv-brad-pitt-ellen-20130416 (accessed 20 December 2017).

78   http://www.rajanzed.org (accessed 20 December 2017).

79   http://www.sitasingstheblues.com (accessed 20 December 2017).

the student blog post written by Jared Powell,[80] for more analysis of Paley's film.) Interspersed in the film are semi-autobiographical parallels to Paley's life and difficult break-up. Particularly since Paley identifies as neither Hindu nor Indian, some have opposed the movie because of the way it retells the story, even accusing her of theft. The accusation here has ideological elements related to gender roles and theological issues about the nature of Rama. Thus, the accusation of cultural appropriation here becomes a way to restrict critique and interpretation and reinforce particular values as Hindu.

Cultural appropriation, then, can become an act of power and identification when people identified with one community (typically a dominant community) employ a stereotyped minority image to emphasize, among other things, their dominance; but the accusation of cultural appropriation can also reflect the desire to control a story, image, artifact, or practice and determine the proper use of that element, both within and outside a community. A blanket restriction on cultural appropriation can serve to limit the range of voices, even within minority communities, as those in positions of authority within minority communities can use charges of cultural appropriation to limit representations and discipline community members. As you prepare your costume, consider the dynamics of power, the power of stereotyped images to diminish minority communities as well as the power of some to assert authority and ideology in the guise of charges of cultural appropriation.

24. Cultural Entrepreneurs[81]

Steven W. Ramey

Accusations of cultural appropriation have been especially prevalent recently. The depiction of Jeff Bezos as Vishnu on the cover of

---

80   https://religion.ua.edu/blog/2015/10/28/sita-sings-the-universal-blues/ (accessed 20 December 2017).

81   Ed. Note: Posted on 11 February 2016, https://edge.ua.edu/steven-ramey/cultural-entrepreneurs/ (accessed 20 December 2017).

Fortune magazine elicited complaints[82] from some people who identify with Hinduism, as did the Krewe of Galatea[83] parading their court as Hindu deities during Mardi Gras festivities. The recent Coldplay/Beyoncé music video release "Hymn for the Weekend"[84] also has generated complaints about its depiction of India and the ways some artists profit off of these images.

Images of India have been used for decades, from the 007 film *Octopussy* to *Indiana Jones and the Temple of Doom*, and the complaints that they have spawned have basis in the colonialism and neocolonialism of India and the global inequality that such images—in their construction of India as some place totally different—reinforce. One critique[85] of the Coldplay/Beyoncé music video expressed concern for artists profiting from images of Indians always throwing colors, as if every day was Holi. However, the author's own discussion actually suggests one limitation of claims of cultural appropriation:

> Just understand that in the age of Twitter and think pieces, the days in which white musicians could use black and brown people as props without expecting widespread scrutiny, mockery or pushback are rapidly drawing to a close.

The problem, as many comments on the commentary noted, is that the artists involved were not simply "white people," as Beyoncé, with her mixed race heritage (Louisiana Creole and African-American) is seldom labeled "white." While including a person of color does not give a video producer freedom to do anything that they want, the

82   http://www.hindustantimes.com/world/it-s-offensive-jeff-bezos-on-the-fortune-cover-as-lord-vishnu-irks-hindus/story-Rh5l9tT2OYejLp7u7Y-aA7I.html (accessed 20 December 2017).

83   http://www.shreveporttimes.com/story/news/2016/02/01/local-krewe-apologizes-dismayed-hindus-over-costuming/79637294/ (accessed 20 December 2017).

84   https://www.youtube.com/watch?v=YykjpeuMNEk (accessed 20 December 2017).

85   https://www.npr.org/sections/codeswitch/2016/02/01/465163237/dear-white-artists-making-music-videos-in-india-lay-off-the-holi-powder (accessed 20 December 2017).

commentary either constructs Beyoncé as white or writes her out of the artistry and production of the video, making her just another "prop," with the resultant issues of gender and ethnic diminution.

This idiosyncratic application of the label "white" reminds us of the malleable nature of such labels that are not fixed, natural categories. Even in more typical usage, the labels, whether ethnic, cultural, national, or religious, overwrite the diverse nature of any grouping, making them into an "imagined community," to use Benedict Anderson's phrase. Accusations of cultural appropriation, though, rely on a generalized unity of those who become identified with a culture, however that is defined.

Along with his critique of the use of the category "ethnicity," Rogers Brubaker in his book *Ethnicity Without Groups* (Harvard University Press, 2004) employs the label "entrepreneur" for various actors, including "ethnopolitical entrepreneurs" and "memory entrepreneurs." The term references people who create/manage ethnicity or memory to gain access to resources. Brubaker asserts: "Reifying groups is precisely what ethnopolitical entrepreneurs are in the business of doing. When they are successful, the political fiction of the unified group can be momentarily yet powerfully realized in practice." And their constructions enable these entrepreneurs to "live 'off' as well as 'for' ethnicity."

So, in addition to those appropriating cultures to make money, "cultural entrepreneurs" can refer to those who use claims of cultural appropriation to reinforce their own position. Rajan Zed,[86] who has produced press releases decrying various appropriations (see Appendix #23, p. 229 above) of what he identifies with Hinduism, also requests donations to support his mission to protect Hinduism. His position and funding rely on a construction of a unified Hindu culture that needs protection from (other) cultural entrepreneurs like those behind *Fortune* magazine or the music video. Of course, it is a competitive field, as the Hindu America Foundation has rejected the critique of this video,[87] preferring to focus attention on the "theft" of

---

86 http://www.rajanzed.org (accessed 20 December 2017).

87 http://religionnews.com/2016/02/10/coldplay-appropriate-hindu-themes-latest-music-video-commentary/?utm_medium=twitter&utm_source=twitterfeed (accessed 20 December 2017).

yoga. Various sets of entrepreneurs live "off" culture in different ways that overgeneralize and reify the unity and image of any single cultural designation.

So, take a look at the Coldplay/Beyoncé "Hymn for the Weekend" and consider both how it constructs an exotic India and how those who critique it for appropriating their culture also construct a generalizable unity of Indianness that connects them with the people and places depicted.

ACTS OF COMPARISON

25. Kids Drink Pop, So What?[88]

Russell T. McCutcheon

I think it's worth pausing for a moment to ask why the image[89] of a young Tibetan Buddhist monk (or at least someone dressed up like one) drinking so casually from a pop bottle, and which I recently used as the cover image on the Culture on the Edge Facebook page, "works." Given the theoretical goals of the Culture on the Edge research group, what do we assume it "says," and about whom?

For example, consider another image that I found online: Steve McCurry's photograph of a monk sitting inside an old tea shop, in the Indian city of Bodh Gaya, with a bottle of Coke in his hand while a big Coca Cola advertisement is painted on the wall behind him.[90]

What I find intriguing about such photographs is how firmly they re-entrench traditional stereotypes despite seeming to undermine them (a problem I find in many current studies of identity). For what presumably makes the situation worth framing in distinction from the

88 Ed. Note: Posted on 11 June 2013, https://edge.ua.edu/russell-mccutcheon/kids-drink-pop-so-what/ (accessed 20 December 2017).

89 A photo originally found in this site: http://fuckyouverymuch.dk/post/52082199117/we-are-thirsty (accessed 20 December 2017).

90 https://pro.magnumphotos.com/Asset/-2K7O3R3UXD2R.html (accessed 20 December 2017).

limitless, centerless, and thus ambiguous background that comprised the setting that day—i.e., what made the photo worth taking—were sets of assumptions about religious people in general, and Buddhist monks in particular, being somehow other than human, historical subjects—for they're set apart from "the outside world," meditative, detached, passionless, spiritual, etc. Without these assumptions, I'm not sure a picture of someone sitting in a teashop drinking a soda, regardless the locale, is all that compelling. For it likely happens across the globe millions and millions of times each day.

This problem of conserved assumptions is made all the more evident in the caption that appears along with that photo:

> Young monk in a tea-shop, Bodh Gaya, India, 2000. On a cloudy day, [Steve] McCurry[91] wandered into a tea-shop and happened upon this incongruous image of two contrasting cultures. One epitomizes the search for some higher truth that characterizes the young Buddhist's journey. The other represents the strident commercialism of a multinational corporation. Holding a bottle of the well-known fizzy drink, the monk seems lost in his own thoughts.

Speculations on the young man's tranquil inner state are evidence of how the captionist, the observer, is the one who creates the impression of incongruity, as opposed to it being a found object in the wild. For without the set of assumptions that we bring to the situation—assumptions reproduced in almost any world religions class—I'm not sure there is a contrast here between two things characterized as distinct cultures. Instead, there is just an apparently thirsty man making the mistake of taking a break in front of a tourist with a camera.

If this is how we choose to view it, seeing instead just a thirsty man, then the photo likely loses much of its appeal—for its edgy provocativeness depends upon the viewer reinscribing assumptions of Buddhism and Tibet as unique, faraway places, freed from the mundane concerns that occupy us in the rest of the world. *The Cup*, a 1999 motion picture, also comes to mind as an example of this problem—for seeing the main character, also a monk, as just an avid

---

91 http://stevemccurry.com/galleries/portraits

football (i.e., soccer) fan, working hard to get to a TV that broadcasts the match, is not sufficient to give the narrative its edge.

"Far from the influence of the outside world …" opens the trailer's narration, with the strategic pause before revealing that, contrary to the viewer's likely expectation about enlightenment and detachment comprising the young boy's "destiny," soccer is instead "his one true love." This contradiction of otherworldly pursuits and World Cup desire, and how the boy overcomes it, is the narrative's hook. While all sorts of people likely have not been able to watch the soccer finals, for all sorts of reasons, their stories are probably not worth telling. But this one is—and it is because of the reinscribed assumptions that many think are being shaken off in this film's efforts to humanize these social actors.

Of course what I've said here is little different from what Donald Lopez argued back in 1998 in his book *Prisoners of Shangri-La*; "Tibetans," he writes in his introduction, making reference to the classic film *Lost Horizon* (1937), "are portrayed as ancient conservators of a timeless wisdom in a timeless realm, now thrust from their snowy sanctuary into history."[92] Ironically, Lopez finds this same portrait still exists today—and it is in contrast with this image (which is none other than a strategically useful impression, perpetuated by a variety of social actors for a variety of purposes) that the Coke sign and the pop bottle can be judged as constituting incongruity.

So what *is* happening in that cover photo on our Facebook page? My hope is that it doesn't simply communicate incongruity to observers (the same incongruity that prompts political observers to be puzzled by the motives of Buddhist protestors in, say, Myanmar[93] or in China[94]) or be seen as curiously humanizing that young initiate. I also hope that it doesn't represent two cultures bumping into one another (i.e., the old "East meets West" genre). Instead, I hope that it prompts

---

92   Donald Lopez, *Prisoners of Shangri-La: Tibetan Buddhism and the West* (Chicago: University of Chicago Press, 1998), 8.

93   http://www.nytimes.com/2013/05/30/world/asia/religious-violence-myanmar.html?_r=0 (accessed 20 December 2017).

94   https://www.voanews.com/a/buddhist-monks-selfimmolate-in-tibet-protest/1648325.html (accessed 20 December 2017).

viewers to consider the role that they, as observers, play in creating the impression of incongruity and why that young boy (or should we call him a young monk? That's the question!) would even need humanizing in the first place—as if he wasn't already human, already in the world, and thus always in history to begin with. For worldwide, kids now drink what I grew up calling pop, simple as that. That we see this particular young boy, dressed in this particular manner, as worth noticing, as worth framing and thereby distinguishing from the rest of the world around him, says far more about us than it does about that thirsty kid.

26. Look Who's Talking![95]

K. Merinda Simmons

In the initial post[96] responding to the Reza Aslan/Fox News interview,[97] Craig Martin brought our attention to the ways in which similar logic can be used to launch competing identity claims. Particularly resonant for me is a quick anecdotal move in his post that contains much when considered carefully. He notes, "When I go to the American Academy of Religion annual meeting, I see lots of scholarship production tied to scholars' identities, and much of it is very political." I know exactly what he means.

I am a literary theorist by training whose research emphasizes sites of production regarding gender and race, especially in the American South. With this kind of academic background, conferences have always been something of a sticky wicket for me. One of my professors in graduate school advised me, "The academy is one big cocktail

95   Ed. Note: Posted on 1 August 2013, https://edge.ua.edu/k-merinda-simmons/look-whos-talking/ (accessed 20 December 2017).

96   https://edge.ua.edu/craig-martin/identity-claims-play-out-on-fox/ (accessed 20 December 2017).

97   https://www.buzzfeed.com/andrewkaczynski/is-this-the-most-embarrassing-interview-fox-news-has-ever-do?utm_term=.rv4XXqMpGQ#.qdEllABPog (accessed 20 December 2017).

party. You find the group that interests you, head to their corner, and join in on the conversation." A hopeless introvert, I don't mind admitting that her metaphor terrified me. I've never really learned the art of seamless conversational entrances and exits. I imagined the whole experience of carving out my academic niche among other people to be like speed dating … except with all of the awkward anxiety and none of the romance. However, I was also a plucky grad student at the time, very eager to do some productive networking and find some scholarly comrades of like mind. "That's how opportunities find you," my PhD faculty mentors assured me.

So I struck out like Goldilocks, experimenting outside the Modern Language Association (MLA) with a few different conferences for each of my specific areas of interest in order to find the one or two that would be "just right." I presented work at meetings focusing solely on the American South, on popular culture, on Black and Diaspora Studies, on Women's Studies, and even on interdisciplinarity as a topic in itself. I'll spare you the hits and misses of particular conference experiences, which include a presentation that consisted entirely of a string of Ani DiFranco lyrics in a PowerPoint slide show that was supposed to make the audience realize that music can … wait for it … have feminist themes! (the nods of serious consideration from the crowd made this feminist want to swallow my Bic pen). Suffice it to say that I was left with some productive scholarly exchanges and business card swapping but nonetheless dissatisfied that I had not found my corner of the cocktail party.

Ultimately, once I found myself working in a Department of Religious Studies at the University of Alabama, I realized that the next group with whom I should flutter into conversation was congregating annually at the American Academy of Religion. At this point, several writing projects and a few years of nomadic conference-going had me thinking less about this or that specific piece of data and much more about sets of questions I had regarding how those data were treated by various discourses, including and often especially academic ones. Pragmatic concerns of money and time kept me focused for a couple of years on presenting primarily at the National Women's Studies Association (NWSA) and the American Academy of Religion

(AAR). These were the big ones, after all! Plus, they would allow me to tease out some of the finer points I had been working on in relation to thematics of "women and religion," a topic on which I was teaching and writing. I had finally settled into a good conference groove, swimming in the soothing waters of intense academic engagement … I thought. Here's what I found instead.

I went to the NWSA, presenting on a panel entitled "Women and Religion." This was my chance. I'd finally get to pick the brains of feminists who were incorporating studies of religion into their work and see how they were tackling the intersection. I was giving a paper that dealt with some of the issues of category claims and classification politics in "women and religion" courses/syllabi. I was eager for feedback. I went first. The other person on the panel (ours was touted as a special session, kept purposefully small for the sake of good discussion on a complex topic) gave a presentation on what she called "heart-centered pedagogy." Her point as I understood it was that yogic practice and ideology can make for better learning environments. Women, of course, are particularly suited for this, as our abilities for compassionate touching and empathy provide a safe space for students to express themselves. I was stunned. While eager questions followed up on my fellow panelist's talk, asking her to explain how she uses the technique in other classroom contexts (she had explored it to great success, she said, in prisons), the questions that came my way primarily pressed the point of why it is exactly that I do not give ample attention in my syllabus to "the experiences of real women." I spent some time reading the huge NWSA program book after my panel was over. Every mention of "religion" was advertising scholars who were participants in a particular faith community talking descriptively about women in that faith community. Muslim women convened for a panel discussing the politics of the hijab in various parts of the world. Jewish women organized to discuss strands of Jewish feminism. I found a panel on goddess movements and one critiquing the patriarchy of Christian doctrine. And so on. In this setting of scholars, "religion" referred to something specific and real—and decidedly experiential.

I realized that I had developed a very different reading of our feminist mainstay "the personal is political"[98] from many of my colleagues working in the discipline. If what we identify as "the personal" is an invariably political act, then there is no sense privileging this or that experiential claim or participant viewpoint. Rather, we might more productively set about the business of examining how various—often competing—notions of identity ("the personal") appear as political claims and contestations.

At the AAR, something interesting happened. While scholars at times (certainly not always) talked about "religion" in more nuanced ways—at least giving a nod to calling it a category—"women" referred to an exceedingly specific, often biological, phenomenon. Conversations about "women and religion," then, took the shape of focusing on descriptive anthropological accounts on this or that group of women in this or that country performing this or that ritual. The importance or relevance of the topic was taken to be self-evident—such work's motivation was one of awareness-building and a global humanism cast beneath a tent of well-intended liberalism. Between sessions, I made a point of talking with various people about the topic of women and religion vis-à-vis pedagogy. This time, the questions put to me dealt with how to give ample time in the semester to various religious traditions.

Okay, okay, these are just anecdotal gripes about a genre of academic performance wherein we are often trotting out very rough drafts of ideas that haven't yet been polished, right? Maybe, but I think the discussions among academics still offer telling moments that we might think about when considering how it is that we go about articulating certain claims to one another. After all, if Reza Aslan's few short minutes in an online interview are able to spark such debate, then surely more concentrated and focused speaking moments in academia—like the structured spaces of conferences—might give us a nice case study that can spell out (at least in useful nutshells) the broad trends in studies of religion and identity. For instance, and perhaps most relevant to the Aslan v. Fox discussion, we might ask

98   http://www.carolhanisch.org/CHwritings/PIP.html   (accessed   20 December 2017).

why some claims to experiential authority are valued and others criticized. At a recent regional AAR meeting, our academic panels coincided with a meeting of a group of Christians of some charismatic or evangelical stripe. Scholars easily poked kind (and occasionally not so kind) fun at the affable group of religious followers (they were our data, after all), only to conduct panels on their own analyses of "authentic" ritual performances or of a "proper" reading of a passage in the Bible. Strikes me that both groups are simply making competing identity claims using the same logic that supposes a way to access a "true interpretation" of something. Or, for another example, how is it that we decide when, like Aslan did, to make heavy note of our scholarly credentials and when to distance ourselves as far as possible from the academy? After all, many engage in the latter when attempting to distinguish the "ivory tower" from the "real world" (and socially conscious PhDs that we are, we certainly don't want to appear aristocratic!). In the pages of *Method and Theory in the Study of Religion*, for example, I recently had a debate with a scholar accusing me of not appreciating what she claimed were the real experiences of folks on the ground. I'll repeat: she made this critique of academic navel-gazing *in the pages of an academic journal*. How does the irony of our own claims in the contexts we make them so often escape us?

The so-called personal is *always* political. It is, indeed, a highly politicized claim to talk about a domain of "the personal" in the first place. What's amazing to me is how often it seems like scholars want to be self-referential without being self-reflexive. We want to lay claim to experiential authority or be detached descriptivists when it suits us, all the while pointing to the "scope of our research" to explain our intellectual projects rather than the politics that motivate our studies.

Among those with similar curiosities and frustrations, I guess I *did* eventually find a group of people to talk to at the proverbial cocktail party. It's just that, instead of huddling in the corner of one of the rooms, they turned out to be standing on the lawn outside, talking about the house.

27. Trick or Trick?[99]

Monica R. Miller

A recent occurrence of misrecognition reminded me of a Culture on the Edge blog post written this past summer[100] in which Russell McCutcheon wrote about what it might mean to see the ordinary as curious. In the post, McCutcheon asked a simple question underneath a picture of Baka people performing for Pope Benedict XVI as he departed for Angola—"who is wearing a costume?"

If we take serious theories of performativity and the role of the discursive in processes of identification as forcefully articulated by thinkers such as Judith Butler, then we know that something like Halloween occurs every day where we un/consciously present who we are/aren't/want to be to the social world in which we participate. In other words, the minute we wake up and start dressing and adorning ourselves (who will we *be* today?), we're all in costume—the process of identification thus begins. But, that's a conversation for another post.

This past weekend I had dinner with a Lehigh University colleague at the Hotel Bethlehem. Given the Bethlehem tradition of always celebrating Halloween on the last Friday in October, the hotel was hosting a Halloween bash on the same evening and thus we found ourselves in the midst of a costume party. We had not, or thought we had not, dressed up for the occasion.

Until, on our way out, partygoers thought my colleague had dressed up for the costume party (he was wearing African printed pants). Quickly noting that he had not, the classifier, seemingly dressed up *in* costume for the party, had quickly reappropriated the misfire of his discursive gaze by noting of himself, "This is not a costume either."

This scene of misrecognition reminds us that the "thing" we often call identity doesn't as much speak to a thing in and of itself, but

99   Ed. Note: Posted on 31 October 2013, https://edge.ua.edu/monica-miller/trick-or-trick/ (accessed 20 December 2017).

100   https://edge.ua.edu/russell-mccutcheon/seeing-the-ordinary-as-curious/ (accessed 20 December 2017).

rather, the perceived *costume* of identity becomes concretized in the very performative "expressions" thought to be the result of the category itself.

So, as McCutcheon asked a number of months back, "who is wearing the costume?"

28. Trainwreck Spotting: How We Insist on Not Working on the Railroad and Instead Tie Ourselves to the Tracks[101]

K. Merinda Simmons

A few days ago, my Facebook feed lit up with various threads all linking to the latest academic critique of the academy. The discussions that afternoon amounted mostly to well-intentioned and kindly commiseration based on the various levels of dissatisfaction among my scholarly nears and dears. Now, the fact that we were all chatting on our computers through Facebook in the middle of a weekday (myself sipping hot tea in the process) is not unimportant. But I'll come back to that after telling you about this article: "'I Quit Academia,' an Important, Growing Subgenre of American Essays." [102]

It is the most recent *Slate*[103] post by Rebecca Schuman, a disgruntled self-described "emotional trainwreck"[104] whose experience with

101 Ed. Note: Posted on 4 November 2013, https://edge.ua.edu/k-merinda-simmons/trainwreck-spotting-how-we-insist-on-not-working-on-the-railroad-and-instead-tie-ourselves-to-the-tracks/ (accessed 20 December 2017). This was among the most popular posts on the Culture on the Edge site with a total of 2,819 views by 14 January 2018.

102 http://www.slate.com/blogs/browbeat/2013/10/24/quitting_academic_jobs_professor_zachary_ernst_and_other_leaving_tenure.html (accessed 20 December 2017).

103 http://www.slate.com/authors.rebecca_schuman.html (accessed 20 December 2017).

104 http://www.slate.com/articles/life/culturebox/2013/04/there_are_no_academic_jobs_and_getting_a_ph_d_will_make_you_into_a_horrible.html (accessed 20 December 2017).

the academy has left her with a fear and loathing she feels it incumbent upon her to share with as many who will listen. Not that she's done badly for herself. After all, as her blurb states, she's the author of an academic book under advance contract with an esteemed university press (Northwestern, to be exact). And that book isn't bound to be what I'd call a mass-market bestseller. It's entitled *Kafka and Wittgenstein: The Case for an Analytic Modernism*. She's thus been successful at navigating the tricky terrain of academic publishing—no small feat for those in early career stages. Further, she's got quite a mighty soapbox in *Slate*, which, despite the fuzzy math of web traffic,[105] boasts millions of readers. Millions. How many folks will wade through her case for an analytic modernism? Who knows—maybe a bunch. But not millions. So, the writing skills she gained in the system of higher education against which she now rails have given her the platform of *Slate* to help her launch these critiques.

So what's the latest piece about? It adds Zachary Ernst's recent "Why I Jumped Off the Ivory Tower" to the growing list of an "important subgenre" of academic writing to which she refers as the "I Quit Oeuvre."

What makes Ernst interesting to Schuman is that he left an already-tenured post as a philosophy professor. In this way, he joins the company of others who were willing to give up tenure. Schuman cites Terran Lane and Anne Trubek as ones who share this dubious distinction. Academics leave the job because, according to the piece, "Academe is a profession full of erudite free-thinkers who feel disillusioned by a toxic labor system in which criticism is not tolerated." She goes on to compare academe to "a fundamentalist religion (or … cult)." Ultimately, her conclusion is that "Ernst's farewell should offer those outside the university a powerful glimpse into why a successful academic would want to add another entry to the I Quit Canon."

While part of a recent trend in writings by what many perceive to be brave academics, willing to spread the *real truth* and expose the maniacal wizard behind the curtain of academic labor, the critique is not a new thing. In the chorus of complaint about professional

---

105 http://www.slate.com/articles/technology/webhead/2006/02/slate_has_8_million_readers_honest.html (accessed 20 December 2017).

woes—finding a "work/life balance"; juggling the triad of research, teaching, and service; and pitching oneself on the competitive job market in the first place—Schuman and those offering similar writings try to warn up-and-comers from making what they see to be the huge mistake of pursuing a graduate degree ... especially in the humanities.

In our worry and (in Schuman's case, outright anger) over the current state of academe, though, it's easy to lose sight of a very important fact: *professional academicians have it pretty darn good.* I'm not at all suggesting that the increase in and reliance on adjunct positions and lectureships isn't a lamentable fact of the institutional matter. And I'm not saying that the market isn't a difficult territory to traverse. But difficult according to whom and compared to what? Is it as difficult as collecting garbage during hot Alabama summers? Is it as difficult as working the graveyard shift as a 911 operator?

But wait—these are unfair comparisons, right? *Those* people made choices to follow other careers or were unable for one reason or another to access the academic institutions that would suggest the professoriate as a possible path of professional development. *We,* on the other hand, are hapless victims of an exploitative system that manipulates us for its own gain. Right? Nah, I don't buy it. We're making choices, too. And, by bemoaning the long hours and small pay in the name of pursuing some nebulous idea of personal fulfillment, we imply not so subtly that we are special and that we deserve to experience a kind of happiness that apparently comes only when we are debt-free and when the academy thanks us for our sacrificial service to the greater good. Two things about that. First, our seeming specialness as academics carries with it the notion that the cashier working multiple shifts at the local grocery store is *not* wrestling with the same questions of workload and self-worth. Or, if she is, it somehow makes sense (or at least, it doesn't bother us nearly so much) for her to do so. Second, clutching the proverbial brass ring— getting a job and/or earning tenure—is not what will make a person happy. Frankly, I don't see what's so provocative or strange about that. Of *course* it's not what will make someone happy.

As my colleague Russell McCutcheon noted in a post elsewhere[106] responding to a different web article on the same subject, the idea that the academy should work to make us happy bears a remarkable degree of entitlement. After all, no job or degree or work environment is *in and of itself* more or less interesting or fulfilling than any other. To suggest as much would be appealing to a series of essences inherent to various career pursuits. And didn't graduate school teach us to be wary of essentialist claims? Scholars like Schuman strike me as akin to Alfred Tennyson's poem "Ulysses,"[107] fancying themselves far too important for the quotidian drudgery that greets them upon completing the graduate school gauntlet. They find, like he does, that the arch of experience and uncharted adventure seems only to fade as they move closer to it.

Sure, that can be frustrating, if not disillusioning. But, you know what? It's 12:55 on a Tuesday, and I'm sitting here with my laptop and another cup of tea comparing contemporary frustrations with those of literary lore. And, yesterday, I was able to steal away an hour's coffee klatch with a historian colleague of mine to catch up and trade descriptions of our busy lives. I didn't even have to punch a clock. I got paid that whole time.

Those tenured folks Schuman mentions who got fed up with academe aren't doing so terribly themselves. Terran Lane kissed the University of New Mexico goodbye for Google. Anne Trubek found that freelance writing could float her. And our Odyssean hero Zachary Ernst is now enjoying a nice salary in the private sector. To suggest, as Schuman does in the blurb for a piece earlier this year (called "Thesis Hatement")[108] that "getting a … Ph.D. will turn you into an emotional trainwreck, not a professor" is not only to (quite arrogantly)

106 https://religion.ua.edu/blog/2013/10/27/isnt-that-special/ (accessed 20 December 2017).

107 https://www.poetryfoundation.org/poems/45392/ulysses (accessed 20 December 2017).

108 http://www.slate.com/articles/life/culturebox/2013/04/there_are_no_academic_jobs_and_getting_a_ph_d_will_make_you_into_a_horrible.html (accessed 20 December 2017).

extrapolate from one's own experience a universal claim about others but also to give ultimate power to the very system one seeks to subvert.

In other words, I would never be so bold as to say that the academy *made me* neurotic, pessimistic, or cynical. I already watched Woody Allen movies and had a heaping spoonful of those traits in my personality without the academy's help. I also like to think, though, that I've learned that we never ultimately move through the ever-receding arch of experience—that happiness is not a by-product of a certain fate ("once I get this or that job, *then* ..." or "once I publish with this or that press, *then* ..."). But the academy didn't show me that. Adulthood did. I'm grown and get to make choices about what I do with myself. Sometimes those choices come with fortuitous outcomes. Sometimes they come with unfortunate ones. Isn't that kinda just Life 101? The old shooting-for-the-stars-and-feeling-anxious-about-the-outcome routine isn't a narrative that should continue to rivet us in our career pursuits. It's best left to the folks on the set of the 1980s film *Fame*. Or the American musical comedy-drama TV series *Glee* (2009–15). It works for that show, too. Know why? Because they're both set in high school. When you're 18, it's easier to play Barbara Streisand.

After a while, we have to stop insisting that no one rain on our parades[109] and start admitting there are no guarantees. A PhD in literature resulted in my working—very happily but very unexpectedly—in a Religious Studies department. Schuman's PhD landed her with a book contract and a *Slate* readership. And my friends who shared her work on Facebook have, despite a wide variety of professional circumstances, been able at the very least to participate in discussions that interest them on computers or smart devices. That is a level of privilege that, while not suggesting in its own right some universal law or categorical imperative, might allow us to pause in our busy day doing whatever we did or didn't expect to be doing with our careers and think about what vast number of things had to fall exactly into place for us catch a reference about Kant's categorical imperative.

109 https://www.youtube.com/watch?time_continue=20&v=8xuID-brZv4g (accessed 20 December 2017).

29. The Luxury of Nuance[110]

Vaia Touna

The first time I came to Edmonton, Canada, was in March of 2010, in order to give a paper at a conference, and, since I had applied for a PhD at the University of Alberta, to also see the city—not knowing though whether I was yet accepted at the program or not. That was the first time I had been so far north and the only thing I knew for sure was that Canada is cold (that the temperature could get as low as –30°C [–22°F] was beyond what my imagination could grasp). As I said, it was mid-March when I arrived and to my surprise what I saw—as we were descending into the International Airport in Edmonton—didn't look like Spring to me at all (Culture on the Edge's Monica Miller knows what I'm talking about, given that she visited me last March!); everything was covered in a thick white blanket, so much snow I've never seen in my life. At the airport Willi Braun, my supervisor now, came to pick me up and as we got out of the airport I remember saying something about how cold it was (I can't recall now what the temperature was, of course—but for those who are not from Canada, or some place north, when I say everything was covered with snow, well it's not that difficult for you to imagine that it was cold), at which point Willi corrected me, saying that it was not cold but just chilly. I wasn't really sure what to make of his correction at the time, and this subtle distinction, because to me chilly still felt cold and that was my first encounter with Edmonton's weather.

Oh, during my stay, they were also saying something about the "windshield," too, but I couldn't figure that one out; maybe you needed a shield to protect you from that wind!

A few months later I would return as a PhD candidate, and around October—although they called it Autumn it did feel like Winter to me (though it is of no surprise that our "Winter Semester" is from January to April)—I would occasionally ask Willi if it was yet legitimate for

---

110 Ed. Note: Posted on 24 February 2014, https://edge.ua.edu/vaia-touna/the-luxury-of-nuance/ (accessed 20 December 2017).

me to say "it's cold," and with his refusal I was offered yet more adjectives. One time I emailed him:

> *Me: Well is it cold yet?*
> *Willi: You will have to wait a bit longer, my dear. I would call this biting or sharp. Both words imply pain. But when it is cold the pain is gone.*
> *Me: But if the pain is gone ... oh no!*
> *Willi: Yes, one could speak more positively. You might revive the old dog metaphor for measuring temperature on the minus end of the thermometer. In the olden days up here in the northern lands, cowboys, ranchers and hunters would have to sleep with their dogs to keep warm. To this day you might hear people around here speak of a "one-dog night" (you need to sleep with one dog to keep warm) or a two-dog night, and so on. I would say we are in the one-dog night range. Definitely not in the hot dog range. That would be Alabama.*

Over the years I've learned that the weather can change from "cool," to "crisp," "brisk," "nippy," to "biting" and "sharp" (as my Professor described it), then to "cold," "frigid," and "freezing cold" or even counting the cold with dogs! Not to mention that it doesn't just snow, there are "scattered flurries," "flurries," "freezing rain," "wet snow," and who knows what else. And I also learned that it's not enough to know that it's −16°C (3.2°F) because, depending on the "wind chill" (not the windshield as I initially thought) it could easily feel like −26°C (−14.8°F) and that's "cold," though not "frigid" or "freezing cold," as is more usually the case in the prairies of Saskatchewan, at least according to the regular Facebook updates I see on William Arnal's wall, for example: "Negative 34. Wind chill, negative 51. Think I'll stay in today."

As you might understand, describing "cold" is a complex and certainly a necessary taxonomy in my neck of the woods, because without such distinctions the weather here would simply be cold eight months of the year, and believe me that's not good.

What this story of distinction may tell you is that insiders have the luxury of nuance, a process that marks their place. It enables a narrative—moving from nippy to freezing—that helps, in some ways, people here to cope with the long-lasting winters. It is hopeful to say "it's a chilly day" and not "it's a cold day" and it's dreary to think that the worst is yet to come. But I suppose there is something to be gained by this movement from cool to freezing, because, as you know, it can always get worse: "freezing cold" for a day or two (or even a bit longer) is not that bad, as you also know that it will be "balmy" (as Marcia Hay-McCutcheon, a good friend in Alabama, once described it for me) when it goes back to –5°C (23°F), and that's a hopeful thought. Our narratives, our classifications, our distinctions, if you will, therefore don't necessarily describe some natural reality out there, instead, they allow us to cope with the everyday, to make sense of it and live in it. That's why I guess when I say to my friends in Greece that –15°C (5°F) is actually nice—"it's a different cold"— they look at me with distrust, because for them it's just "cold"; but we don't have the same things at stake, do we? I mean, they don't have to live where I live so the nuances of "cold" are of no relevance to them.

After four winters in Edmonton I not only have all this vocabulary in mind to cope with the winter wonderland, but I also feel more of an insider, that is, being able to distinguish between these subtle gradations of coolness. So when it is only starting to get a bit chilly in early October and I hear newcomer students (often from warmer climates like myself)—in "International House" the University's residence where I live—complaining about how cold it is, I immediately tell them that they should do well by reserving that word for January and February or even March, and that they shouldn't forget the wind chill.

30. Does My "Wife" Have a "Job"?[111]

Craig Martin

Six years ago I took an academic post at a liberal arts college with a heavy teaching load about 4 hours away from Syracuse, New York,

111 Ed. Note: Posted on 25 June 2014, https://edge.ua.edu/craig-martin/ does-my-wife-have-a-job/(accessed December 20, 2017). This was among the most popular posts on the Culture on the Edge site with a total of 1,543 views by 14 January 2018.

where my wife works as a middle school teacher and where we own a home. Consequently, I commute back and forth every week during the fall and spring semesters. Many of my academic friends and colleagues ask me, "Can't your wife get a job where you work?" or "You've got a good publication record; why don't you apply for jobs at more research-oriented universities?" Arguably, there are some latent sexist or patriarchal assumptions underlying these questions.

Presumably as someone who identifies as an academic, I have a career—perhaps even a "vocation"—whereas my wife, a public school teacher, has a *mere* job. Careers have trajectories and involve planning, nurturing, the accumulation of social capital, networking, and so on. A job by contrast could be picked up or discarded for another job, which would be its functional equivalent. Why can't she just swap jobs so I can pursue my career?

Two key questions come to my mind. First, is there a latent assumption of male privilege, that my career would be more important than hers? Or is it assumed that as a woman, my wife can't have a "career"? Is it that men have careers, but women have jobs? Second, if it is the case that a woman could in fact have a career, is it nevertheless automatically assumed that academic careers are more important than careers in public education? Is it possible that primary and secondary school teaching is belittled in contrast to college teaching because the former is traditionally and historically populated by women and the latter by men? Are primary and secondary teaching roles feminine and college professorships masculine—making the latter more important?

It turns out that my wife does, in fact, have a career. She's nurtured her career through involvement with regional and state organizations (the Central New York Council for Social Studies and the New York State Council for Social Studies), for which she's served as an officer, helped plan conferences, etc.; she's earned tenure at her school and has a level of seniority that protects her from layoffs due to budget cuts; she has developed social capital as a union representative in her district; and so on. Because college-level academic disciplinary networks are national, my social capital and career could easily transfer to a new institutional context within the same nation; however, because of the local structural organization of school districts and teacher networks, my wife's social capital would not transfer, for instance, to a new state within the same nation. If we moved to a new state—while I might be able to carry on, as before, with my career—her career would more or less have to start from scratch; she would need to build an all-new local network of colleagues, involve herself anew in regional organizations, etc.

Reading assumptions into casual conversations is a precarious endeavor, and the questions I've asked above are just that—questions. I'm really not sure how to answer them. A part of me is tempted to chalk it up to the fact that of course people talking to *me* focus on me rather than my wife. However, my wife has pointed out to me—interestingly—that while in general people ask both of us about whether she will follow me (i.e., they will directly ask her why she doesn't take a job where I work), I have *never* been asked why I haven't left my position to follow her.

For all of these reasons, there is something odd about the way otherwise progressive colleagues ask me questions about my "wife" and her "job," questions that certainly *seem* to have some latent sexist baggage. How different would it be if they asked about my "partner" and her "career"?

31. The Most Disgusting Picture Ever[112]

Leslie Dorrough Smith

True confession: As I am prone to do every semester, I have once again tarnished the innocence of young adults by forcing a group of students to look at a particular photo of a woman which shows her abundant armpit hair. It is, I am told, "the most disgusting picture ever."

It turns out that my students' near ubiquitous sense of disgust with this image is not unique, for scholar Breanne Fahs has recently shown

112 Ed. Note: Posted on 20 February 2015, https://edge.ua.edu/leslie-dorrough-smith/the-most-disgusting-picture-ever/ (accessed 20 December 2017). This has been one of the most popular posts on the Culture on the Edge site with a total of 6,538 views by 14 January 2018.

that despite many women's nonchalant attitudes towards underarm and other body hair as mere "personal choice" when discussed hypothetically, a diverse group of her female students who opted to forego hair removal as part of an in-class experiment reported almost universal feelings of social pressure, helplessness, disgust, and anger, not only in the way that they felt about themselves, but also in the way that their families and peers treated them.[113]

There have been ample articles written about the history of hair removal, not to mention how the Western preoccupation with relatively hairless women came about (if we're looking at specific trends, it appears that shortened hemlines and sleeveless clothing had something to do with it). But knowing why a certain body modification came into vogue is not the same as discussing its social ramifications or how those dynamics work, so my interest here is not to discuss whether this "really" is disgusting, nor to provoke arguments on the relative merits (or lack thereof) of body hair. Rather, my interest lies in asking about our tolerance of the boundaries of the category "natural."

What intrigues me about this photo is the manner in which it typifies Candace West and Don Zimmerman's famous remark that when one transcends a gender boundary, the artificiality of that boundary is rarely interrogated or noticed, but the person who transgressed it is.[114] To put it differently, the common reaction to this photo is not that our standards about underarm hair are strange or unnecessary, but that this particular woman's choice to sport underarm hair is what is strange and unnecessary.

So while there have been numerous popular commentators who have asked why adult women's body hair drives a rather common cultural revulsion, what is often missing from those discussions is a realistic look at the dynamics that shape disgust in the first place.

113 Breanne Fahs, "Perilous Patches and Pitstaches: Imagined Versus Lived Experiences of Women's Body Hair Growth," *Psychology of Women Quarterly* 38(2), 2014: 167–80, http://www.breannefahs.com/uploads/1/0/6/7/10679051/2014_psychology_of_women_quarterly_fahs.pdf (accessed 20 December 2017)

114 Candace West and Don Zimmerman, "Doing Gender," *Gender and Society* 1(2), 1987: 142.

As Julia Kristeva reminds us, that which is disgusting is not self-evident; it must be taught and then emotionally cultivated.[115] Like any other social preference, the degree of our disgust typically reflects the degree to which the act or artifact challenges the power-based structures that invisibly define our lives.

In this sense, despite American culture's current love affair with all things "natural," there are certain forms of "natural" that transgress other social codes that are otherwise considered inviolable, even if we are unconscious of their presence. Let's consider for a moment that a woman's shaven body is seen as particularly "feminine" in part because it signifies difference from men (who can generally wear their body hair without judgment), but also for its similarity with children, in the sense that children are, generally speaking, the only other relatively hairless humans around. A very long line of social critics have pointed out that everything from the grouping of "women and children" together in emergencies to the continued popularity of the sexy schoolgirl motif has not only, in the case of the former, likened women to weak and innocent children, but in the latter, also sexualized them precisely because of their comparative weakness.

While few of us may overtly associate this disgust with body hair with the concurrent infantilization and sexualization of women, one of the most important social principles to recognize is that just because we are not conscious of the roots of the social dynamics that define us does not mean that they are not at work.

In other words, I don't have to know the history of how Western women have been deemed sexually desirable in order for the connections of "hair," "female," and "disgusting" to make an impact on my life. As Fahs puts it, "… body hair is a 'gateway drug' into topics that carry loftier and more serious consequences for women," for if the personal is always the political in the sense that there is no individual untouched by society, then we physically become society's mirror reflection, what Susan Bordo has called the process by which "the body becomes the medium of culture."[116]

115 Julia Kristeva, *Powers of Horror: An Essay on Abjection* (New York: Columbia University Press, 1985).

116 Susan Bordo, *Unbearable Weight: Feminism, Western Culture, and the Body* (Berkeley: University of California Press, 1993), 165.

This is why I have great sympathy for Fahs' position that discussions about body hair are neither silly nor less important than other gripping issues, since diminishing them as such is yet another method to render society's forces invisible. As Fahs concludes:

> Body hair represents an avenue into tougher and more painful discussions about gender, bodies, power, social control, invisibility of patriarchy, the fusions between heterosexism and sexism (seen vividly in men's and family members' reactions to women's body hair), and overlaps among classism, racism, ageism, homophobia, and sexism. In the classroom, body hair opens doors to rich discussions about intersectionality (e.g., "My mother tells me I'm a 'dirty Mexican' when I have leg hair"), privilege ("My hair is blond, yours is black, so we're already dealing with different things at stake"), misogyny ("My boyfriend said I need his permission to grow my body hair"), power ("How can I be a radical if I can't even grow body hair? "), and the internalization of oppression ("Even though no one says anything, I feel disgusting when I have armpit hair"). Conversations about body hair hold up a mirror to otherwise unseen aspects of gender and sexuality, making the seemingly benign ("fluffy tufts," "fuzzy patches") suddenly endowed with the power to unsettle and transform. (178)

32. Identifying Threats of Violence[117]

Steven W. Ramey

With discourses surrounding terrorism and gun violence, which have become prominent again in the wake of Charleston and Chattanooga, people want to find patterns that illustrate the source of the threats of violence. Looking for these patterns, people engage in an act of comparison, which, as we have discussed on this blog previously, is more about the person constructing the comparison than some reality outside of him/her. For example, I have seen various social media

117 Ed. Note: Posted on 22 July 2015, https://edge.ua.edu/steven-ramey/identifying-threats-of-violence/ (accessed 20 December 2017).

posts recently that include lists of acts of violence, ranging from 9/11 and the storming of the U.S. Embassy in Iran to the Chattanooga shootings, all attributed to people who identified as Muslims. While these posts appear to be direct descriptions of reality, they reflect the choices of the creator of the list as to which acts of violence to include and which identifications to include.

Of course, most of those individuals identified as Muslims and even in some cases made direct connections between their under-standing of Islam and their actions, so the designation is not some-thing fabricated by the person constructing the comparison. Yet, this willingness to accept the self-descriptions of the violent offenders is a choice rather than something automatic. For example, a member of the KKK who connects their ideas and practices to Christianity is often seen as shocking, and commentators clarify or critique those claims in ways that are not always done in relation to Muslim self-descriptions. Accepting self-representations only works when the identification allows the dominant communities to distance them-selves from the perpetrator.

The *New York Times*[118] last month emphasized a different compar-ison of extremist violence in the U.S. A study from New America[119] concluded that non-Muslims engaging in "ideological violence" have committed more attacks and killed more people in the United States than attacks attributed to Muslim extremists. Of course, to make that claim, they restrict the analysis to events after 9/11, thus their choices also influence the outcome. The New America study also limited attacks to those identified as ideologically-driven based on their pre-sentations of radical ideological views in social media posts or online manifestoes or something of that sort. The *New York Times* further noted that violent attacks that the study excluded because no ideo-logical motive was evident "have cost more lives than those clearly tied to ideology." So, if those non-ideological attacks (as determined in such studies) are more of a threat than ideological attacks by any

118 https://www.nytimes.com/2015/06/25/us/tally-of-attacks-in-us-challenges-perceptions-of-top-terror-threat.html?_r=0 (accessed 20 Dec-ember 2017).

119 https://www.newamerica.org/in-depth/terrorism-in-america/ (accessed 20 December 2017).

group, why should we focus on "Muslims" or the broader category of "extremists"?

We can easily identify a different commonality (and others have said this before). From the bombings in Oklahoma City and the 1996 Olympics to shootings in Aurora, Colorado, Virginia Tech, and a Sikh Temple in Wisconsin, the most obvious commonality is gender. Another dataset[120] that focuses on U.S. mass shootings (thus excluding events like bombings) finds that over 90% of the incidents involved male shooters, and around 75% were in the age range from teenagers to 40. So, perhaps instead of suggesting greater law enforcement scrutiny for people who are identified as Muslim or efforts to counter "radicalization," law enforcement should be profiling all young men, and society should question the ways we socialize males.

Neither politicians nor social media posts, though, focus much on young males in the rhetoric following such events. The identification of patterns in these horrific events often serves to distance us from the perpetrators, and this commonality fails to do that, as most of us who are not young men have young men whom we know and love (significant others, children, siblings, nephews, etc.). It is much less emotionally satisfying to see ourselves or our loved ones in the image of the perpetrators, so instead of focusing on the most obvious commonality, we emphasize their radicalization, their mental problems, or their minority religion. In that sense, the ways we construct the comparison is often more about us than about the data that we analyze.

33. Innumerable Shades of Grey[121]

Russell T. McCutcheon

Yes, about a week ago there was yet another mass shooting in the U.S., this time at a Planned Parenthood clinic in Colorado Springs,

120 http://specialprojects.myajc.com/graphics/mass-shootings/#panel2 (accessed 20 December 2017).

121 Ed. Note: Posted on 3 December 2015, https://edge.ua.edu/russell-mccutcheon/innumerable-shades-of-grey/ (accessed 20 December 2017).

CO. (I won't go into the even more recent mass shootings in Georgia or California yesterday.)

There're not too many details in the public domain yet (at least when I wrote this post), but we know that a middle-aged, white male suspect was apprehended after a stand-off with police, that three people (including a cop) were killed, and that several more were wounded.

The few details that are now available (more are slowly being released)[122] concerning his motive, read as follows—

> Suspected Colorado Springs Planned Parenthood shooter Robert Lewis Dear mentioned "baby parts" to investigators and in later interviews expressed anti-abortion and anti-government views, a law enforcement official briefed on the investigation told CNN.[123]

—which makes this episode easily linked to ongoing criticisms across the U.S. of Planned Parenthood's efforts to provide reproductive health services to women. For, as Colorado Spring's mayor, John Suthers, was quoted as saying:

> People can make "inferences [about the motive] from where it took place" ... .[124]

But there's more: the fact that the man arrested was white and is accused of committing such a violent crime is also something that easily attracts some people's attention these days, what with the number of African-American males who are annually killed by police for doing far less than this. For the fact that he was taken alive, allowed to surrender, is itself cited as but one more instance of white privilege. (Compare it to how Laquan McDonald was treated by police in Chicago, back in October of 2014, for example.)

122 https://www.nytimes.com/2015/12/02/us/robert-dear-planned-parenthood-shooting.html (accessed 20 December 2017).

123 http://www.cnn.com/2015/11/28/us/colorado-planned-parenthood-shooting/ (accessed 20 December 2017).

124 https://www.nytimes.com/2015/12/02/us/robert-dear-planned-parenthood-shooting.html (accessed 20 December 2017).

And for yet others, it's tough not to think about the manner in which so-called mainstream members of American (assumed to be Christian) society seem not to feel a compulsion to disavow this act of violence, what with the way that a crime perpetrated by someone who seems Muslim is now an occasion for the media to call on all Muslims to condemn the act. In fact, a quick search online will actually find people supporting his alleged actions, as if anyone in that clinic deserved what they got.

What's more, the fact that we don't yet know many details of the accused shooter's motives is itself a curious thing (much like the care with which the authorities are now treating the 2 December 2015 San Bernardino shooting), for whenever we believe a crime is committed by someone unlike us we rather quickly decide on a narrative to account for their acts (whether or not that narrative holds water once the details are actually disclosed)—thus the ease of how we sometimes use that designator "terrorist"; yet, in this case, the media keeps reporting (as phrased by CNN the other day):

> Law enforcement officials caution it's too early to determine a motive in the case until all evidence is gathered and examined. That process is still ongoing.[125]

Slow and steady wins the race when the accused is judged to be like us—for then we introduce all manner of nuance to accomplish two things: (1) account for the crime in a way that isolates it to the perpetrator (the old "one bad apple" mode of explanation) and thereby (2) distance ourselves from it. But when the crime is committed by those judged unlike us, those we fear or despise, well, we predictably do the opposite, of course, for then we account for the crime by appealing to broad generalities about others that portray "them" as homogeneously uniform and thereby lacking the fine-grained distinctions we routinely afford to ourselves.

Only "we" have innumerably nuanced shades of grey.

My point?

---

125 http://www.cnn.com/2015/11/28/us/colorado-planned-parenthood-shooting/ (accessed 20 December 2017).

For anyone interested in comparison—its motives, how to carry it out, and the practical effects of doing it in different ways—the way that not just the police and media respond to such events, but also the way that we ourselves narrativize them, are all instructive examples that deserve study. For these moments afford us a glimpse into how that continuum whose opposite ends are known as affinity and estrangement (to hearken back to terms Bruce Lincoln used in what is arguably his most influential book)[126] is self-beneficially managed by people, thereby revealing how the value of sameness is either extended to or withheld from people around us.

Update: That the San Bernardino suspects now turn out to be a man who worked at the facility named Syed Farook and a woman (seemingly his partner) named Tashfeen Malik[127] means that we are afforded yet another tragic moment to study how quickly terms such as terrorism and presumption of a religiously-inspired motive are or are not invoked by media.

34. Competing Discourses on Life and Death[128]

Craig Martin

According to this news story[129] from a few years ago, a "living" man from Ohio was legally ruled "dead":

> A US man declared dead after he disappeared nearly three decades ago cannot now be declared officially alive, though he has returned home and is in good health, a judge has ruled.

---

126 Bruce Lincoln, *Discourse and the Construction of Society: Comparative Studies of Myth, Ritual and Classification* (New York: Oxford University Press, 1989).

127 http://www.latimes.com/local/lanow/la-me-ln-san-bernardino-shooting-live-updates-htmlstory.html (accessed 20 December 2017).

128 Ed. Note: Posted on 21 April 2016, https://edge.ua.edu/craig-martin/competing-discourses-on-life-and-death/ (accessed 20 December 2017).

129 http://www.bbc.com/news/world-us-canada-24486718 (accessed 20 December 2017).

Donald Miller of Ohio left behind a wife, two children and significant debt when he fled his home in 1986.

He was declared legally dead in 1994, then re-emerged in 2005 and attempted to apply for a driving license.

A judge this week found death rulings cannot be overturned after three years.

Judge Allan Davis handed down the ruling in Hancock County, Ohio, probate court on Monday, calling it a "strange, strange situation," according to media reports.

"We've got the obvious here. A man sitting in the courtroom, he appears to be in good health," he said, finding that he was prevented by state law from declaring Mr Miller legally alive.

"I don't know where that leaves you, but you're still deceased as far as the law is concerned."

What we have seems to be a case of competing discourses. If this man went to the hospital, it seems unlikely that the doctors would direct him to the morgue. On the other hand, from the court's perspective he is dead and thus not eligible to get a driver's license.

Given that he is medically alive, on what grounds, then, does the court find him to be dead? When we include the concerns of the IRS, Child Services, and the Social Security Administration, the plot thickens:

By 1994, Mr Miller's back child support payments amounted to more than $25,000 … and the family had heard no word from him.

With Mr Miller declared dead, his "widow" was entitled to Social Security death benefits to support their children.

As Mr Miller remains legally deceased, Ms Miller does not have to return those funds to the government.

It remains unclear if she would have been able to collect back child support had he been declared living.

In *A Critical Introduction to the Study of Religion* (1st edition, Routledge, 2014), I suggested that rather than ask questions of authenticity—is this man authentically alive or authentically dead—it is better to ask "(1) *who* is identified by (2) *whom* as (3) *what*, and (4) with what *effects*" (161).

Here it's quite clear:

(1) This man identifies (2) himself as (3) alive, with the hope that (4) he can get a driver's license.

(1) This man's former wife identifies (2) him as (3) dead, with the hope that (4) she does not have to repay his social security benefits paid out to her by the state.

However, we can ask the further question: whose identity claim is authoritative? Here it appears that his ex-wife's lawyers were successful in persuading the state to authorize her claim rather than his claim. Not surprisingly, authoritative institutions can always trump common sense; even though the judge said the man appears "in good health," the institution of the law—or at least those parts of it that assign the determination of "death" for legal purposes—is authoritatively binding. While it's an unusual story, it's not difficult to understand.

Compare, then, this case to last year's story[130] about a "200-year-old Buddhist monk [who was] found mummified in Mongolia," and ruled to be "still alive … and nearing a state of Nirvana." In this case, it appears much the same is going on: an authoritative institution—in this case, a Mongolian Buddhist monastery—can rule that the "Lama is sitting in the lotus position vajra, the left hand is opened, and the right hand symbolizes of [sic] the preaching Sutra … . This is a sign that the Lama is not dead, but is in a very deep meditation according to the ancient tradition of Buddhist lamas." With what consequence? The man who found the body cannot sell it on the black market, despite the fact that it might have earned him an "enormous sum."

So despite what may appear here to be "self-evident," i.e., Mr Miller's apparent vitality or the Lama's post-mortem mummification, the persistent question remains: Who has the authority to make claims, about whom, and to what end? Instead of refereeing the opposing truth claims being presented in each of these examples, we should look to the strategic moves being made and the implications such moves have. As it turns out, these competing claims

130 http://www.ibtimes.co.uk/mummified-buddhist-monk-still-alive-after-200-years-nearly-buddha-1486570 (accessed 20 December 2017).

about authoritative discourses are more often tied to varying material interests rather than notions of truth. In looking at these examples as discourses on authority, we can begin to see strategic moves being made—and not self-evident claims—by groups with (sometimes) competing interests at stake in much larger social agendas.

35. Shoots, Stabs, or Farts: Some Thoughts on Child's Play[131]

Leslie Dorrough Smith

My three school-aged children recently stayed with grandma for the week, and while there, she took them to the dollar store. Going to the dollar store is one of my kids' favorite rituals (so popular that they practice it with both sets of grandparents); among other things, it is a pilgrimage that feeds their unending appetites for cheap plastic stuff. Although we actively discourage violent play with our children, have never purchased them violent toys, and talk consistently in our house about the danger of weapons, my sons' favorite dollar store items are almost always plastic guns, grenades, and knives.

So it was little surprise when grandma texted me to tell me how, upon entering the store, my 8-year-old son had declared that he was interested in "anything that shoots, stabs, or farts." After I recovered from that proud parenting moment, I began to consider Michael Kimmel's observation that male violent play is not a matter of genetic destiny. As much as we may love to utter the following words to one another, this is not an inherently "boys will be boys" situation, for, as Kimmel and other gender scholars have amply shown, violent play is a phenomenon caused by specific cultural patterns and power arrangements rather than an inbred trait of boys.[132]

<del>131 Ed. Note: Posted on 18 August 2016, https://edge.ua.edu/leslie-dorrough-smith/shoots-stabs-or-farts/ (accessed 20 December 2017).
132 Michael Kimmel, "The Gender of Violence," in *The Gendered Society* (4th Edition, Oxford: Oxford University Press, 2011), 381–407.</del>

Rather, what Kimmel demonstrates is that rates of male violence
—and the popularity of gendered violence more generally—are
positively correlated with the degree of traditional gender author-
itarianism within a culture (384–5). In other words, the popularity
of violence and violence-type imagery increases in circumstances
where masculinity is seen as something not just starkly separate
from femininity, but where men are seen as more authoritative than
women. This data is closely akin to Bruce Lincoln's observation that
one telling sign of the volatility of a person or group's authority is
that they resort to physical force.[133] That is, Lincoln notes, because
authority is the mental effect of having granted someone power, being
pushed to make power physical is, as such, the sign of the erosion of
that effect. In physical force we thus find the response to the breaking
point, the social seams, wherein arguments on the naturalization of
power begin to falter.

If we keep in mind that virtually all people seek out avenues of
social status and power, then it's not difficult to consider the allure of
a toy gun to a person without authority (such as a child, and particularly a child whose parents have made that thing relatively taboo).
Regardless, it gives me pause to consider how few popular languages
for my son's gendered self-expression are readily recognizable by
others in the way a weapon is; weaponry (not to mention flatulence)
is a very efficient way for his gender to become culturally legible.

It may seem on the surface that farting and killing are quite separate things, but if we imagine that the entire dollar store were laid
out in a Venn diagram, both acts help to build an identity strategy
carved out of rule defiance (for as we know, neither farting nor killing
are generally considered socially appropriate). Of course, one might
think, what does any of this matter, for it's all in jest—it's just child's
play! And yet it is interesting that, in navigating the gendered life of
my older daughter, very rarely have the outlets of imaginative play
that have been offered to her in mainstream social settings tinkered
with rule-breaking in ways that have been culturally commonplace

133 Bruce Lincoln, *Authority: Construction and Corrosion* (Chicago and
London: University of Chicago Press, 1994), 4–5.

for my sons. While none of my children has been consistently gender-conforming, I cannot think of anything that even comes close for my daughter in the mélange of "girl stuff" that is baby dolls, makeup (her dollar store go-to), dressing up, and the like. In short, the subtle work of play reinforces the freedom/constraint double standard that is so intimately tied up with traditional gender roles.

For those of us intrigued with the dynamics of gender development, toys reveal several interesting things, not the least of which is the fact that children bear the imprint of our society precisely because society cannot survive without turning its most impressionable members into itself. Perhaps it is thus easier to see how even the most mundane and seemingly insignificant cultural practices ever so subtly inculcate and encourage attitudes, behaviors, and dispositions that create the patterns we willingly naturalize, if only because such naturalization hides both our own culpability and perceived helplessness.

Craig Martin is Professor of Religious Studies at St Thomas Aquinas College. His research concerns theory and method in the study of religion and culture, specifically focusing on discourse analysis and ideology critique. His recent books include *Capitalizing Religion: Ideology and the Opiate of the Bourgeoisie* (Bloomsbury 2014) and *A Critical Introduction to the Study of Religion, Second Edition* (Routledge 2017).

Russell T. McCutcheon is Chair of the Department of Religious Studies at the University of Alabama. Author or editor of a variety of books and resources, his interests involve theories of religion, the politics of classification systems, and social theory of identity formation.

Monica R. Miller is Associate Professor of Religion and Africana Studies, and Director of Women, Gender and Sexuality Studies at Lehigh University in Bethlehem, PA.

Steven W. Ramey is a professor in the Department of Religious Studies at the University of Alabama, where he also directs the Asian Studies program. He works on contested identifications in contemporary India and beyond and has published three books, *Hindu, Sufi, or*

Sikh (Palgrave 2008), *Writing Religion* (University of Alabama Press 2015), and *Fabricating Difference* (Equinox 2017), along with a variety of articles.

K. Merinda Simmons is Associate Professor of Religious Studies and Graduate Director of the Religion in Culture MA program at the University of Alabama. Her books include *Changing the Subject: Writing Women across the African Diaspora* (Ohio State University Press, 2014), *The Trouble with Post-Blackness* (co-edited with Houston A. Baker, Jr., Columbia University Press, 2015) and *Race and Displacement* (co-edited with Maha Marouan, University of Alabama Press, 2013). She is working on a monograph tentatively entitled *Sourcing Slave Religion: Theorizing Experience in the American South*, as well as two co-authored books: *Race and New Modernisms* (with Andy Crank, Bloomsbury) and *Gender: A Critical Primer* (with Craig Martin, Equinox). She is the editor of the book series *Concepts in the Study of Religion: Critical Primers*.

Leslie Dorrough Smith is Associate Professor of Religious Studies and Director of the Women's and Gender Studies Program at Avila University. She is author of *Righteous Rhetoric: Sex, Speech, and the Politics of Concerned Women for America* (Oxford University Press, 2014) as well as a forthcoming book (also with Oxford) about political sex scandals and American religion. Her research focuses on the interplay between gender, sex, reproduction, and the politics of American evangelical groups and conservatives more broadly.

Vaia Touna is Assistant Professor in the Department of Religious Studies at the University of Alabama. She is author of *Fabrications of the Greek Past: Religion, Tradition, and the Making of Modern Identities* (Brill, 2017). Her research focuses on the sociology of religion, acts of identification and social formation, as well as methodological issues concerning the study of religion and the past in general.

Index

www.ingramcontent.com/pod-product-compliance
Lightning Source LLC
Chambersburg PA
CBHW061003280326
41935CB00009B/821